*Schiller's "On Grace and Dignity" in Its
Cultural Context*

Studies in German Literature, Linguistics, and Culture

Schiller's "On Grace and Dignity" in Its Cultural Context

Essays and a New Translation

Edited by
Jane V. Curran and Christophe Fricker

CAMDEN HOUSE

First published 2005
by Camden House

Camden House is an imprint of Boydell & Brewer Inc.
668 Mt. Hope Avenue, Rochester, NY 14620, USA
www.camden-house.com
and of Boydell & Brewer Limited
PO Box 9, Woodbridge, Suffolk IP12 3DF, UK
www.boydellandbrewer.com

ISBN: 1–57113–305–4

Library of Congress Cataloging-in-Publication Data

Schiller's "On grace and dignity" in its cultural context: essays and a new
    translation / edited by Jane V. Curran and Christophe Fricker.
        p. cm. — (Studies in German literature, linguistics, and culture)
    Includes bibliographical references and index.
    ISBN 1–57113–305–4 (hardcover : alk. paper)
        1. Schiller, Friedrich, 1759–1805. Über Anmut und Würde. 2.
    Aesthetics, German — History. 3. Grace (Aesthetics) — History. 4.
    Dignity — History. 5. Grace (Aesthetics). 6. Dignity. I. Curran, Jane
    Veronica. II. Fricker, Christophe. III. Schiller, Friedrich, 1759–1805.
    Über Anmut und Würde. English & German. IV. Title. V. Series:
    Studies in German literature, linguistics, and culture (Unnumbered)

B3086.S33U2237 2005
111′.85–dc22

                                                    2005003339

A catalogue record for this title is available from the British Library.

This publication is printed on acid-free paper.
Printed in the United States of America.

Contents

The Cultural Context

The Text

Acknowledgments

WE ARE GRATEFUL TO Dr. Fritz Heuer for alerting us to the need for a new translation of Schiller's essay on grace and dignity, and for his financial support. We owe thanks to Carolyn and Klaus Schulte for their financial support of this volume.

Thanks are also due to Camden House, especially to James Hardin and James Walker, for being open to and supportive of this project, and to Verlag Hermann Böhlaus Nachfolger for permission to reproduce Schiller's text.

Notes on References and List of Abbreviations

ENGLISH VERSIONS OF quotations from "On Grace and Dignity" are taken from the translation in this volume. In all other cases they are by the author of the respective chapter if a source for the translation is not explicitly stated.

All italics in quotations are original.

AEM   Schiller, Friedrich, *On the Aesthetic Education of Man in a Series of Letters,* ed. and trans. with an introduction, commentary, and glossary of terms by Elizabeth M. Wilkinson (Oxford: Clarendon Press, 1967).

DVjs   *Deutsche Vierteljahresschrift*

GY   *Goethe Yearbook*

JbDSG   *Jahrbuch der Deutschen Schiller-Gesellschaft*

JWGV   *Jahrbuch des Wiener Goethe-Vereins*

LJb   *Literaturwissenschaftliches Jahrbuch*

NA   *Nationalausgabe der Werke Schillers*

Volume 20, *Philosophische Schriften Tl. 1,* unter Mitw. von Helmut Koopmann, ed. by Benno von Wiese (Weimar: Böhlau, 1962), includes "Ueber Anmuth und Würde" (251–308). We have modernized the title in the essays.

SHb   *Schiller-Handbuch.* Edited by Helmut Koopmann (Stuttgart: Kröner, 1998).

WGS   Christoph Martin Wieland, *Gesammelte Schriften,* ed. Deutsche Akademie der Wissenschaften (Berlin: Akademie, 1909–76).

ZphF   *Zeitschrift für philosophische Forschung*

Introduction

Jane V. Curran and Christophe Fricker

PYGMALION CREATES STATUES marked by a certain majesty but lacking grace. Only when the goddess of beauty appears to the artist in a dream is he capable of making statues so perfect that he wishes them to come alive. This eventually happens, and the figure moves gracefully. This version of the myth of Pygmalion with its notable opposition of two characteristics comes from the French Enlightenment author André-François Boureau-Deslandes.[1] It speaks to us even today: we still talk about dignity of bearing and about grace if we are attracted to a person because of a special air about him or her. At first glance, the concepts seem to be complementary.

For millennia, philosophers and poets have tried to define grace. The discussion usually starts by referring to grace as a gift granted by a divine being for a limited time. This gift becomes visible in the posture and movements of a person. It has thus to be interpreted primarily from an aesthetic viewpoint. The connection with a transcendental sphere changes its meaning in the eighteenth century; it loses its religious dimension but remains important as a reference point. The transcendental becomes the vanishing point for concepts unable to come to terms with undeniable and attractive appearances. This inadequacy of definitions, this *je ne sais quoi*, is ever present. Grace, in an Enlightenment context, becomes a "kulturphilosophische Heilskategorie"[2] (a cultural and philosophical road to salvation). It thus fulfills the function of an educational standard in a time when bourgeois society is trying to define itself. The concrete relevance of grace for society reaches its intellectual peak with Schiller's essay "Über Anmut und Würde" (1793). Gerd Kleiner calls it the "elaboriertesten philosophischen Entwurf des Zeitalters"[3] (the most elaborate philosophical essay of its era).

In his exposition of grace, Schiller uses the myth of Venus as a starting point. He does not introduce the discussion of dignity with a myth but asserts that it is acceptable to have recourse to the physical when present-ing this concept to the understanding: "Streng genommen ist die morali-sche Kraft im Menschen keiner Darstellung fähig, da das Übersinnliche nie versinnlicht werden kann. Aber mittelbar kann sie durch sinnliche Zeichen dem Verstande vorgestellt werden" (*NA* 20:294; strictly speaking, moral strength in humans is not capable of being represented, because the suprasensuous can never be made sensuous. But it can be presented to the understanding in an indirect way through sensuous signs). A Greek myth, however, will not do, since dignity, a complex consisting of free will, incli-nation, duty, moral strength, and natural impulse does not sit comfortably with the eighteenth-century view of the Greek world. A quintessentially modern mythical figure, Don Juan, would make a better choice. If Schiller had been in a position to act on this recommendation, the thematic link to Pygmalion would have been provided by the statue that comes alive. This time, the statue (of the Commendatore, who is offended and roused to life and action by Don Juan's treatment of women and his insolence) repre-sents the commanding moral force that keeps ephemeral impulses in check.

Don Juan himself appears as the epitome of natural impulse. He oscil-lates between desire's demands and the short-lived pleasure of desire fulfilled. He also possesses pure will, that quality that raises human beings above animals. Freedom of will allows him to act in contradiction to reason and to remain, despite his freedom, in the natural realm. Some versions of Don Juan's story are didactic and moralizing tragedies, but myth has always had an organic, metamorphic capacity that allows for endless recon-stitution. Molière even feels justified in calling his celebrated stage version a comedy. His protagonist is in a constant state of contradiction; his defin-ing obsession with sensual pleasure leads him through a series of amorous conquests, and yet Don Juan has, at some point before the play begins, embraced holy matrimony. Still, whenever he appears on stage, it is as a man whose will denies reason, law, and custom, who rejects power and allies himself with nature.

Immutable, implacable, and larger than life, the stone statue is more than a match for Don Juan, with his puny "heart of stone." And yet it demonstrates the capacity for change that we look for in Don Juan. The statue's monolithic force must crush Don Juan in the end, since the restoration of harmony within him is out of the question. Inclination will never align itself with duty; he will never freely choose to limit desire by the exercise of moral strength. Don Juan's impulses constantly overpower his will, keeping spiritual freedom within strict limits. With the intervention of the statue, moral fortitude gains the upper hand, to keep the impulses in check. Only through that encounter and the necessary control it exercises does the phenomenon of dignity emerge.

There is a long tradition of looking at grace and dignity in conjunction with one another. But there is a turning point in this tradition. Rhetoric and courtly style from Quintilian to Tasso and Castiglione postulate that both virtues can be acquired by learning, just like other norms for behavior and communication. But in the Enlightenment and especially in Schiller's essay, other aspects become more important: the appearance of grace and dignity as phenomena becomes a subject of interest, as does the basis of their connectedness.

Schiller's Argument

Grace is defined as "*bewegliche* Schönheit" (*NA* 20:252, *movable* beauty) in a human being. It cannot be produced according to explicit rules and it cannot be consciously repeated. It is part of the object in which it appears. It appears before us not only in space but also in time. It is part of an object for a brief moment only and disappears as soon as reason, in amazement, tries to explain it.

What kinds of movement can be graceful? Schiller introduces the idea of a "moralischer Empfindungszustand" (*NA* 20:267; moral sensibility of the person) governing those parts of a voluntary movement that are not determined by intention. A person's character can be interpreted on the basis of the visibility of his or her moral attitude. His or her being becomes visible as temporal.

How is reason's interest in grace to be understood? Reason has to be receptive with regard to what it encounters, to what provokes amazement and raises questions. This underlines the links between "Vernunft" (reason) and the etymologically related verb "vernehmen" (to hear). The question arises: according to which laws can one be receptive to the appearance of grace? Reason does not use the charm influencing it as a means of controlling the effects of grace to its own ends. But how can one, through reason, approach what is perceived? If what is beautiful becomes a product of the activity of reason in the process of appearing, then reason may have had a prior concept of beauty. This idea would now enable reason to recognize what is beautiful. In this case, thinking recognizes that one aspect of its own activity, the inquiry into what is beautiful, is not at its disposal. By acknowledging this, reason recognizes its own indeterminacy. This is how the task of being human can be fulfilled at the highest level: once the appearance of the beautiful as subject to laws has been thought, an arena for human freedom has been built.

One cannot be certain of appearance because one cannot re-enact its production. This is why it is also impossible to be sure that another onlooker responds the same way. But it seems as though beauty is universally pleasing to the senses. Each person assumes or hopes that what he finds pleasing is also pleasing to others. This universality cannot be conceptualized. Observation does not affect beauty, but the common sense of a valid sensation arises from beauty perceived. The object itself radiates the way it is to be treated: beauty, with respect. Life accommodates its environment to itself here as well. Thus recognition of the law governing beauty becomes the model for finding the way in a world accessible to the senses.

Grace becomes visible in movements that are "moralischsprechend" (*NA* 20:277; morally expressive). They hint at their moral origin and they are beautiful at the same time. Schiller resolves this contradiction between sensual and non-sensual origin by introducing an image of something like a playing-field: Morality sets the limits within which the sensual is permitted to appear. Thus, mind does not produce beauty or grace but makes it possible. Graceful movements are thus both unmediated expression in the sensual realm and representation to be interpreted within the moral realm. Recent scholarship has labeled this paradoxical constellation "Vermittlung von Unmittelbarkeit"[4] (transmitted immediacy).

As could be expected, the paradox illustrates that a system of philosophical devices has limits. The commentator has to acknowledge paradox as the final outcome. But one also has to acknowledge that some object of interest still lies behind these boundaries. One needs to be cautious when labeling grace itself as paradoxical.[5] This would entail claiming that the inadequacies of one's concepts and ways of reasoning are in fact inherent in the object. Grace itself is not paradoxical. But a way of thinking that assumes it can completely explain grace will lead to paradox.

Dignity appears as sublimity when the balance between the sensual and the moral, endangered by the force of emotions, collapses. In the second part of his essay, Schiller now contrasts grace and dignity. This passage is central to his argument and is also characteristic of the author's style. Hence we will quote it at some length:

> Anmuth liegt also in der *Freyheit der willkürlichen Bewegungen;* Würde in der *Beherrschung der unwillkührlichen.* Die Anmuth läßt der Natur da, wo sie die Befehle des Geistes ausrichtet, einen Schein von Freywilligkeit; die Würde hingegen unterwirft sie da, wo sie herrschen will, dem Geist. Ueberall, wo der Trieb anfängt zu handeln, und sich herausnimmt, in das Amt des Willen zu greifen, da darf der Wille keine *Indulgenz,* sondern muß durch den ausdrücklichsten Widerstand seine Selbstständigkeit (Avtonomie) beweisen. Wo hingegen der Wille *anfängt,* und die Sinnlichkeit ihm *folgt,* da darf er keine Strenge, sondern muß Indulgenz beweisen. Dieß ist mit wenigen Worten das Gesetz für das Verhältniß beyder Naturen im Menschen, so wie es in der Erscheinung sich darstellet. (*NA* 20:297)

> [Grace, then, lies in the freedom of *intentional movements,* dignity in the mastery of *instinctive ones.* Grace leaves nature with the appearance of free will where she carries out the commands of the mind; dignity, by contrast, subjugates her where she wants to be in command, to the mind. Whenever instinct begins to act and takes the liberty of encroaching on the offices of the will, the will may not allow indulgence, but must demonstrate its independence (autonomy) through the most insistent opposition. If, on the other hand, the will begins, and the sensuous follows it, then it should not show severity; it must show indulgence. This, in brief, is the law for the relationship between the two natures in humans, as represented in appearance.]

Schiller reaches conclusions to this argument only in the fifteenth of his letters "Über die ästhetische Erziehung des Menschen" (On the Aesthetic Education of Man, 1795). With reference to the statue known as Juno Ludovisi, he explains that the statue's extraordinary effect is based on the fact that neither grace nor dignity can be found in her "herrlichen Antlitz" (glorious face), but "beydes zugleich" (*NA* 20:359; both at the same time). This raises the question concerning a basis for the connection between grace and dignity. Dignity is a necessary corrective whenever emotions threaten to overcome the authority of the moral. But when dignity appears as the force re-establishing this authority, a new area in which grace can appear opens up.[6] This interpretation of dignity is very close to the text of "Über Anmut und Würde," but it does not take the temporal character of grace itself into account. Schiller's first statement is that grace is bestowed by the goddess of beauty for a limited time. It is thus impossible to think of grace without considering time. Its disappearance is a part of its essence. Thus, the balance between the sensual and the moral is not conceivable as anything other than temporal. This becomes clearer when one looks at the other specifications Schiller makes about the proper constitution of humanity, which is to occur through the union of grace and dignity.

In the fourteenth Aesthetic Letter he speaks of annulling time in time — "*Zeit in der Zeit* aufzuheben" (*NA* 20:353). This occurs when the sensuous impulse and the impulse to form are united and constitute the play impulse. The force that brings about sensations in time and binds one to the material is what Schiller calls the sensuous impulse. It unfolds human characteristics, whereas the impulse to form brings them to fulfillment. The timeless spirit of a human being asserts personhood. The key here again lies in the various dispositions of the two impulses to time: "Der sinnliche Trieb will, daß Veränderung sey, daß die Zeit einen Inhalt habe; der Formtrieb will, daß die Zeit aufgehoben, daß keine Veränderung sey" (*AEM* 97; The sense-drive demands that there shall be change and that time shall have a content; the form-drive demands that time shall be annulled and that there shall be no change). What is needed in order for the two to be united, for time to be annulled in time, and for grace and dignity to become simultaneous and lasting, is not primarily a corrective to sensuousness but the superior powers of history. This is the point where we need to look at dignity.

In the teleological perspective of Schiller's philosophy of history, grace hints at a future state where the highest possibilities of man are realized. We would like to replace the term "Vermittlung" (transmission) by describing grace as meaningful immediacy. It carries meaning because it opens up a perspective that allows us to see the sensual and the moral united in the future. But it is still immediate because its appearance cannot be inferred from an interpretation of the conditions of the present. If Schiller regards the simultaneity of grace and dignity as human perfection, then dignity has to be seen as a means of protection against emotions, protection needed because emotions would mean an incursion on the part of time. Dignity is the expression of resistance against impulse and revolution. Wilcox rightly argues that dignity is present in grace as the mechanism by which the impetus of the sensual has been adjusted. Simultaneity of grace and dignity always implies the simultaneity of different conceptions of time: historical time, constructed and understood by reason, and that other concept of time that is essentially mythical and aesthetically interpretable. It is not because of a particularly challenging political, social, or intellectual situation that dignity is needed[7] but because of the temporal nature of human existence. By illuminating this through the question of grace, one can see the role of dignity more clearly.

Creative Reception

Schiller shows that grace and dignity form part of a person for a limited time and will then dominate the overall impression of the person. Generations of poets have been influenced by this notion of grace and dignity as inextricably intertwined. Even a brief glance at writings from the past two centuries reveals a great number of illustrations. They do not form a consistent tradition; it would be wrong to infer one on the basis of shared terminology alone. But the following three quotations might serve as an index to the phenomenon.

In *Des Meeres und der Liebe Wellen* (1831), Franz Grillparzer's dramatic rendering of the love story of Hero und Leander, Leander's friend Naukleros describes the impression that the two have of Hero:

> Der Anmut holder Zögling und der Hoheit,
> Des Adlers Aug', der Taube süßes Girren,
> Die Stirn so ernst, der Mund ein holdes Lächeln,
> Fast anzuschauen wie ein fürstlich Kind,
> Dem man die Krone aufgesetzt noch in der Wiege.
>
> (verses 626–30)

[The noble child of grace and majesty, / Eye of the eagle, the dove's sweet coo, / Her brow so grave, her mouth a noble smile, / Almost looking like a royal child, / Whose crown is laid already in the cradle.][8]

The close connection between the two central ideas is underlined by the fact that their attributes are named in reverse order: In verse 626, grace is named before majesty, whereas in the following line the eagle is mentioned first and only then the pigeon. Majesty is thus illustrated before grace. The two friends gain a deep insight into a personality through its momentary appearance.

A poem by Friedrich Hebbel (1813–63) exemplifies the temporal dimension of grace and dignity. Hebbel occupies himself with the image that also formed the concluding image in Schiller's argument.

JUNO LUDOVISI

Du lässest uns die Blüte alles Schönen
Und seines Werdens holdes Wunder sehen;
Die Stirn' ist streng, man sieht's in ihr entstehen,
Wo es noch ringen muß mit herben Tönen.

Die Wange will sich schon mit Anmut krönen,
Doch darf sie noch im Lächeln nicht zergehen,
Der Mund jedoch zerschmilzt in süßen Wehen,
Daß Ernst und Milde sich im Reiz versöhnen.

Erst keusches Leben, wurzelhaft gebunden,
Dann scheuer Vortraum von sich selbst, der leise
Hinüberführt zur wirklichen Entfaltung;

Und nun ist auch der Werdekampf verwunden,
Man sieht nicht Anfang mehr, noch Schluß im Kreise,
Und dieses ist der Gipfel der Gestaltung.[9]

[You let us see all the blossoms of beauty / And the wonders of its growing; / The brow is severe; one sees in it the sign / Of struggles to come against the bitter sounds. // Her cheek is pleased to crown itself with grace, / But may not yet dissolve into a smile, / Her mouth, however, melts in sweet travail, / Thus gravity and mildness join in charm. // First, life is shy, and bound by roots, / Then modest dreams of self lead softly / Onward to the point of true unfolding; // And now the need to strive is over, / The circle has no start, it has no end, / This is now the peak of all formation.]

Verses 2 and 3 speak of beauty as something that needs to unfold. This only happens as a struggle against opposing forces. The traces of this struggle appear as harshness. These first signs of beauty and the fact that they are seen together with the opposing forces is appealing. The image is ambiguous: grace itself must not "zergehen" (dissolve) but needs a certain kind of resistance. This is how grace as a prelude to beauty is anchored in time. Grace is beauty's "scheuer Vortraum von sich selbst" (modest dreams of self) and will eventually lead to the transcendence of beginning and end.

In the work of the poet Stefan George (1868–1933), grace and dignity are mentioned at a turning point: in the first stanza of "Zeitgedicht" (Time Poem). This is the opening poem of the collection *Der siebente Ring* (The Seventh Ring, 1907) and marks the beginning of the second half of George's oeuvre. George himself designs the poem as strategically important. He starts with a look back at comments made about him. Many believed him a

> [. . .] salbentrunknen prinzen
> Der sanft geschaukelt seine takte zählte
> In schlanker anmut oder kühler würde
> In blasser erdenferner festlichkeit.
>
> (verses 5–8)

[. . . prince drenched in salves / Who counted his measures, softly swayed, / In graceful slimness or grew cooler· / In pale remote festivity.][10]

Apparently, both these characteristics were used in a derogatory sense. He was seen as a dreamer detached from ordinary life. Now that he goes back to the people as a prophet of change in society and as a teacher, he seems to undergo a profound change. But he assures the readers: "Ihr sehet wechsel · doch ich tat das gleiche" (verse 28; You see change, but I still did the same). He does not refute the attributes formerly ascribed to him but indicates that they are relevant for him regardless of his views on art and its role in life.[11] He also fulfills his new role by keeping grace and dignity as his ideals. This might seem a very limiting view of George, but it is confirmed by the fact that he uses the twin concepts several times in works published after the *Siebente Ring* and each time they are clearly used both as a point of orientation and an example.[12]

Scholarly Reception

Four questions have gained particular attention among those who have written commentaries on Schiller's essay:[13] Is the work's argument consistent, and if not is it still valid? How does Schiller employ traditional rhetorical techniques, and what role do they play? What is the influence of Kant and of other philosophers? And, finally, does Schiller intend the essay to have an effect on society?

The philosophical rigor of the work has been called into doubt many times. Käte Hamburger's essay is the prime example of this. She questions Schiller's many syntheses: first, she doubts the legitimacy of the ambition to find an expression of a person's moral attitudes on the basis of outward appearance; she holds strong views against any attempts to reconcile anthropology and aesthetics.[14] This attempt is related to Herder's concept of kalokagathia, which designates the unity of moral goodness and aesthetic beauty as appearance.[15] She identifies the character of Schiller's anthropology as a demand linked to the idea of kalokagathia and as the reason for his logical and theoretical failure. Second, she relates the alleged contradictions in his argument back to the discrepancies among Schiller's models. Third, she accuses him of failing to distinguish between metaphorical and analytical language.

This position has been weakened mainly by the findings of rhetorical approaches. Elizabeth M. Wilkinson has shown that tensions between individual terms can be resolved by seeing them as parts of underlying schemes of argumentation (which she visualizes in diagrams).[16] She argues that Schiller is not greatly concerned with a discussion along the lines of clearly defined concepts; instead, he tries to reassess certain experiences with the help of language. Because of the very nature of the reassessment as an exercise carried out in language, this approach facilitates changes in one's way of living. The way of arguing, in her view, is itself aesthetic education. Wilkinson repeatedly exemplifies how poetic and philosophical language overlap.[17] Numerous commentators, however, find this supposedly unclear language irritating, an "indigestible brew of literary philosophizing."[18] Klaus L. Berghahn even declares the whole enterprise of defining beauty a failure. He is led to this conclusion not by looking at Schiller's main result, namely the definition of beauty as freedom in appearance, or perceptible freedom, but by denying the validity of Schiller's development of the thought process.[19]

Much has been made of Schiller's apparent dependence on Kant, and it is certain that exposure to the philosopher's Critiques had a tremendous impact on him. A letter he wrote in 1791 testifies to this fact: "Seine Kritik der Urteilskraft reißt mich hin durch ihren neuen, lichtvollen, geistreichen Inhalt und hat mir das größte Verlangen beigebracht, mich nach und nach in seine Philosophie hineinzuarbeiten" (*NA* 26:77; His Critique of Judgment fascinates me, with its new, enlightening, and profound content, and it has led me to long to immerse myself in his philosophy). In "On Grace and Dignity," Schiller veers off and establishes his own direction, and at one point explicitly mentions what he finds inadequate about Kant's position. For his part, Kant is capable of expressing admiration for "On Grace and Dignity" and for its author, while pointing out their differences — not irreconcilable, according to Kant — on the question of morality. Fritz Heuer's study on Kant and Schiller has set the framework for further discussions.[20] It has recently been challenged by Frank-Peter Hansen,[21] who claims an even wider Kantian influence than Heuer had shown.[22]

A glance at "On Grace and Dignity" will also confirm the importance of the works of Rousseau, Home, and Shaftesbury. Many commentators have shown how comprehensively Schiller was acquainted with English and French Enlightenment thought. Henry Home uses the twin concepts of grace and dignity in his work *Elements of Criticism* (1762–65) and is one of the fathers of the *je ne sais quoi* attitude towards grace as a phenomenon resisting conceptual definition — an attitude Schiller courageously refutes. Home, along with Fichte, prepares the ground for Schiller's view that human beings constitute their identity in reaction to unmediated sensuous impressions. Shaftesbury's ideas of "moral grace," widely believed to be a source of inspiration for the concept of the beautiful soul, were available to Schiller through Herder and conversations with Wieland. Schiller's attempt to combine anthropology and aesthetics thus found its reference points well before he occupied himself intensively with Kant's Critiques. In the late stages of German Enlightenment thinking, Schiller goes back to anchoring morality in the interplay between instincts and rationality rather than solely in the latter. It is here that the openness of the ever-changing nature of man becomes the basis for aesthetics. Moral education becomes almost a prerequisite for the appearance of grace.

The importance of historical context is a fourth aspect crucial to the proper understanding of Schiller's achievement. It must be set against the backdrop of the Reign of Terror. This leads into questions about the task of Enlightenment thinking. Although "On Grace and Dignity" is a work ostensibly about aesthetics, the political flavoring is impossible to overlook. A broadly conceived historical backdrop is provided by David Pugh's look at Schiller as a citizen of his time.[23] Taking Schiller's initial interest in and ultimate reservations about the French Revolution into consideration, Pugh explores the use of political metaphor and analogy in "On Grace and Dignity." He argues that rationality and freedom are just as important as components of the human disposition as they are in their function as guarantors of harmony in the state. Art offers the possibility of a moral freedom in reason, one that corresponds to the harmony that constitutes the aim of the modern state.

Translation

Commenting on a perceived inability of Schiller's to blend the poetic with the philosophical in his essays, his Danish patron, Prince Friedrich Christian of Holstein-Sonderburg-Augustenburg, remarks: "Er bedarf einen Übersetzer"[24] (he needs a translator). Speaking more generally, one could say that any attempt to clarify the conceptual formulation of any subject matter is a type of translation. In this case, it is especially true because the discussion is about the boundary between the operations of understanding and sensuousness, between the things one can be sure of conceptually and the things to which one has to be receptive. Understanding is conscious of what is outside it. Traditional positions permit themselves to be queried. Understanding is able to recognize the conditions for realization that pertain to pure concepts and their objects. But if reason wishes to have access to the sensuous world, it has to put into question its own receptivity, its limits. This is where the importance of imagery in presenting grace and dignity becomes clear. Helmut Pfotenhauer establishes the constitutive importance of the reference to the statue of Juno Ludovisi and calls plastic art the realm beyond reason. In the attempt to join up what is categorically separate, in epistemological terms, sensuousness and reason, the particularity and the generality of taste, the work of art becomes a transitory telos of a dynamic way of thinking that aims to combine sense impression with the constant search for concepts. Schiller's argument can only be understood as this type of constant process of synthesis, behind which the inexpressibility topos is implied. The driving force is fear of the inability to create and comprehend aesthetically.[25]

More than two hundred years later, the statement that Schiller needs a translator still holds true. In the controversy provoked by Schiller's refusal to publish Fichte's essay *Über Geist und Buchstab in der Philosophie*, Fichte's polemic includes the claim: "Ich muß alles von Ihnen erst übersetzen, ehe ich es verstehe"[26] (I have to translate everything you write before I can understand it). Fichte's bitterness notwithstanding, this principle readily applies to the act of translating Schiller's works into another language. As one might suspect of a dialectical procedure such as translation, the principle works in two directions: at several points, statements that in the original appeared self-evident become problematic when they must be translated, and, on the other hand, occasionally, a translation can serve to elucidate a murky formulation in German.

Schiller's essay "Über Anmut und Würde" does indeed need a translator, as the Danish prince's statement, admittedly quoted out of context, suggests. Two nineteenth-century translations, one by C. J. Hempel (1861), the other unattributed (1884), stood unchallenged until 1988, when the self-styled Schiller Institute, in an effort to counteract what it perceived as a tradition of propaganda-based mistranslations of Schiller's works, published its own version. Although this version has its merits, it is marred by instances of archaism and bowdlerization. A doctoral dissertation by Leon R. Liebner, dated 1979, consists of a translation of "Über Anmut und Würde," with commentary, but this has never been published. The volume of Schiller's essays published in the series *The German Library* (1993) does not include "On Grace and Dignity," although there are a number of references to it in footnotes.[27]

One example will suffice to show why it is that the nineteenth-century versions of Schiller's essay are in need of replacement. Schiller writes: "Weil nun die Sittlichkeit des Weibes gewöhnlich auf Seiten der Neigung ist, so wird es sich in der Erscheinung eben so ausnehmen, als wenn die Neigung auf Seiten der Sittlichkeit wäre" (*NA* 20:289). The anonymous nineteenth-century translator translates as follows: "Precisely because the moral nature of woman is generally on the side of inclination, the effect becomes the same, in that which touches the sensuous expression of this moral state, as if the inclination were on the side of duty" (204–5). This is a consciously interpretative translation, complete with an added remedial phrase: "in that which touches the sensuous expression of this moral state" has no equivalent in the original German sentence. The first word, "precisely" is more emphatic than "weil nun," and it suggests a causality that is arguably absent from Schiller's opening. Notable also is the fact that the translator has rendered "Sittlichkeit" in the first instance as "moral nature" and in the second instance as "duty." Translator's license often has to permit more than one English equivalent for a German term, and this is particularly true in the case of a word such as "sittlich," partly because there does not seem to be an English equivalent that captures all the connotations present in an eighteenth-century German setting. There is also the grammatical problem that, having chosen an English equivalent, such as "moral," one finds that it does not support the same number of grammatical mutations as "sittlich" does. It is often necessary, then, to employ more than one English term, particularly when a German word is used in a variety of contexts. The anonymous translator, however, has used two different translations for "Sittlichkeit" within a single sentence, and much damage has been done to the delicate balance of Schiller's rhetoric. If the translator had not been quite so determined to hammer home the moral point, he would have been able to appreciate the sentence for what it is: a masterpiece of construction, with a fine chiasmus consisting of three elements. "Sittlichkeit . . . Seiten . . . Neigung . . . Neigung . . . Seiten . . . Sittlichkeit."

Reservations about the unpublished translation of the essay (1979) begin with the title itself. Liebner translates this as "Gracefulness and Dignity" and notes that he has suppressed "Über" as unnecessary. He adds that the choice of the word "gracefulness" in the title, rather than "grace," which he often uses in the body of the text, was based partly on the fact that, in his judgment, the meter of the English title corresponds more closely to that of the German one. Through these two decisions, he demonstrates a radical misapprehension of the genre of the text he is trans-lating. Schiller's use of the word "Über" tells his readers that this is an essay, that is to say, something slightly tentative and unsystematic, even possibly inconclusive. It is not a treatise or an exhaustive exposition. To suppress the preposition is to misrepresent Schiller's intentions. Further evidence that this choice of preposition was by no means arbitrary or empty can readily be gleaned from a survey of the titles Schiller gives to his essays: "Über naïve und sentimentalische Dichtung," "Über den Grund des Vergnügens an tragischen Gegenständen," "Über das Pathetische," "Über die ästhetische Erziehung des Menschen in einer Reihe von Briefen," "Über die notwendi-gen Grenzen beim Gebrauch schöner Formen," "Über das Erhabene." This list is confined to those titles that begin with "über." In other titles the preposition appears midway through, for example, in "Gedanken über den Gebrauch des Gemeinen und Niedrigen in der Kunst."

A further lack of understanding is evident in Liebner's defense of the word "gracefulness" on metrical grounds. While Schiller himself admitted that he could never hold his poetic and philosophical natures in strict sep-aration from one another, it would be absurd to reason that the translation of an essay would be more faithful to its original if it captured the metrical features of the German.

The present translation is based on the text provided by the standard edition of Schiller's works, the *Nationalausgabe*. The editors of that edition based their text on the original publication of the essay in Schiller's own journal *Neue Thalia* (1793) and on a very slightly revised text that appeared in volume two of Schiller's *Kleinere prosaische Schriften* (1800). The latest scholarly edition of the text is the *Frankfurter Ausgabe*. Its editors provide an annotated text, history of publication, brief paragraphs on Schiller's sources of inspiration, and a bibliography. A small sample of reactions to the essay by contemporary writers is also included. More affordable but with a less generous apparatus is the Reclam edition, which combines our text with the correspondence between Schiller and Christian Gottfried Körner on the topic of an objective standard by which to judge beauty: "Kallias oder über die Schönheit."

Although often referred to in works on aesthetic theory, the German Enlightenment or Weimar Classicism, the essay "On Grace and Dignity" remains unavailable to the English-speaking world in a reliable, reader-friendly, and scholarly form that uses contemporary idiom. Less substantial than the better-known "On Naïve and Sentimental Poetry" or "Letters on the Aesthetic Education of Man," "On Grace and Dignity" is nevertheless anything but marginal in the topics it covers. Freedom, outward beauty as it relates to inner morality and the connections between body and soul in the aesthetic realm are questions that have stood at the centre of philosophical inquiry since Plato. In addition, Schiller's essay points to a way forward in aesthetic thinking after Kant's *Critique of Judgment,* a way of loosening the hold that Kant's treatise had taken on the contemporary critical mind.

Notes

1 André-François Boureau-Deslandes, *Pigmalion, ou la statue animée* (London [i.e. Amsterdam?]: Samuel Harding, 1742).

2 Gerd Kleiner, "Anmut/Grazie," in *Ästhetische Grundbegriffe: Historisches Wörterbuch in sieben Bänden* (Stuttgart, Weimar: Metzler, 2000–), 203.

3 Kleiner, "Anmut/Grazie," 202.

4 Janina Knab, *Ästhetik der Anmut: Studien zur "Schönheit der Bewegung" im 18. Jahrhundert* (Frankfurt am Main: Peter Lang, 1996), 16.

5 Knab, *Ästhetik der Anmut*, 19.

[6] Kenneth Parmelee Wilcox, *Anmut und Wuerde: Die Dialektik der menschlichen Vollendung bei Schiller* (Frankfurt am Main: Peter Lang, 1981), 125.

[7] Hans Richard Brittnacher, "Über Anmut und Würde," *SHb*, 590 (Stuttgart: Kröner, 1998).

[8] Franz Grillparzer, *Werke* (Frankfurt am Main: Deutscher Klassiker Verlag, 1987), 3:33.

[9] Friedrich Hebbel, *Werke* (Munich: Hanser, 1965), 3:114.

[10] Stefan George, *Sämtliche Werke*, vol. 6/7 (Stuttgart: Klett-Cotta, 1986), 6.

[11] Cf. Dirk von Petersdorff, "Wie viel Freiheit braucht die Dichtung? 'Das Zeitgedicht' im 'Siebenten Ring' " (*George-Jb*. 5, 2004/05), 45–62.

[12] Cf. Christophe Fricker's article in this volume.

[13] For a comprehensive and diligently annotated overview of the scholarship on Schiller's aesthetic essays, see Lesley Sharpe, *Schiller's Aesthetic Essays: Two Centuries of Criticism* (Columbia, SC: Camden House, 1995).

[14] Käte Hamburger, "Schillers Fragment 'Der Menschenfeind' und die Idee der Kalokagathie," *DVjs* 30 (1956): 367–400.

[15] Cf. Johann Gottfried Herder, *Werke* (Frankfurt am Main: Deutscher Klassiker Verlag, 1985), 1:312–23.

[16] Elizabeth M. Wilkinson, "Reflections after Translating Schiller's *Letters on the Aesthetic Education of Man*," *Schiller: Bicentenary Lectures* (London: Intern. Univ. Booksellers, 1960), 46–82.

[17] Cf. Jane V. Curran's essay in this volume.

[18] Michael T. Jones, "Schiller Trouble: The Tottering Legacy of German Aesthetic Humanism," *GY* 10 (2001): 223.

[19] Klaus L. Berghahn, "Nachwort," *Kallias oder über die Schönheit: Über Anmut und Würde* (Stuttgart: Reclam, 1971), 166.

[20] Fritz Heuer, *Darstellung der Freiheit: Schillers transzendentale Frage nach der Kunst* (Cologne: Böhlau, 1970).

[21] Frank-Peter Hansen, "Die Rezeption von Kants *Kritik der Urteilskraft* in Schillers Briefen *Über die ästhetische Erziehung des Menschen*," *LJb* 33 (1992): 167–88.

[22] Cf. Fritz Heuer's essay in this volume.

[23] Cf. the essay in this volume.

[24] Quoted from Hans Schulz, *Schiller und der Herzog von Augustenburg in Briefen* (Jena: Diederichs, 1905), 153.

[25] Helmut Pfotenhauer, *Um 1800: Konfigurationen der Literatur, Kunstliteratur und Ästhetik* (Tübingen: Niemeyer, 1991), 171.

[26] Johann Gottlieb Fichte, *Gesamtausgabe der Bayerischen Akademie der Wissenschaften*, vol. 3/2, ed. by Reinhard Lauth and Hans Jacob (Stuttgart and Bad Cannstatt: Frommann, 1970), 339. Letter from Fichte to Schiller, 27 June 1795.

[27] Friedrich Schiller, *Essays*, ed. by Walter Hinderer and Daniel O. Dahlstrom (New York: Continuum, 1993).

Schiller Editions and Translations

"On Loveliness and Dignity." In *Schiller's Complete Works*, edited, with careful revisions and new translations, by Charles J. Hempel, M. D. Philadelphia: I. Kohler, 1861, 1:459–78.

"On Grace and Dignity." In *Essays Aesthetical and Philosophical*, by Friedrich Schiller, newly translated from the German. London: George Bell & Sons, 1884, 168–223.

"Ueber Anmuth und Würde." In *Schillers Werke: Nationalausgabe*, vol. 20: Philosophische Schriften 1, edited by Benno von Wiese and Helmut Koopman. Weimar: Böhlau, 1962, 251–308.

Kallias oder über die Schönheit: Über Anmut und Würde. Edited by Klaus L. Berghahn. Stuttgart: Reclam, 1971, 67–136.

Liebner, Leon R. *Schiller's Treatise "Über Anmut und Würde": An Annotated Translation into English*. PhD diss., Northwestern University, 1979.

"On Grace and Dignity." Translated by George Gregory. In *Friedrich Schiller: Poet of Freedom*. Schiller Institute: Washington DC, 1988, 2:337–95.

"Über Anmut und Würde." In *Werke und Briefe in zwölf Bänden, Bd. 8: Theoretische Schriften*. Edited by Rolf-Peter Janz, Hans Richard Brittnacher, Gerd Kleiner, and Fabian Störmer. Frankfurt am Main: Deutscher Klassiker Verlag, 1992, 330–94.

Works Cited

Boureau-Deslandes, André-François. *Pigmalion, ou la statue animée*. London (i.e. Amsterdam?): Samuel Harding, 1742.

Brittnacher, Hans Richard. "Über Anmut und Würde." In *SHb*, 587–609. Stuttgart: Kröner, 1998.

Fichte, Johann Gottlieb. *Gesamtausgabe der Bayerischen Akademie der Wissenschaften*. Edited by Reinhard Lauth and Hans Jacob. Stuttgart and Bad Cannstatt: Frommann, 1962–.

George, Stefan. *Sämtliche Werke*. Stuttgart: Klett-Cotta, 1982–.

Grillparzer, Franz. *Werke*. Edited by Helmut Bachmaier. Frankfurt am Main: Deutscher Klassiker Verlag, 1986–87.

Hamburger, Käte. "Schillers Fragment 'Der Menschenfeind' und die Idee der Kalokagathie." *DVjs* 30 (1956): 367–400.

Hansen, Frank-Peter. "Die Rezeption von Kants *Kritik der Urteilskraft* in Schillers Briefen *Über die ästhetische Erziehung des Menschen*." *LJb* 33 (1992): 167–88.

Hebbel, Friedrich. *Werke*. Edited by Gerhard Fricke, Werner Keller, and Karl Pörnbacher. Munich: Hanser, 1963–67.

Herder, Johann Gottfried. *Werke*. Edited by Martin Bollacher et al. Frankfurt am Main: Deutscher Klassiker Verlag, 1985–2000.

Heuer, Fritz. *Darstellung der Freiheit: Schillers transzendentale Frage nach der Kunst*. Cologne: Böhlau, 1970.

Jones, Michael T. "Schiller Trouble: The Tottering Legacy of German Aesthetic Humanism." *GY* 10 (2001): 222–45.

Kleiner, Gerd. "Anmut/Grazie." In *Ästhetische Grundbegriffe: Historisches Wörterbuch in sieben Bänden,* edited by Karlheinz Barck et al, 193–208. Stuttgart, Weimar: Metzler, 2000–.

Knab, Janina. *Ästhetik der Anmut: Studien zur "Schönheit der Bewegung" im 18. Jahrhundert*. Frankfurt am Main: Peter Lang, 1996.

Petersdorff, Dirk von. "Wie viel Freiheit braucht die Dichtung? 'Das Zeitgedicht' im 'Siebenten Ring.'" *George-Jb.* 5 (2004/5): 45–62.

Pfotenhauser, Helmut. *Um 1800: Konfigurationen der Literatur, Kunstliteratur und Ästhetik*. Tübingen: Niemeyer, 1991.

Schiller, Friedrich. *Essays*. Edited by Walter Hinderer and Daniel O. Dahlstrom. New York: Continuum, 1993.

Schulz, Hans. *Schiller und der Herzog von Augustenburg in Briefen*. Jena: Diederichs, 1905.

Sharpe, Lesley. *Schiller's Aesthetic Essays: Two Centuries of Criticism*. Columbia, SC: Camden House, 1995.

Wilcox, Kenneth Parmelee. *Anmut und Wuerde: Die Dialektik der menschlichen Vollendung bei Schiller*. Frankfurt am Main: Peter Lang, 1981.

Wilkinson, Elizabeth M. "Reflections after Translating Schiller's *Letters on the Aesthetic Education of Man*." In *Schiller: Bicentenary Lectures,* edited by F. Norman, 46–82. London: International University Booksellers, 1960.

The Cultural Context

Schiller's Essay "Über Anmut und Würde" as Rhetorical Philosophy

Jane V. Curran

IF THEIR LETTERS ARE TO BE considered reliable evidence, relations between Schiller and Kant remained cordial and gentlemanly, despite the fact that Schiller's essay "On Grace and Dignity" was written partly as a corrective to Kant's position in the *Critique of Judgment*. Schiller's premise, if not his structural point of departure, taken from the formula he had earlier established, already demarcates the margin that separates his views from Kant's moral didacticism: "Schönheit ist . . . nichts anders als Freiheit in der Erscheinung" (*NA* 26:183, Beauty is nothing other than freedom in appearance). Liberated from the need to settle aesthetic questions in terms of subjective judgment or taste, Schiller begins his analysis of grace as present in the unconscious movement of a morally conscious (and beautiful) being. In a letter to Kant (13 June 1794; *NA* 27:12) Schiller describes how he intended to soften the severity of the philosopher's theories and make his views more accessible to the public. Kant's inquiry into a universal standard by which beauty can be judged and recognized is singularly devoid of examples, and nowhere does he try out his principle by applying it to any of the fine arts. In diplomatic mood, Schiller expresses the wish not to be regarded as an opponent of Kant's, and is relieved by Kant's apparent disinclination to see him in this light.

Schiller evidently made a deliberate decision to treat the definitions of beauty and dignity, and the aesthetic questions which arise from them, in a style that not only reflected but actually embodied his subject matter. He avoids the confines of a purely deductive method of presentation, but still preserves its advantages. His choice of examples and the descriptive language in which he couches their exposition are a distinctive feature of his aesthetic writings. For example, to support his observation that grace is more frequently found in women than in men, Schiller writes that only a storm can set the stronger, masculine constitution in motion. The feminine essence is made of more sensitive stuff: "Die zarte Fiber des Weibes neigt sich wie dünnes Schilfrohr unter dem leisesten Hauch des Affekts. In leichten und lieblichen Wellen gleitet die Seele über das sprechende Angesicht, das sich bald wieder zu einem Spiegel ebnet." (NA 20:288–89; The delicate fiber of a woman bends like a thin reed at the slightest breath of emotion. The soul glides in light, delightful waves over the expressive face, which soon becomes as calm as a mirror again.) The sustained imagery of a body of water, the reeds that grow at its edge, and the storm that can stir up its surface not only demonstrates Schiller's concept of natural grace by analogy, but actually embodies it in image, rhythm, and sound. Moreover, the passage specifies one further characteristic, that of movement, and reinforces the contention that inanimate phenomena are incapable of graceful movement. The passage is neither simply an argument nor the mere illustration of an argument. Schiller both introduces a feature of grace and describes its appearance in strikingly graceful and poetic language. In two sentences he uses simile ("wie dünnes Schilfrohr" [like a thin reed]), metaphor ("Fiber" [fiber], "Hauch des Affekts" [breath of emotion], "Wellen" [waves], "Spiegel" [mirror]), onomatopoeia ("Hauch" [breath]), and alliteration ("leichten und lieblichen" [light, delightful]).

To clarify the concept of false grace, Schiller contrasts it with simulated or learned grace, the kinds cultivated in drama or dance. This artificial grace, he says, is analogous to the beauty produced by cosmetics and artificial aids: "Sie ist ein würdiges Gegenstück zu derjenigen Schönheit, die am Putztisch aus Karmin und Bleiweiß, falschen Locken, Fausses Gorges und Wallfischrippen hervorgeht" (NA 20:269; It is a worthy counterpart to the beauty produced at the dressing table from rouge and white lead, hairpieces, bust enhancements, and whalebone corsets). By listing five tools of the trade, rather than just one example, Schiller insinuates the futility of a quest for true beauty through artificial means. He also includes two pairs of contradictions: the red color of rouge aims at an effect opposite to Bleiweiss, a make-up that feigns an immaculate whiteness; "fausses gorges" give false size to one feature, while the corset squeezes in another to create the illusion of dainty, slim girlishness. The list, with its inherent contradictions, is a stylistic device that gives shape and form not only to the body itself, but also to the hopelessness of an unending succession of attempts to counterfeit the real thing.

Throughout the essay, Schiller's imagery, descriptive detail, poetic and rhetorical flourishes, mythology, and even dramaturgical craft transform a potentially systematic but lifeless analysis of the subject into a seamless amalgam of theory and practice. Subtly nuanced phrasing sometimes displays epic grandeur, as in the following sentence, which echoes the opening myth: "Das Feuer, welches die himmlische Venus entzündete, wird von der irdischen benutzt, und der Naturtrieb rächt seine lange Vernachlässigung nicht selten durch eine desto unumschränktere Herrschaft" (*NA* 20:304; The fire that heavenly Venus ignited is used by the earthly Venus, and natural instinct not infrequently seeks to avenge its long neglect by means of a domination that is all the more uninhibited). Elsewhere, Schiller draws on his stagecraft and sense of drama to build up in the reader a feeling of mounting tension. After the first four paragraphs of the essay have set out the myth, he inserts a dramatic pause, then reopens the action within a broader frame, to speak about the Greeks in general. It is as though, at the end of a scene or act, a new backdrop had been let down and had altered the appearance of the stage.

The poetic energy with which Schiller invests his philosophical investigation disarms any temptation to dismiss his stylistic variation as inconsistency or as evidence of a lack of philosophical rigor in his method. In this work, devoted to the characteristics of the beautiful, Schiller consistently combines discussing the topic in an analytical way with putting it into practice in the style he adopts.[1] If grace is to imprint itself on the public consciousness as an ideal, and if readers are to develop an appreciation for Schiller's discussion of it, then much hinges on its textual presentation. Stark rationality cannot be left to make the desired impact; it must express itself with the natural ease of an unreflected gesture. Schiller repeatedly voiced the desire to focus on the reading public and to be guided by his wish to convince readers rather than simply to outline an argument methodically. In 1785 he writes, à propos the launching of his journal *Rheinische Thalia*, "Das Publikum ist mir jetzt alles, mein Studium, mein Souverain, mein Vertrauter." (*NA* 22:94; The public is everything to me, my object of study, my sovereign, my confidant). In the context, Schiller's statement is a declaration of independence: he is not beholden to any princely patron. He also does not mean to depict himself as a writer who succumbs to the reading public's every whim. After all, his journal would fall into the hands of a rather small percentage of readers in any case. His sensitivity to their needs amounts to the decision to adopt a more aesthetically pleasing presentation of the contents of his argument. The public, in Schiller's judgment, was less likely to respond to the structure and strict divisions of Kant's *Critiques,* to their clinical precision, than to the essayistic style he himself practiced.

In a footnote passage where Schiller makes explicit reference to Kant in "On Grace and Dignity," a stylistic analysis makes this difference in attitude clear. Schiller writes "Achtung (nach ihrem reinen Begriff) geht nur auf das Verhältnis der sinnlichen Natur zu den Forderungen reiner praktischer Vernunft überhaupt, ohne Rücksicht auf eine wirkliche Erfüllung" (*NA* 20:303; Respect [in its purest sense] only applies to the relation of sensuous nature to the demands of pure practical reason, without regard for their actual fulfillment). He then quotes Kant: "Das Gefühl der Unangemessenheit zu Erreichung einer Idee, die für uns Gesetz ist, heißt Achtung" (The feeling of inadequacy as regards the attainment of an ideal that we accept as law is called respect). Schiller reasonably enough begins his sentence with the term to be defined, but then immediately makes what on the stage would be an aside, a parenthetical remark. The word "nur," balanced in the next phrase by "ohne," heightens the emphasis of the definition. He provides two parallel, balanced phrases, constructed from the following elements: abstract noun, adjective, concrete noun: "Verhältnis . . . sinnlichen Natur" and "Foderungen . . . praktischer Vernunft." The sentence culminates in one final phrase of a similar construction in which, however, the third element has been elevated from concrete to abstract: "Rücksicht . . . wirkliche Erfüllung." A brief glance at the line he quotes from Kant is sufficient to establish that Kant keeps his readers waiting to the end of the sentence to discover what his actual subject is. Nor does he feel the need for adjectives. Yet, before going any further, it is worth checking the original, because what Kant actually wrote is a little different. "Das Gefühl der Unangemessenheit unseres Vermögens zur Erreichung einer Idee, *die für uns Gesetz ist,* ist *Achtung*"[2] (The feeling of the inadequacy of our ability to attain to an idea *that is a law for us* is *respect*). Schiller has simplified Kant's phrasing by omitting the reference to our ability, but he has also made it more abstract. By supplying "heißt" as a replacement for Kant's repeated use of "ist," Schiller has greatly improved the euphony of the sentence, which marks a gain in the persuasive force of its language. No doubt Schiller was quoting from memory, so that the changes he introduces are unconscious, but it is interesting that he makes Kant's definition easier to grasp by removing an element already implied by the context, and that in doing so he makes Kant's style more arid and even more charmless than it actually is.

In order to evaluate the differences between Kant's writing style and Schiller's, some clarity on the question of genre is necessary. It is fairly evident that Kant's *Critiques* are philosophical treatises, but pinpointing Schiller's composition is a trickier undertaking. In a discussion of genre distinctions germane to the present task, Walter Benjamin separates philosophical writing, which exists in isolation from the problem of representation, from the didactic authority that resides in the truth of language. Benjamin identifies the "esoteric essay" as an alternative. The admixture of philosophical, poetic, and rhetorical features, as well as Schiller's ability to grant a tight structure to some passages while leaving the outer contours ill-defined, point to the essay genre as the best fit for "On Grace and Dignity." In an essay, presentation, rather than system, is important, and the less directly the individual components of that presentation relate to the central idea the more highly they are valued.[3] Benjamin compares this to a mosaic whose beauty as a whole depends on the somewhat arbitrary constellation of the pieces. Thus also, truth as an intellectual whole is grasped by a process of immersion in the details of the subject under discussion. He also sees the shifts and new beginnings (typical of Schiller's style) as a quintessential feature of thought's progression.

The essay as an independent genre owes much to Michel de Montaigne, whose *Essais* (1580) display a liberal attitude towards form that one also recognizes in Schiller's essays on aesthetics. Montaigne insists on his right to start wherever he pleases, given the fact that everything is connected. In Adorno's defense of the essay as form, he takes the further step of characterizing both the opening and the conclusion of an essay as being entirely determined by the author's preferences. According to Adorno, the essay "fängt nicht mit Adam und Eva an sondern mit dem, worüber er reden will; er sagt, was ihm daran aufgeht, bricht ab, wo er selber am Ende sich fühlt und nicht dort, wo kein Rest mehr bliebe" (starts not with Adam and Eve but with what it wants to talk about; it says what occurs to it in that context and stops when it feels finished rather than when there is nothing left to say).[4] Schiller famously chooses to begin this essay by presenting a myth that makes vivid the qualities of grace that he wishes to isolate. The same myth occurs in two of his poems, "Die Götter Griechenlands" and

"Die Künstler." Schiller judges that by opening with a well-known example, one to which, incidentally, Kant himself refers in passing in his "Beobachtungen über das Gefühl des Schönen und Erhabenen" (1764), he will effortlessly draw his readers into the argument. He explicitly protects the myth from possible charges that its only function is decorative, by asserting its importance for the task of the philosopher, which is nothing more exalted than seeking out concepts to describe the discoveries made by the senses, or "die Bilderschrift der Empfindingen zu erklären" (*NA* 20:252; explaining the figurative language of sensations).

The reflections on grace that arise out of that opening image undergo a systematic process of division, inspection, and qualification as Schiller seeks ever more precision in defining the distinguishing characteristics of grace. In the pages that follow he carefully delineates its relation to beauty, to the senses, and to reason. He establishes movement as a decisive feature, then restricts this to willed movements dictated not by nature but by a moral sensibility, and he explains the crucial participation of reason before determining the precise extent to which the senses participate in grace. Schiller the philosopher is methodical and dialectical and thorough.[5]

Thus, although Schiller refuses to concede to philosophy any discoveries that were not first intuited by the senses and revealed by poetry, although, in other words, he assigns no special, privileged position to philosophy, he nevertheless brings its methods to bear on the task of defining beauty to good effect. Schiller is careful to ensure that beauty is a clear concept in his readers' minds before he relates it to grace. His method is to present the conundrum that beauty belongs to the order of the senses and should therefore be of no real interest to reason, and yet reason does take pleasure in beauty. How then does a beautiful appearance relate to reason's concept of perfection? Schiller confronts this contradiction, and reasons his way out of it by positing a dual role for reason. On the one hand, it may find the idea in the appearance, on the other, it bestows the idea on the appearance. Schiller refers to the first instance as objective perfection and the second as subjective beauty. Although beauty cannot originate with reason, and is independent of reason, reason interprets and uses it.

Prose fiction is not a substantial component of Schiller's oeuvre, and so the narrative techniques one encounters in his essays are not attributable to the novelist within but to the linguistic habits engrained in the dramatist. An intermittent feature of his analysis is his use of the first person to signal a new stage in the argument or to sum up progress made so far.

Schiller writes, "Ich habe mir bis jetzt darauf eingeschränkt . . ." (Up until now I have restricted myself . . .) or "es sei mir erlaubt . . ." (I permit myself . . .). He sets up a kind of dialogue with his reader from time to time. In order perhaps to avoid excess in the employment of this direct appeal to the readers, Schiller also frequently resorts to using *Sperrdruck*, a typesetting convention of the day that sets extra space between the letters of a word (much in the manner in which italic type is now used to show emphasis; indeed Schiller's *Sperrdruck* is rendered as italics in the translation provided here) and, occasionally, inserts quotation marks for a similar purpose: accentuation. He guides his readers by pointing out the main emphases of his sentence or by identifying and highlighting terms that relate to one another, either through contrast or as individual features of the same phenomenon. In the following sentence the contrast between true grace and false grace is conveyed by the two verbs in italics: "Die echte Anmut *gibt bloß nach* und kommt entgegen, die falsche hingegen *zerfließt*." (*NA* 20:306; True grace *simply yields* and *accommodates;* false grace, on the other hand, *flows away*).

Towards the end of his essay, Schiller abandons the style of sustained argument in favor of a succession of shorter, gnomic statements. He adopts the rhetorical practice of employing aphorism to reinforce a conclusion. What he loses in conventional rigor of argumentation he gains in transparency, vigor, and persuasive force. For example, "Wahre Schönheit, wahre Anmuth soll niemals Begierde erregen" (True beauty, true grace should never arouse desire). "Der höchste Grad der Anmuth ist das *Beza-ubernde;* der höchste Grad der Würde die *Majestät*" (*NA* 20:305–6; The highest grade of grace is the *enchanting;* the highest grade of dignity is *majesty*). This clarity characterizes the section on dignity in particular. The actual ending of an essay, as Adorno accurately observed, does not ring with the tone of finality. This is typical of Schiller's essays. He does not, for instance, round it off with a myth, as he was to do only once, for "Über Matthissons Gedichte," to balance and match the myth of Venus's girdle at the beginning. Neither does he glance back at the opening myth. True dignity is distinguished in the last sentence from false dignity by the degree and area of control nature exercises in each. But Schiller seems then to sense the inadequacy of this ending and attaches a footnote to the very last word. Here he talks about ceremonial and its usefulness in preparing a proper reception for subject matter of great moment. Apparently moved by the desire to do everything in his power to help his readers grasp the final clarification, Schiller adds to this an illustration taken from the analysis of music and finally moves on to the effects produced by music in a liturgical setting. Yet he still does not present a satisfying or conclusive finale.

When contrasted with Kant's, Schiller's style can appear rhetorically disciplined and poetically inspired but conceptually lax. Some commentators have gone so far as to maintain that the paradoxical, even contradictory character they believe to have identified in this work is a sign that Schiller had incorrectly understood Kant.[6] Schiller himself recognizes dual inclinations vying for ascendancy in himself: the drive towards philosophical analysis on the one hand, and, on the other, the need to express ideas poetically. He writes to Goethe (31 August 1794): "gewöhnlich übereilte mich der Poet, wo ich philosophieren sollte, und der philosophische Geist, wo ich dichten wollte" (the poet usually overtook me when I was supposed to philosophize, and the philosophical spirit when I wanted to write poetry). Although Schiller appears to be presenting this, both here and in a letter to Körner in the same year, as a difficulty, elsewhere he seems determined not to sacrifice either of these two modes — in other words, to preserve both the image and the concept, to use presentation to bring the content alive. Only in this way can Schiller achieve his goal of producing a work corresponding to the wholeness of human nature, its harmony of understanding and imagination.[7] In the same way, grace celebrates the human ideal of unity of body and mind, and the form of Schiller's essay fits together with and consciously strives to resemble its content.[8]

Commentators feel impelled to analyze and classify Schiller's seemingly somewhat elusive use of vocabulary. Instances in Schiller's works of the word "Natur," for example, go beyond the imprecision generally characteristic of eighteenth-century usage and vary according to whether they fall into the pre-Kantian, the Kantian, or the post-Kantian and final period of his writing. The essay "On Grace and Dignity," it is said, adds to the repertoire a new, more positive connotation, suggesting a more stable entity, not susceptible to arbitrariness, while still preserving earlier senses.[9] This implies that Schiller's method of expression should not be condemned as idiosyncratic and unsystematic; rather, his use of language brings more to the table than the limitations of conceptual thinking allow. By adding to this the persuasive appeal of rhetoric, Schiller offers his readers more, in his essays, than the systematic philosopher can. Schiller's style does not impoverish clarity; it enriches it.

On the whole, Schiller's usages are far from consistent even within a single work; he consistently takes liberties, and this tendency naturally militates against the ability to establish clear and distinct ideas of a Cartesian variety. A term such as "Anschauung," for example, sometimes means visual perception and sometimes intuition, and his uses of "Vorstellung" divide along similar lines, sometimes purely intellectual, at other times more empirical. For example, when Schiller refers to a "Vorstellung der Vollkommenheit" (*NA* 20:259) he means a "conception of perfection," but in the following sentence he means something concrete, an image: "Man erlaube mir dieß durch eine bildliche Vorstellung zu erläutern" (*NA* 20: 278, With permission, I shall illustrate this with an image). He neither establishes nor holds ɔ any pedantically exact distinction among the terms "Anmut," "Grazie," and "Reiz." Because Schiller is more concerned with the relation of the concepts to one another than with isolating the meaning of a single term, he frequently uses more than one word to designate the same idea.[10] These features of Schiller's style of writing make translation into another language a daunting prospect, fraught with pitfalls. Yet it was a translator who most staunchly defended Schiller on this score. Demonstrating a clear understanding of Schiller's intentional productive tension between form and content, Wilkinson describes the instability and constant revisions of Schiller's vocabulary as analogous to the "perpetual process of the inner life."[11] The other side of this coin is redeemed by Adorno's defense of equivocation as a way of drawing attention to the affinities existing in unlikely places: if the same word is used with two meanings, this subtly suggests a kinship between these designations. In a sense then, the "more" that Schiller offers is a new, hitherto unimagined way of shaping the inherently formless mass of content.[12]

Venue is as important an issue as genre. For those writers who, like Kant, remained uncomprehending of the benefits to be derived from the exchange of ideas and experimentation with literary forms that took place in the regular gatherings of the salons of early Romanticism, an alternative means of presenting their views offered itself in a huge variety of journals. Kant does ultimately appear to have become conscious of the need to satisfy the curiosity of the subscribers by trying to discover what sorts of questions he should be handling in his essays. And Erich Biester, editor of the journal *Berlinische Monatsschrift*, writes to him in diplomatic tone, encouraging him to make his views more widely known through that publication: "gebrauchen Sie bald unseren Mund, um durch uns Ihre Rede ans

Publikum zu bringen"[13] (use us as a mouthpiece to bring your argument to the public). Other writers, notably Wieland and Schiller, were not dependent on the goodwill of an editor; their own experience in journal production intensified their motivation to engage the public, driven as they were by the desire to ensure the success of the publishing enterprises they themselves had launched. A letter from Schiller in 1784, advertising the forthcoming *Rheinische Thalia*, pragmatically recommends the journal to circles where art is appreciated and people are prepared to pay for it (cf. *NA* 23:159).

It is no doubt true that Schiller contributed the lion's share of the most important articles in the *Rheinische Thalia*, a journal he himself edited,[14] and it is likely that essays such as "Über Anmut und Würde" and "Vom Erhabenen" were written with a view to supporting and furthering the journalistic enterprise launched under the title *Neue Thalia*.[15] This was the common belief among Schiller's contemporaries too. Even Humboldt thought that Schiller was driven to write most of his best-known poems purely in order to further the cause of the Musenalmanach.[16] But rather than disparaging the essays as potboilers, the product of a hack, one should surely investigate the spirit that led to the proliferation of this type of journal during the Enlightenment. The Enlightenment's search for reason's truth and its accompanying spirit of propagation for the purposes of moral improvement were the driving force behind these publications.[17] The preface to the 1783 edition of the *Berliner Monatschrift* speaks, in just such terms, of "Eifer für die Wahrheit, Liebe zur Verbreitung nützlicher Aufklärung und zur Verbannung verderblicher Irrthümer" (Zeal for the truth, love for the spread of useful enlightenment and for the banishment of harmful errors). As regards the type and style of contributions to the journal, editors were concerned to offer food for both body and soul. "Gleichwohl werden diese Aufsätze größtentheils aus solchen bestehen, welche den Verstand denkender oder das Herz empfindsamer Leser zu unterhalten geschickt sind" (Nevertheless these essays will for the most part consist of those that are designed to entertain the understanding of readers who think or the heart of those who feel). This is the policy set out for Wieland's periodical, the *Teutscher Merkur* (Vorrede 1773, vol. 1).[18] Schiller aims still more directly at his public in the advertisement for the *Rheinische Thalia* when he undertakes "keine andere Fessel zu tragen als den Anspruch der Welt — an keinen andern Thron mehr zu appellieren als an die menschliche Seele" (*NA* 22:95; to be tied by no other fetter than the world's demands — to make appeal to no other throne than the human soul). This is surely more than financial calculation and concern about possible losses in revenue. By his very choice of words, by setting logical divisions aside in favor of the language of imagery, Schiller both states his intention and carries it out.

Among Schiller's objections to Fichte's submission to *Die Horen* in 1795, under the title "Über Geist und Buchstab in der Philosophie," was, finally, a weakness in the philosopher's presentation of his work. Schiller complains of an unevenness of tone and says that if a work is to have any aesthetic worth, it must demonstrate a relationship between image and concept that he refers to as "Wechselwirkung" (*NA* 27:202; reciprocal interplay). This is not to be confused with the alternation between concept (Begriff) and image (Bild) that often occurs in Fichte's letters. Even for a philosophical contribution to his journal, Schiller demands that the writer pay attention to aesthetic considerations. He requires that an image mold the concept and that the concept in turn shape the image. What is abstract must strive for and attain a concrete clarity, and this is not easily accomplished by simply switching back and forth between two distinct modes. This is Schiller writing as editor of the journal, but it relates directly to his own method of progressive development through restriction and amplification, separation and analogy. Naturally enough, Fichte took offence and retaliated with disparaging references to Schiller's philosophical style: "Sie gehen gröstentheils analytisch, den Weg des strengen Systems; und setzen die Popularität in Ihren unermesslichen Vorrath von Bildern, die Sie fast allenthalben Statt des abstrakten Begriffs setzen"[19] (For the most part you proceed analytically, on the path of a strict system, and you insert popular appeal with your immeasurable store of images, which you put almost everywhere, in the place of abstract concepts). Tellingly, despite his sneering tone, Fichte both acknowledges the philosopher and identifies the intention behind his unsystematic forms of expression and stylistic decisions.

"Das Publikum läßt sich gern alles erklären" (*NA* 27:186; The public likes to have everything explained), Schiller writes to Goethe. He was responding to Goethe's offer to provide explanatory notes to accompany the publication of his "Römische Elegien" and encouraging him to do so. Though it refers to a relatively straightforward practical decision, Schiller's statement resonates with the explicit policies of Enlightenment journals. The public is seen to be receptive, and this makes all the difference: the public has to be receptive if aesthetic judgment is to have an influence on moral disposition. Thus Schiller and Kant part company on the objectivity of aesthetic judgment, on the need to coat logic in an accessible idiom and on the importance of a public forum in which a direct link between aesthetic and moral questions can be forged. In his decisions about layout, his interest in choice of typeface, and his views on scholarly apparatus, Schiller demonstrates his adherence to the principle that the content of a text can be enhanced by a well-planned presentation.[20] Similarly, the rhetorical features of his style, both here and in his plays and poems, smooth the path for readers and make their progress towards enlightenment easier.

Only if one is cognizant of the proliferation of journals in eighteenth-century Germany as a distinguishing feature and tool of the Enlightenment can one see how rhetoric must be a basic component of any discussion of a Schillerian essay on aesthetics. It is a prominent feature of the Enlightenment that aesthetic theory evolves from its prescriptive, regulating function to one that demonstrates the creative process itself. With the shift in emphasis in the plastic arts, as described in Lessing's *Laokoon*, from artistic imitation of the object to a process that leaves a mark on the observer, a parallel change of focus among writers of poetic theory takes place. With this new axis, the passive, descriptive exercise is left behind; the definition of art becomes inseparable from the practice of art, and the reader abandons the role of dispassionate observer. So while the formal art of rhetoric was falling into disrepute among Schiller's generation of writers, the integration of its techniques into their critical writings and its benefits for the range of their influence are tangible.[21]

Since the methods of the rhetorician aim at persuasion, the art of rhetoric is a natural ally of logic. But if this assertion is to make the transition from theory to practical application, there needs to be some evidence that, in Schiller's case for example, he actually expected his work to exercise this type of power. Were the rhetorical devices, so clearly detected on the printed page, also intended as an aid to rhetoric in its literal and practical application, to reading aloud? Perhaps Schiller's actual intentions cannot be established with certainty, but one learns from his correspondence with Goethe that, rather than sending his friend a copy of his "Briefe über die ästhetische Erziehung" before they were due to meet, he anticipated reading them out to him: "so hoffe ich Ihnen meine Briefe noch vorher lesen zu können" (*NA* 27:186; I hope to be able to read my letters to you beforehand). In a letter to Augustenburg in 1793, Schiller explains that a writer who sets out to please his readers must conceal the logic used to guide their minds. He identifies three categories of teacher, and it is not difficult to determine which one he considers himself to be. "Der *dogmatische* Lehrer, könnte man sagen, zwingt uns seine Begriffe auf, der *sokratische* lockt sie aus uns heraus, der Redner und Dichter gibt uns Gelegenheit, sie mit scheinbarer Freiheit aus uns selbst zu erzeugen" (*NA* 26:321; The dogmatic teacher, one might say, forces his ideas on us; the *Socratic* one coaxes them out of us; the speaker and poet gives us the opportunity to produce them out of ourselves with apparent freedom). Schiller conceals his logic, but it is still present underneath. He combines the arts of poetry and rhetoric in his concealment, and the most important element of the disguise is the appearance of freedom.

The story of Schiller's career as an editor of journals is not one of unmitigated good fortune.[22] However, after the closing down of the *Wirtembergisches Repertorium der Litteratur*, after the financial collapse of the *Rheinische Thalia* and its resurrection as *Thalia*, after the unsuccessful plans to join this journal with Wieland's *Teutscher Merkur* and its second resurrection, at the instigation of the publisher Göschen, with the title *Neue Thalia*, and after Schiller's loss of interest in *Neue Thalia* in favor of plans for a new journal, *Die Horen*, we still find the same intentions expressed in the invitation he sent out to potential contributors to this latest enterprise. He neither intends this new journal to interest scholars exclusively, nor wants simply to amuse a popular readership. Schiller's outlook as editor is of a piece with his style in the essays on aesthetics. Truth and beauty must both be present, and if they are, the limitations of merely conceptual thinking have been superseded.

Notes

[1] Andreas Wirth, *Das schwierige Schöne: Zu Schillers Ästhetik; Auch eine Interpretation der Abhandlung "Über Matthissons Gedichte" (1794)* (Bonn: Bouvier, 1975), 119.

[2] Immanuel Kant, "Kritik der Urteilskraft," § 27, *Immanuel Kants Werke* 5, ed. Otto Buek (Hildesheim: Gerstenberg, 1973), 328.

[3] "Der Wert von Denkbruchstücken ist um so entscheidender, je minder sie unmittelbar an der Grundkonzeption sich zu messen vermögen …" (Walter Benjamin, *Ursprung des deutschen Trauerspiels* [Frankfurt am Main: Suhrkamp, 1974], 10).

[4] Theodor W. Adorno, "Der Essay als Form," in *Noten zur Literatur* (Berlin and Frankfurt am Main: Suhrkamp, 1958), 9–49. The English translation is taken from

Theodor W. Adorno, *Notes to Literature,* vol. 1, ed. Rolf Tiedemann, trans. Shierry Weber Nicholsen (New York: Columbia UP, 1991).

[5] Else Löns refers to "Schillers logisch aufgebaute und gegliederte Prosa." See Else Löns, "Schillers Abhandlung 'Über Anmut und Würde' — Bindings Novelle 'Der Opfergang,'" *Deutschunterricht* 1 (1948–49): 57.

[6] Dieter Henrich, "Der Begriff der Schönheit in Schillers Ästhetik," *ZphF* 11 (1957): 539.

[7] Herman Meyer, "Schillers philosophische Rhetorik," in *Begriffsbestimmung der Klassik und des Klassichen,* ed. Heinz Otto Burger, 464 (Darmstadt: WBG, 1972).

[8] Kerry writes: "Schiller at the same time expresses, and in some sense resolves, the dichotomy of which he is aware in himself between the regions of intuition and intellect." See S. S. Kerry, *Schiller's Writings on Aesthetics* (Manchester: Manchester UP, 1961), 4.

[9] Olive Sayce, "Das Problem der Vieldeutigkeit in Schillers ästhetischer Terminologie," *JbDSG* 6 (1962): 151.

[10] Kenneth Parmelee Wilcox, *Anmut und Würde: Die Dialektik der menschlichen Vollendung bei Schiller* (PhD diss., Ohio State, 1977), 21.

[11] Elizabeth Wilkinson, "Reflections after Translating Schiller's *Letters on the Aesthetic Education of Man,*" *Schiller: Bicentenary Lectures,* ed. F. Norman (London: International University Booksellers, 1960), 68.

[12] Adorno, "Der Essay als Form," 36.

[13] Quoted from *Immanuel Kant und die Berliner Aufklärung,* ed. Dina Edmundts (Wiesbaden: Reichert, 2000), 65.

[14] Fritz Alexander Maria Berresheim, *Schiller als Herausgeber der Rheinischen Thalia, Thalia und neuen Thalia und seine Mitarbeiter* (PhD diss., Breslau, 1913), 25.

[15] Michael Groß, *Ästhetik und Öffentlichkeit: Die Publizistik der Weimarer Klassik* (Hildesheim: Olms-Weidmann, 1994), 35.

[16] Mix points to ways in which the form of publication influences the compositions destined for inclusion in it. See York-Gothart Mix, "Geselligkeitskultur, Gattungskonvention und Publikumsinteresse: Zur Intention und Funktion von C. M. Wielands und J. W. v Goethes *Taschenbuch auf das Jahr 1804* und O. J. Bierbaums *Modernem Musen Almanach,*" *JWGV* 97/98 (1993–94): 35–45.

[17] "Der Gedanke, daß der Umgang mit den schönen Wissenschaften und Künsten ersprießliche moralische Wirkungen hervorrufe, zeigt, wie sehr Schiller in der Aufklärung wurzelt." (Manfred Misch, "Schillers Zeitschriften," in *SHb,* 744).

[18] Christoph Martin Wieland, "Vorrede des Herausgebers," *Der Teutsche Merkur* 1 (January 1771): x.

[19] J. G. Fichte, *Gesamtausgabe* (Stuttgart: Frommann, 1970), vol. 3.2, 338–39.

[20] From the letter to Goethe (18 May 1795) about publishing the "Elegien": "Wenn wir zu den Ueberschriften der einzelnen Elegien recht viel Raum übrig lassen, so können wir jede auf einer eigenen Seite anfangen, ohne daß sie zu hoch oben aufhört. Ich werde denselben Druck wie bey den Episteln dazu nehmen lassen" (*NA* 27:186; If we leave a large amount of space above the titles of the individual poems we will be able to begin each one on its own page without having them end too far up).

[21] Gert Ueding, *Schillers Rhetorik: Idealistische Wirkungsästhetik und rhetorische Tradition* (Tübingen: Niemeyer, 1971), 4.

[22] Manfred Misch remarks that Schiller's style was influenced by his involvement in journal publishing. "So unbefriedigend diese Nebenbeschäftigung gewesen sein mag, unergiebig war sie nicht. Abgesehen davon, dass sie Schillers Blick für stilistische Phänomene schärfte" (*SHb*, 744; However dissatisfying this sideline may have been, it was not without profit. Besides the fact that it sharpened Schiller's eye for stylistic phenomena).

Works Cited

Adorno, Theodor W. "Der Essay als Form." In *Noten zur Literatur*. Berlin and Frankfurt am Main: Suhrkamp, 1958. In English, *Notes to Literature*. Vol. 1. Edited by Rolf Tiedemann, translated by Shierry Weber Nicholsen. New York: Columbia UP, 1991.

Benjamin, Walter. *Ursprung des deutschen Trauerspiels*. Frankfurt am Main: Suhrkamp, 1974.

Berresheim, Fritz Alexander Maria. *Schiller als Herausgeber der Rheinischen Thalia, Thalia und neuen Thalia und seine Mitarbeiter*. PhD diss., Breslau, 1913.

Edmundts, Dina, ed. *Immanuel Kant und die Berliner Aufklärung*. Wiesbaden: Reichert, 2000.

Fichte, Johann Gottlieb. *Gesamtausgabe*. Stuttgart: Frommann, 1970, vol. 3.2: 338–39.

Groß, Michael. *Ästhetik und Öffentlichkeit: die Publizistik der Weimarer Klassik*. Hildesheim: Olms-Weidmann, 1994.

Henrich, Dieter. "Der Begriff der Schönheit in Schillers Ästhetik." *ZphF* 11 (1957): 527–47.

Kerry, S. S. *Schiller's Writings on Aesthetics.* Manchester: Manchester UP, 1961.

Koopmann, Helmut. "Denken in Bildern: Zu Schillers philosophischem Stil." *JbDSG* 30 (1986): 118–250.

Löns, Else. "Schillers Abhandlung 'Über Anmut und Würde' — Bindings Novelle 'Der Opfergang.'" *Deutschunterricht* 1 (1948–49): 57–63.

Meyer, Herman. "Schillers philosophische Rhetorik." In *Begriffsbestimmung der Klassik und des Klassichen,* edited by Heinz Otto Burger, 413–67. Darmstadt: WBG, 1972.

Misch, Manfred. "Schillers Zeitschriften." *SHb,* 743–57.

Mix, York-Gothart. "Geselligkeitskultur, Gattungskonvention und Publikumsinteresse: Zur Intention und Funktion von C. M. Wielands und J. W. v Goethes *Taschenbuch auf das Jahr 1804* und O. J. Bierbaums *Modernem Musen Almanach.*" *JWGV* 97/98 (1993–94): 35–45.

Sayce, Olive. "Das Problem der Vieldeutigkeit in Schillers Ästhetischer Terminologie." *JbDSG* 6 (1962): 149–77.

Ueding, Gert. *Schillers Rhetorik: Idealistische Wirkungsästhetik und rhetorische Tradition.* Tübingen: Niemeyer, 1971.

Wilcox, Kenneth Parmelee. *Anmut und Würde: Die Dialektik der menschlichen Vollendung bei Schiller.* PhD diss., Ohio State, 1977.

Wilkinson, Elizabeth. "Reflections after Translating Schiller's *Letters on the Aesthetic Education of Man.*" In *Schiller: Bicentenary Lectures,* edited by F. Norman, 46–82. London: International University Booksellers, 1960.

Wirth, Andreas. *Das schwierige Schöne: Zu Schillers Ästhetik; Auch eine Interpretation der Abhandlung "Über Matthissons Gedichte" (1794).* Bonn: Bouvier, 1975.

Schiller as Citizen of His Time

David Pugh

WHILE IT WOULD BE HARD to maintain that "Über Anmut und Würde" has much in the way of overt political content, the treatise was certainly written at a time of high political tension. In late 1792 and early 1793, Schiller had started drafting a theory of beauty in a series of letters to his friend Christian Gottfried Körner, while at the same time considering an intervention in the trial of King Louis XVI in Paris.[1] It is unknown what precisely he was proposing to say, but it is certain that it would have included a plea to spare the King's life. The trial was arousing a high level of attention in Germany, with opinion shifting away from the sympathy that had originally been shown to the revolutionaries towards a disdain for their apparent descent into lawlessness. With Louis's life at stake, Schiller wrote to Körner on 21 December 1792 of a dual benefit that could result from his (Schiller's) intervention at this time. First, a statement by a prominent foreigner might make an impression on "diese richtungslosen Köpfe" (these disoriented minds). Second, however, Schiller speculated that such a statement might have a positive effect at home as well:

> Außerdem ist gerade *dieser* Stoff sehr geschickt dazu, eine *solche* Vertheidigung der guten Sache zuzulassen, die keinem Mißbrauch ausgesetzt ist. Der Schriftsteller, der für die Sache des Königs öffentlich streitet, darf bei dieser Gelegenheit schon einige wichtige Wahrheiten mehr sagen, als ein anderer, und hat auch schon etwas mehr Credit. Vielleicht räthst Du an mir zu schweigen, aber ich glaube, daß man bei solchen Anlässen nicht indolent und unthätig bleiben darf. Hätte jeder freigesinnte Kopf geschwiegen, so wäre nie ein Schritt zu unserer Verbesserung geschehen. Es giebt Zeiten, wo man öffentlich sprechen muß, weil Empfänglichkeit dafür da ist, und eine solche Zeit scheint mir die jetzige zu sein. (*NA* 26:172)

[Besides, this topic is particularly suitable to permit a defense of the good cause, a defense of a kind that is not capable of abuse. On this occasion, the writer who speaks up openly in the king's cause is permitted to utter a few more important truths than someone else, and he has more credit. You will perhaps advise me to be silent, but I believe that one must not be indolent and inactive on such occasions. If every free-minded person had remained silent, no step would ever have been undertaken for our improvement. There are times when one must speak publicly, because the receptivity is there, and the present seems to me to be such a time.]

This is a tantalizing passage that hints at more than it says, and it indicates that Schiller felt he had to be careful about committing his political thoughts to paper. The background to the letter, however, would certainly have been an ongoing discussion that he and Körner conducted when they met in person. Schiller's discretion here and in the rest of his correspondence, unfortunately, means that we have to guess about the details. Also, the King was executed on 21 January 1793, before Schiller could put his plan into effect, and on 8 February he vented his disgust to Körner: "Ich kann seit 14 Tagen keine *französischen* Zeitungen mehr lesen, so ekeln diese elenden Schindersknechte mich an" (*NA* 26:183; For a fortnight I have not been able to read any French newspapers, so disgusted am I with these miserable thugs). For the rest of the month he devoted himself to his theory of beauty, which he aimed to present in a dialogue to be called "Kallias oder Über die Schönheit," but which survives only in the form of the "Kallias Letters" to Körner. In the spring he turned to "Über Anmut und Würde," which he published in the *Neue Thalia* in June. In the summer, however, he began the series of letters to the Duke of Augustenburg that formed the first draft of the treatise "Über die ästhetische Erziehung des Menschen in einer Reihe von Briefen" (On the Aesthetic Education of Man in a Series of Letters), which was published in the *Horen* in 1795. It was here, and particularly in the letter of 13 July 1793, that he proposed a political significance for his theory of beauty. The apparent turn away from politics on 8 February is therefore not final. If the political references in the "Kallias Letters" and "Über Anmut und Würde" are somewhat sparse, that does not mean that Schiller had banished all thoughts of the political situation from his mind.[2]

Returning to the quoted passage from the letter of 21 December 1792, we must infer that by "die gute Sache" (the good cause) Schiller means what we might call the progressive cause, taken in a very broad sense. His calculation is that, by calling for mercy for the French King, he will be able to earn enough credit with the German authorities to tell some "important truths." What might these truths be? Surely that monarchs who rule wisely and in accordance with the wishes of their subjects do not find themselves in Louis's situation. In order to learn something more specific, we must turn to the letter of 13 July 1793 to the Duke of Augustenburg, which expresses Schiller's aspirations in a negative form. If, he writes, the French Revolution had realized certain goals, which it has not, then he would be willing to lay poetry aside and devote his energies to the construction of "[das] herrlichst[e] aller Kunstwerke, [die] Monarchie der Vernunft" (the most glorious of all works of art, the monarchy of reason). He outlines these unrealized goals as follows:

> wäre der ausserordentliche Fall wirklich eingetreten, daß die politische Gesetzgebung der Vernunft übertragen, der Mensch als Selbstzweck respektiert und behandelt, das Gesetz auf den Thron erhoben und wahre Freiheit zur Grundlage des Staatsgebäudes gemacht worden, so wollte ich auf ewig von den Musen Abschied nehmen. (*NA* 26:261–62)

> [if the extraordinary circumstance had really occurred that political legislation had been entrusted to reason, that man was respected and treated as an end in himself, if law had been placed on the throne, and true freedom been made the foundation of the state structure, then I would want to bid farewell to the Muses for ever.]

Assuming we are right to combine the two passages, then, we can take the "good cause" to consist of a simple list of objectives, all of them fairly standard tenets of the Enlightenment as manifested in political thought: government by laws rather than by men, rationality as the criterion of good legislation, freedom and respect as the portion of the individual citizen. However, as in the letter to Körner of 8 February, Schiller expresses an extreme disillusionment with the way in which events are developing in France: "ich bin so weit entfernt an einen Anfang einer Regeneration im Politischen zu glauben, daß mir die Ereignisse der Zeit vielmehr alle Hoffnungen dazu auf Jahrhunderte benehmen." (*NA* 26:261–62; I am so far from believing in the start of a political regeneration that the events of our time actually take away my hopes of such a thing for centuries). Although he remains vague as to which events he means, we should recall that the Jacobins had staged their coup d'état at the beginning of June and that the Revolution had therewith entered its most radical and bloody phase.

In considering the context of "Über Anmut und Würde," therefore, we have to bear three things in mind: first, Schiller's adherence in principle to the political aspirations of the Enlightenment; second, his conviction that these aspirations were suffering disastrous reverses in France; and third (this perhaps more implied than stated openly), his decision to investigate questions of theoretical aesthetics as a response to the unpromising situation. We thus cannot escape the question whether the absence of political content in the essay represents a flight from politics as such, or whether it rather contains hints of the argument of the "Augustenburg Letters" and their later published version. This argument, as it is normally understood, is that a theoretical analysis of aesthetic concepts can provide the foundation for a form of aesthetic education that in turn, and in the long term, can help to bring about the political objectives of the Enlightenment. To pose the question more bluntly, we need to know whether "Freiheit in der Erscheinung" (freedom in appearance), Schiller's definition of beauty in the "Kallias Letters," is supposed to serve as a means of creating political freedom or as a substitute for it.

In "Über Anmut und Würde," after Schiller has introduced the notion of grace, and as he approaches the exposition of the beautiful soul, which for many readers is the climax of the treatise, he introduces a memorable and suggestive political metaphor. Grace, he tells us, rests on a surprising coincidence of the demands of nature and reason, and can only be explained as a "Gunst" ("favor") shown by the latter to the former. The associations of the term "Gunst," as a gratuitous act of favor shown to a social inferior, seem then to prompt Schiller to illustrate the point by means of a socio-political analogy:

> Wenn ein monarchischer Staat auf eine solche Art verwaltet wird, daß, obgleich alles nach eines Einzigen Willen geht, der einzelne Bürger sich doch überreden kann, daß er nach seinem eigenen Sinne lebe und bloß seiner Neigung gehorche, so nennt man dieß eine liberale Regierung. (NA 20:278)

> [When a monarchic state is run in such a way that, although everything proceeds in accordance with the will of one person, the individual citizen can still persuade himself that he is living according to his own lights and simply following his inclinations, one calls this a liberal government.]

After the lengthy and somewhat arid analyses of architectonic beauty and of the types of movement that are capable of grace, this is a passage that catches our attention.

Schiller returns to the political analogy a few pages later. The human individual, he has told us, consists of two parts, a sensual and a rational one, and these can stand in three relations to each other. The rational can dominate the sensual, the sensual can dominate the rational, or else they can exist in harmony; in Schiller's words, "oder die Triebe des letztern [i.e., des sinnlichen Teils] setzen sich mit den Gesetzen des erstern [i.e., des vernünftigen Teils] in Harmonie, und der Mensch ist einig mit sich selbst" (*NA* 20:280; or the impulses of the sensuous settle into harmony with the rules of the rational and human beings are at one with themselves). Some exegesis follows, in which Schiller explains that neither form of disharmony is conducive to beauty, but he portrays the dominance of sensuality in the most outspoken terms as not only aesthetically but also morally repulsive. However, in order to grasp the ramifications of the passage we should note that Schiller alludes to the realm of artistic production and appreciation in order to explain why the sensual individual is aesthetically displeasing: "auch der *ästhetische* Sinn, der sich nicht mit dem bloßen Stoffe befriedigt, sondern in der Form ein freyes Vergnügen sucht, wird sich mit Ekel von einem solchen Anblick abwenden, bey welchem nur die *Begierde* ihre Rechnung finden kann" (*NA* 20:281; also the aesthetic sense, which is not satisfied with mere matter, and seeks free enjoyment of form, will turn away in disgust at such a sight, in which *desire* alone is accommodated). The moral constitution of the individual, which depends on the balance of forces between reason and sensibility in the soul, is thus analogous to a work of art, which is a balance of form and matter, and will (we can infer) appeal equally to the rational and sensual parts of the spectator's soul. Indeed, in "Über die ästhetische Erziehung des Menschen," Schiller goes so far as to define the two parts of the soul as "form-" and "matter-impulse" ("Form-" and "Stofftrieb"), terms that allude unmistakably to the forming process engaged in by the artist.

The political metaphor reappears now. The domination of the rational and the sensual parts of the soul, Schiller tells us, is reminiscent respectively of a monarchy and an ochlocracy (that is, rule of the mob). He does not give us a political analogue for the state of harmonious balance, but in the light of the earlier passage there can be no doubt that this must be what Schiller has called the liberal state. He thus affirms the idea of this state at the outset of his celebrated critique of Kant's moral theory in the name of nature and grace in "Über Anmut und Würde" (*NA* 282–89), and so, even if only subliminally, the reader must associate Schiller's plea

for a more generous attitude to natural sentiment with the political concept of liberalism.

For many scholars, this association of grace with the term "liberal" has
presented an irresistible temptation, and a temptation that reveals a great
deal about the discipline of Germanistik in the post-1945 period. So overwhelming has been the awareness of the baleful traditions that led to the
German catastrophe that scholars have tended to approach the great writers of the past in a somewhat constrained spirit, asking in effect if a particular author or work must be rejected as belonging to or fostering the
authoritarian and nationalistic culture from which Nazism sprang. In the
case of Schiller, strong attacks came from the Marxist quarter. Friedrich
Engels coined the phrase "überschwengliche Misere" (high-flown
wretchedness) for the idealistic spirit of the later dramas, and Georg Lukacs
attacked Schiller's aesthetic writings as being essentially a diversion of
energy into an irrelevant direction and a compensation for the social revolution that ought to have occurred in Germany but did not.[3] These accusations continue to hang over Schiller's work today. Indeed, even a
non-Marxist might well wonder why Schiller chose to devote six weeks to
an analysis of grace in deportment and beauty of moral character at a time
when, as he well knew, the followers of Robespierre and Brissot were
engaged in a life-and-death struggle for domination of the Assembly, a
struggle whose outcome was fraught with consequences for Germany also.
But discussions by non-Marxist writers, anxious to present their author in
the best possible light, all too often have an apologetic or affirmative character.[4] Rather than a balanced analysis of the socio-political significance of
these writings, which is actually rather ambiguous, what is offered is all too
often a rather hasty and one-sided justification. Selective quotation is preferred to the structural examination of arguments. Textual passages that
seem to support the picture of Schiller the liberal tend to find favor;
passages that cast doubt on this image are all too often ignored. In this
context, it is hardly surprising that the sentence from "Über Anmut und
Würde" comparing grace to a liberal government is quoted again and
again.

If in the remainder of this essay I seek to qualify this affirmative
approach to the passage and the treatise as a whole, it is not because
I wish to damn Schiller as an intellectual precursor of Nazism. Such an
attack would plainly be absurd. Schiller died in 1805, a year before
Napoleon's invasion of Germany. More than anything else, it was the

French occupation from then till 1813 that formed a kind of axis of German history, setting off the nationalistic reaction and founding the German tradition of illiberalism. Schiller lived out his life in the Germany established by the Treaty of Westphalia in 1648. This Germany was weak and provincial, its politics were dynastic and legalistic rather than national and emotional, the aristocracy dominated its society, and its culture was enlightened and (apart from a short patriotic outburst among the literati in the 1770s) cosmopolitan. If we try to see Schiller within this context, then it becomes possible to read his aesthetic writings in a more dispassionate way and with more realistic expectations as to what political stance he could reasonably have taken.

The first thing to be said is that the term "liberal" did not mean the same thing in 1793 as it meant in the mid-nineteenth century, or as it means today. As a political movement of the mid-nineteenth century, liberalism stood for some very specific things, such as free trade, constitutional government, and universal admission to the professions. One looks in vain for such demands in Schiller's works, as indeed one does for references to specific events of the recent past, such as the suppression of the Illuminati in the 1780s or the Duke of Brunswick's invasion of France in 1792. Schiller's interest in politics is in fact of a highly abstract kind, consisting almost entirely of an adherence to general moral principles. This is true even of his outspoken prose dramas of the 1780s, the reputation of which had earned Schiller his honorary French citizenship. True, these plays contain some references to contemporary scandals and abuses, but their political dimension is largely confined to a conventional denunciation of tyranny. Nineteenth-century liberalism was a movement chiefly of the professional and commercial middle classes and was rooted in their interests. A wide gulf separates Schiller from that very different post-1815 world.

In his letter of 13 July 1793 to the Duke of Augustenburg, Schiller offers a diagnosis of the current social crisis, the essence of which is that the upper and lower classes suffer from forms of depravity that are the mirror-image of each other. The lower classes are thus ruled by their anarchic desires while the upper classes suffer from an excess of culture, in particular a one-sided devotion to theoretical culture, which has sapped their character of all energy. This is a view of society as seen when looking down on it from a great height. It is the analysis of a moralist rather than of a social or political thinker, and a moralist of a somewhat priggish kind.[5] Schiller evinces not a trace of sympathy with the lower classes, nor any suggestion

that their condition might be improved by improved civil rights or economic freedom; he has apparently been so shocked by the reports of mob
violence in Paris that he can only see them as a herd of wild animals. On the
other side, Schiller's portrayal of the "civilized classes" as vicious and cyni-
cal seems to be based on the kind of picture of the French aristocracy that
was drawn by Laclos in his great novel *Les liaisons dangereuses*, which he
had read in 1787.[6]

The conclusion to the whole passage is as follows: "Und so sehen wir
den Geist der Zeit zwischen Barbarey und Schlaffheit, Freigeisterei und
Aberglauben, Rohheit und Verzärtelung schwanken, und es ist blos das
Gleichgewicht der Laster, was das Ganze noch zusammen hält." (*NA*
26:264; And thus we see the spirit of the age swaying between barbarism
and self-indulgence, libertinism and superstition, rawness and effeminacy,
and it is merely the *equilibrium of vices* that keeps the whole thing
together.) The pairs of antithetical terms point to the underlying antithesis
of nature and reason, or matter and form, and, as the diagnosis rests on the
accentuation of the antithesis, it comes as no surprise that a fusion of the
opposites is to provide the cure. What is striking therefore is not only the
non-historical and moralizing method of argument but also the way in
which the diagnosis appears dictated, not by an examination of the patient,
but by the appropriate cure, upon which the doctor has evidently decided in
advance. We know that this is so, because in his speech "Was kann eine gute
stehende Schaubühne eigentlich wirken?" (What Can a Good Permanent
Theatre Really Achieve?), which he wrote before the French Revolution in
1784, Schiller put forward essentially the same argument, namely, that
society and the individual both suffer from a division between the upper
and the lower faculties, and that the enjoyment of art can help to bring
about a middle condition that will be beneficial to both. If we are scrupulous,
therefore, we cannot maintain that Schiller has examined the situation in
France with fresh eyes or come to a conclusion as to the way forward based
on the specifics of the new situation. Rather, in his aesthetic essays he is
developing ideas that had occurred to him during the previous decade, and
in doing so he tailors the facts of the political situation to suit his ideas and
not vice versa.

While the metaphors suggest that Schiller's argument has political ramifications, the basic level of argumentation concerns the contemporary discipline of anthropology, or the investigation of the moral and physiological
constitution of the individual.[7] Schiller had been trained in anthropology

while at the Hohe Karlsschule in Stuttgart, and he has it in mind when, in his exegesis of the beautiful soul, he writes: "Die menschliche Natur ist ein verbundeneres Ganze in der Wirklichkeit, als es dem Philosophen, der nur durch Trennen was vermag, erlaubt ist, sie erscheinen zu lassen." (*NA* 20:286; Human nature is a more coherent whole in reality than a philosopher, who can only achieve results through separation, is permitted to reveal). The sentence catches well the realistic and anti-metaphysical tone of the new discipline and its aspiration to build a progressive science of humanity. Anthropology leaned on medical science and hence rejected the scholasticism that pervaded both the official Wolffian philosophy and still, in a different form, the new Kantian one. It asserted a unified human nature as a fact. It was only the philosopher with his academic distinctions and abstractions who carved man up into a collection of fictitious faculties, or into an alleged dichotomy of nature and spirit. Even assuming that Schiller's political terms are merely metaphors prompted by an anthropological argument, the ethos of anthropology suggests that a political program inspired by it would be humane and progressive. It would be directed towards human needs rather than towards high-flown ideals or supernatural fictions, it would not make distinctions between classes or nations, and it would incline towards generosity rather than severity. Even in the absence of statements about political interests or institutions, and even granting the fact that his ideas derive from the 1780s and not from observing the events of the 1790s, we might still feel inclined to allow Schiller the designation of a liberal if we thought that his politics derived from the anthropological way of thinking.[8]

However, a close reading of "Über Anmut und Würde" and the other essays shows us that Schiller was very much in two minds about anthropology and its aspirations.[9] In a flight of rhetorical pathos, he writes: "Dadurch schon, daß sie ihn zum vernünftig sinnlichen Wesen, d.i. zum Menschen machte, kündigte ihm die Natur die Verpflichtung an, nicht zu trennen, was sie verbunden hat." (*NA* 20:284; In that it made him a rational, sensitive being, that is, a human, nature gave the human being notice of his obligation not to separate what it had bound together). The talk here is of anthropological unity not as a fact but as a moral duty, and a nature that dictates such a duty must be a metaphysical entity rather than an object of scientific investigation. This shift of ground goes to the heart of the ambiguity of this essay and of Schiller's thought in general. A few pages later, after he has performed the peripeteia from the advocacy of moral beauty and physical grace to that of moral sublimity and physical dignity, we read the crucial paragraph:

> Es ist dem Menschen zwar aufgegeben, eine innige Übereinstimmung zwischen seinen beyden Naturen zu stiften, immer ein harmonirendes Ganze zu seyn, und mit seiner vollstimmigen ganzen Menschheit zu handeln. Aber diese Charakterschönheit, die reifste Frucht seiner Humanität, ist bloß eine Idee, welcher gemäß zu werden er mit anhaltender Wachsamkeit streben, aber die er bey aller Anstrengung nie ganz erreichen kann. (*NA* 20:289)

> [Human beings do have the task of establishing an intimate agreement between their two natures, of always being a harmonious whole, and of acting with their full human capacity. But this beauty of character, the ripest fruit of humanity, is only an idea that they can vigilantly strive to live up to, yet, despite all efforts, can never fully attain.]

The roles of reality and fiction are here completely reversed. Reality now entails an ineluctable division and conflict between desire and duty, while unity and harmony have now become an idea and a goal banished to the end of history. The proper context for this kind of unification is not the anthropology of the philosophical doctors, which was essentially materialistic, but the nascent "Vereinigungsphilosophie," that is, the transcendental idealism that one associates with the names of Hölderlin, Schelling, and Hegel.[10] Not the least of the many ambiguities of Schiller's philosophical thought is that he ranges freely back and forth across the border separating these two modes, one of which is deeply metaphysical and the other radically anti-metaphysical.

This equivocation has serious consequences for the political implications of Schiller's thought. If reality entails not harmony but an endless conflict between the upper and lower faculties of the soul, then the appropriate political metaphor, and perhaps the reality also, will not be a liberal harmony but strife between upper and lower classes, and the supremacy of reason will be illustrated by the metaphor of a repressive monarchy. This implication is not spelled out in "Über Anmut und Würde" (although it will be in the fourth letter of "Über die ästhetische Erziehung des Menschen"). However, if we revisit a sentence quoted earlier, we can see that not all is well with Schiller's metaphor of a liberal government. Schiller wrote: "Wenn ein monarchischer Staat auf eine solche Art verwaltet wird, daß, obgleich alles nach eines Einzigen Willen geht, der einzelne Bürger sich doch überreden kann, daß er nach seinem eigenen Sinne lebe und bloß seiner Neigung gehorche, so nennt man dieß eine liberale Regierung" (*NA* 20:278; When a monarchic state is run in such a way that, although everything proceeds in accordance with the will of one person, the individual citizen can still persuade himself that he is living according to his own lights and simply following his inclinations, one calls this a liberal government). A liberal government, we notice first of all, is not a distinct kind of state, but rather a manner in which a monarchy can conduct itself. Monarchy, we recall, is the metaphor for the supremacy of reason. A liberal monarchy is one in which people obey the law of reason while being under the illusion that they are merely following their own inclinations. Schiller's sentence makes it clear that despite this liberal government the supremacy of the monarch is unchallenged, and that the citizens have no real power to alter the monarch's decisions. They merely persuade themselves that they are following their own will.

This impression is confirmed in a later use of the term "liberal," where Schiller has introduced the concept of dignity as the demeanor arising from sublime conflict, whereas grace has its origins in beautiful harmony:

> Bey der Würde also führt sich der Geist in dem Körper als *Herrscher* auf, denn hier hat er seine Selbständigkeit gegen den gebieterischen Trieb zu behaupten, der ohne ihn zu Handlungen schreitet und sich seinem Joch gern entziehen möchte. Bey der Anmut hingegen regiert er mit *Liberalität,* weil *er* es hier ist, der die Natur in Handlung setzt, und keinen Widerstand zu besiegen findet. Nachsicht verdient aber nur der Gehorsam, und Strenge kann nur die Widersetzung rechtfertigen. (*NA* 20: 296–97)

> [In dignity, then, the mind conducts itself in the body as *ruler,* because there it has to assert its independence against domineering instinct, which proceeds to action without it, and would like to escape from its yoke. In grace, on the other hand, the mind governs with *liberality,* because it is the mind that sets nature in action here, and it finds no opposition to quell. Leniency is due only to the obedient, however, and only opposition justifies severity.]

The political metaphors here are even more overt than before, and we find ourselves in a Hobbesian world in which despotic rule is the only means of controlling anarchic passions. Liberality emerges here as a kind of post-civil war settlement, that is, as a conciliatory means of governing subjects whose independent will has been crushed and who hence require no conciliation.

All these passages show that, if Schiller is a liberal, it is only in a non-political sense of the word, for with such arguments we are a very long way indeed from modern notions of civil rights or representative government. Schiller's premises are rather, first, that the purpose of the state is to ensure that the citizens act in a morally right way, but second, that the citizens have no right to participate in the state's determination of what is morally right. Despite the apparently progressive references to morality and reason (as opposed to, say, tradition or dynastic loyalty), the citizens remain to all intents and purposes the subjects of a monarchical state. Here we see more than ever that Schiller is a man of his time, for the proper context for such ideas is Enlightened absolutism; that is, the paradoxical form of eighteenth-century rule that, on the one hand, modified feudalism in the direction of princely autocracy, and, on the other, sought to provide modern and efficient government through the work of trained administrators. Schiller, it is fair to say, is a man of the Enlightenment when it comes to the goals of government but not when it comes to its nature or methods, which he sees as a one-way process from the top down. Sovereignty rests on the self-justifying rationality of the state, not on the consent of the governed.[11]

We can gain another perspective on Schiller's position if we look next at his concentration on harmony in the individual personality. Richard Löwenthal has located the birth of the modern intellectual at the turn from the eighteenth to the nineteenth century, as the old estate-based (*ständisch*) society gave way to the bourgeois one, and the newly won freedom came rapidly to appear as a burden or threat:

> Der erste Schrei der Intelligenz war . . . überall der Ruf nach persönlicher Freiheit und Unabhängigkeit. Doch mit dem zweiten protestierte sie bereits gegen den Zerfall der Gemeinschaft ethischer Werte, gegen die Verkrüppelung des Menschen durch die moderne Arbeitsteilung, gegen die Entfremdung der Arbeit zur Ware durch das Lohnverhältnis, kurz, gegen die rasch fortschreitende Ersetzung persönlicher Beziehungen der Menschen durch unpersönliche Markt- und Geldbeziehungen.[12]

> [The first cry of the intellectuals everywhere was . . . the call for personal freedom and independence. But with the second they were already protesting against the dissolution of the community of ethical values, against the crippling of man by the modern division of labor, against the

alienation of labor from the product through the wage relationship; in short, against the rapidly progressing replacement of personal relations between human beings by impersonal relations of the market and money.]

On the strength of his response to Kant's axiom of moral self-determination, Schiller must certainly count as a representative of Löwenthal's first phase: "Es ist gewiß von keinem Sterblichen Menschen kein größeres Wort noch gesprochen worden als dieses Kantische, was zugleich der Innhalt seiner ganzen Philosophie ist: Bestimme Dich aus Dir selbst." (To Körner, 18 February 1793, *NA* 26:191; There has definitely been no greater word ever spoken by a mortal man than this Kantian one, which is simultaneously the content of his whole philosophy: Determine yourself from within yourself).

As for the second phase (which, using the terms of Ferdinand Tönnies, we can summarize as the protest against *Gesellschaft* in the name of *Gemeinschaft*), we must make some distinctions, for Schiller participates in it only in a qualified sense. The economic grievances cited by Löwenthal belong to a period after Schiller's lifetime, while the nostalgia for communal values is characteristic of Herder and the Romantics but cannot be found in Schiller. However, the attack on the division of labor is quintessentially Schillerian, and its locus classicus is the sixth letter of "Über die ästhetische Erziehung des Menschen."[13] While he espouses freedom as a general principle, Schiller is enough of a prophet to see the administrative and technocratic aspect of the emerging society, and he is too much the artist not to be struck by its menaces rather than by its opportunities.

It is important to be clear here. Schiller's protest against this society does not take the form of nostalgia for the mediaeval community, nor does he indulge in calls for an assertive national spirit. Nonetheless, his advocacy of an integrated personality and of art as the source of recreation from the stresses and strains of bourgeois life stills forms part of an unmistakably anti-modern response. This is the side of Schiller's thought that one cannot think of as liberal in any sense beyond a vague generosity,[14] and the predominantly affirmative scholarship since 1945 has been overwhelmingly blind to it. Although he regards freedom as a good thing, Schiller sees the modernity that freedom engenders as a threat; the individual must seek a refuge from its inhuman mechanism in artistic enjoyment in order to preserve his character. Schiller is thus not interested in the opportunities presented by an emancipated society; we discover nothing of the possibilities of individual self-development by the acquisition of skills or property, by activity in a civil or military profession, or by participation in government. His aesthetic education rather points towards the life of isolated self-cultivation as practiced in Baron Risach's house in Stifter's *Der Nachsommer* (*Indian Summer*, 1857), a sterile rentier existence that has been so devastatingly analyzed by Carl Schorske.[15]

To turn finally to the question I asked earlier: should we understand Schiller's theory of beauty as "freedom in appearance" as a means of gaining freedom or as a substitute for it? The point to recall here is that for Schiller freedom is not an unqualified good. As he writes in "Über Anmut und Würde," "Nur im Dienst einer schönen Seele kann die Natur zugleich Freyheit besitzen, und ihre Form bewahren, da die erstere unter der Herrschaft eines strengen Gemüts, letztere unter der Anarchie der Sinnlichkeit einbüßt." (*NA* 20:288; Only in the service of a beautiful soul can nature possess freedom and at the same time preserve its form, since freedom vanishes under the control of a strict disposition and form under the anarchy of sensuousness). When Schiller speaks of freedom, the menace of anarchy is never far off, and this can be exemplified by two of his most famous poems. In his great elegy "Der Spaziergang" (The Walk), historical progress reaches its crisis when humankind breaks its bonds ("Seine Fesseln zerbricht der Mensch"; 139, *NA* 2/1:312[16]), for in so doing it also casts itself adrift from "holy nature" and places itself at the mercy of its unruly passions, which are symbolized by a stormy sea. The ambiguity of freedom is epitomized here perfectly in the line "Freiheit ruft die Vernunft, Freiheit die wilde Begierde" (141; "Freedom!" reason calls, "Freedom!" calls wild desire).[17] Secondly, in "Das Lied von der Glocke" (The Song of the Bell), the forging of the bell serves to epitomize form as the basis for an ordered human existence, which is set against the formless anarchy of revolutionary Paris. Again, the reader is warned against the siren call of freedom:

> Wo rohe Kräfte sinnlos walten,
> Da kann sich kein Gebild gestalten,
> Wenn sich die Völker selbst befrein,
> Da kann die Wohlfarth nicht gedeihn.
> (349–52, *NA* 2/1:237)

[Where raw forces prevail without sense, there no formed structure can exist; when the peoples liberate themselves, welfare cannot flourish.]

In both poems, the loss of form in society rapidly leads to bestialization: in "Der Spaziergang" human nature rages like a tigress (167), in "Das Lied von der Glocke" the call for freedom and equality turns women into hyenas and panthers (362–69). The foundation for these metaphors can be found in "Über Anmut und Würde," where it is repeatedly stated that human beings who cannot resist their natural desires are no different than animals.[18]

Schiller's attitude to freedom, then, is a mixture of devotion and anxiety, a struggle between his love of freedom allied to reason and his horror of unchained passions. Nature, the master concept of the Enlightenment, stands on both sides of the divide, both as "holy nature" and as "raw nature." The pursuit of art and of aesthetic philosophy appears to Schiller to offer a way off the horns of the dilemma, a way to have the one while keeping the other at bay. "Freedom in appearance," as I have argued elsewhere, is an ambiguous formula with complex implications that appear to grant just this.[19] Whether in the individual or in the artwork, beauty as the harmony of form and matter epitomizes the harmony of reason and nature, and Schiller must certainly have intended that it should stand in some causal relation, no matter how distant, to the realization of a free and liberal society. However, his moral austerity and his contempt for the sensual human masses lead him to conclude that, for the foreseeable future, the expression of freedom by aesthetic means is the closest we may approach to that political freedom for which we may be destined but with which we cannot yet be trusted.

Notes

[1] A persuasive account of this episode can be found in Jeffrey High, "Schillers Plan, Ludwig XVI. in Paris zu verteidigen," *JbDSG* 39 (1995): 178–94.

[2] An authoritative recent book sees "Über Anmut und Würde" as "a sort of preparatory study" for the essay on aesthetic education: "The essay ["Über die ästhetische Erziehung des Menschen"] amounts to an attempt to move from the exclusive concentration on the 'beautiful' individual to the level of the whole social sphere." (Robert Norton, *The Beautiful Soul: Aesthetic Morality in the Eighteenth Century* [Ithaca: Cornell UP, 1995], 244.)

[3] See Engels, Review of Karl Grün, *Über Goethe vom menschlichen Standpunkte*, in Karl Marx and Friedrich Engels, *Über Kunst und Literatur*, ed. Manfred Kliem,

1:457–483; here, 468 (Berlin: Dietz, 1968), and Lukacs, "Zur Ästhetik Schillers," in *Probleme der Ästhetik* (Berlin: Luchterhand: 1969), 17–106.

[4] See most recently Peter-André Alt, " 'Arbeit für mehr als ein Jahrhundert': Schillers Verständnis von Ästhetik und Politik in der Periode der Französischen Revolution (1790–1800)," *JbDSG* 46 (2002): 102–33.

[5] See Michael T. Jones, "Schiller Trouble: The Tottering Legacy of German Aesthetic Humanism," *GY* 10 (2001): 239: "Indubitably, in his personal life, Schiller was a moralistic prig, and that moralism significantly colors the whole of his aesthetic writings." I can find little evidence, however, for Jones's contention (for which he cites the support of Dieter Borchmeyer) that Schiller's political thought is indebted to the tradition of natural law.

[6] See his letter to Körner of 22 April 1787. The German translation of the novel had appeared in 1783, a year after the original. *NA* 24:93.

[7] The discovery of this eighteenth-century discipline is the achievement of Hans-Jürgen Schings in his book *Melancholie und Aufklärung* (Stuttgart: Metzler, 1977). Wolfgang Riedel has investigated Schiller's early thought against this background in *Die Anthropologie des jungen Schiller* (Würzburg: Königshausen, 1985). There is now an extensive literature on the subject.

[8] The tendency to think of politics as a form of medicine, however, has its own dangers. See George Sabine's critique of Plato's political thought in *A History of Political Theory*, 4th revised ed. (Hinsdale: Dryden, 1973), 72. On the neglect of the role of institutions in German political thought, see chapter 1 of Harold James, *A German Identity: 1770 to the Present Day* (London: Phoenix, 2000).

[9] See his letter of 19 February 1795 to Goethe, in which he disparages Kant's early essay "Beobachtungen über das Gefühl des Schönen und Erhabenen" (Observations on the Feeling of the Sublime and the Beautiful, 1764) as "bloß anthropologisch" (*NA* 27:146, merely anthropological). The passage implies that Schiller himself was aiming at something higher than this in his own theoretical writings.

[10] See Dieter Henrich, "Hegel und Hölderlin," in *Hegel im Kontext* (Frankfurt: Suhrkamp, 1971), esp. 12–17.

[11] In this respect Schiller does not follow the constitutional traditions of his home, the duchy of Württemberg, with its balance of authority between duke, estates, and privy council. See James Allen Vann, *The Making of a State: Württemberg 1593–1793* (Ithaca: Cornell UP, 1984). In *Enlightenment, Revolution, and Romanticism: The Genesis of Modern German Political Thought 1790–1800* (Cambridge, Mass.: Harvard UP, 1992), 16, Frederick Beiser identifies the commitment to restricting the paternalistic power of the state as the hallmark of early German liberalism: "Paternalism was the doctrine that the ruler has a responsibility to promote the welfare, religion, and morality of his subjects, and that he, not his subjects,

determines the proper form of that welfare, religion, and morality." If that is so, then the state that Schiller envisages in the fourth "Aesthetic Letter" is a paternalistic and not a liberal one.

[12] Richard Löwenthal, "Zwischen Konformismus und Sezession: Zur Rolle der Intellektuellen in Deutschland," in *Der romantische Rückfall* (Stuttgart: Kohlhammer, 1970), 15.

[13] See however Vicky Rippere, *Schiller and "Alienation,"* (Bern: Lang, 1981), who argues that Schiller's argument in letters 5 and 6 is a modification of a commonplace view of the period.

[14] Schiller applies the term "liberal" in that sense to the philosophy of F. H. Jacobi in his letter of 20 July 1795 to Goethe (*NA* 28:11–12).

[15] See the chapter "The Transformation of the Garden" in Carl Schorske's *Fin-de-siècle Vienna: Politics and Culture* (New York: Vintage, 1981), esp. 281–95.

[16] In this discussion of poems, the first number is that of the line.

[17] See also the original line in "Elegie," the first version of "The Walk": "Freiheit heischt die Vernunft, nach Freyheit rufen die Sinne" (145, *NA* 1:264; Reason demands freedom, the senses call for freedom).

[18] For some later examples of animal imagery applied to the passions of the lower classes, see Blackbourn, "The Discreet Charm of the Bourgeoisie: Reappraising German History in the Nineteenth Century," in David Blackbourn and Geoff Eley, *The Peculiarities of German History: Bourgeois Society and Politics in Nineteenth-Century Germany*, 258 (Oxford: Oxford UP, 1984). Blackbourn comments: "Attitudes of this kind were ubiquitous in the bourgeois liberalism of the 1860s, 1870s and beyond."

[19] David Pugh, *Dialectic of Love: Platonism in Schiller's Aesthetics* (Montreal: McGill-Queen's UP, 1996).

Works Cited

Alt, Peter-André. " 'Arbeit für mehr als ein Jahrhundert': Schillers Verständnis von Ästhetik und Politik in der Periode der Französischen Revolution (1790–1800)." *JbDSG* 46 (2002): 102–33.

Beiser, Frederick. *Enlightenment, Revolution, and Romanticism: The Genesis of Modern German Political Thought 1790–1800*. Cambridge, Mass.: Harvard UP, 1992.

Blackbourn, David. "The Discreet Charm of the Bourgeoisie: Reappraising German History in the Nineteenth Century." Edited by Blackbourn and

Geoff Eley. In *The Peculiarities of German History: Bourgeois Society and Politics in Nineteenth-Century Germany*, 176–292. Oxford: Oxford UP, 1984.

Engels, Friedrich. Review of Karl Grün, *Über Goethe vom menschlichen Standpunkte*. In Karl Marx and Friedrich Engels, *Über Kunst und Literatur*, edited by Manfred Kliem, 2 vols., 1:457–83. Berlin: Dietz, 1968.

Henrich, Dieter. "Hegel und Hölderlin." In *Hegel im Kontext*. Frankfurt: Suhrkamp, 1971, 9–40.

High, Jeffrey. "Schillers Plan, Ludwig XVI. in Paris zu verteidigen." *JbDSG* 39 (1995): 178–94.

James, Harold. *A German Identity: 1770 to the Present Day*. London: Phoenix, 2000.

Jones, Michael T. "Schiller Trouble: The Tottering Legacy of German Aesthetic Humanism." *GY* 10 (2001): 222–45.

Löwenthal, Richard. *Der romantische Rückfall*. Stuttgart: Kohlhammer, 1970.

Lukacs, Georg. "Zur Ästhetik Schillers." In *Probleme der Ästhetik*. Berlin: Luchterhand, 1969, 17–106.

Norton, Robert E. *The Beautiful Soul: Aesthetic Morality in the Eighteenth Century*. Ithaca: Cornell UP, 1995.

Pugh, David. *Dialectic of Love: Platonism in Schiller's Aesthetics*. Montreal: McGill-Queen's UP, 1996.

Riedel, Wolfgang. *Die Anthropologie des jungen Schiller*. Würzburg: Königshausen & Neumann, 1985.

Rippere, Vicky. *Schiller and "Alienation."* Bern: Peter Lang, 1981.

Sabine, George. *A History of Political Theory*. 4th revised ed. Hinsdale: Dryden, 1973.

Schings, Hans-Jürgen. *Melancholie und Aufklärung*. Stuttgart: Metzler, 1977.

Schorske, Carl. *Fin-de-siècle Vienna: Politics and Culture*. New York: Vintage, 1981.

Vann, James Allen. *The Making of a State: Württemberg 1593–1793*. Ithaca: Cornell UP, 1984.

Sensuous-Objective: Beauty in the Realm of Human Freedom: On the Language of Concepts in Schiller's Essay "On Grace and Dignity"

Fritz Heuer

SCHILLER'S THOUGHT CONFRONTS US with the proposition that humans only ever reach the unity of human Being*[1] within the realm of the laws of beauty. The task of cultivating beauty results from this. This is as true for art and the artist as it is for man's relationship with himself. Schiller calls this task "Aesthetische Erziehung" (Aesthetic Education), and his essay "On Grace and Dignity" deals with it too. Professor of Universal History at Jena and citizen of his time (*NA* 20:311),[2] Schiller was concerned about the unfolding of the French Revolution and threw out a broad challenge with his "Aufgabe für mehr als Ein Jahrhundert" (*NA* 20:329; task for more than one century) for modern man who, despite having enlightened concepts for everything, has not learned how to understand the realm of his freedom and still needs to grasp that "es die Schönheit ist, durch welche man zu der Freyheit wandert"[3] (*NA* 20:312; it is through beauty that one arrives at freedom). Schiller knows that the formulation of such a plan stretches back as far as those beginnings of thought in the West that gave the first impulse to the formation of our ideas. Ever since Plato, however, the concepts of grace and dignity, aimed at determining the nature of art and beauty, have been as contentious as the methods of inquiry about the essence of man. Schiller takes up the challenge, conscious of the fact that it is the operations of reflection themselves that make the matter so contentious,[4] because they fall short of revealing the unity of the human in the realm of beauty and art.

Schiller's achievement is to redefine the concept of grace in such a way that the definition compels human commitment. This commitment involves man's action in the world of appearances. The subject of our inquiry is twofold: first, what makes grace — together with dignity — binding; second, how does grace, alone and together with dignity, express itself in man as appearance, once man is adequate to such a commitment in the realm of appearance. Schiller devotes the first part of his essay to the concept of grace. He trains the perspective by means of a universal historical testimony. He invokes mythological images and the way they originally imprinted the human mind. He says that a significant unity can be experienced more concisely and completely in such imagery than through reflection, where the concept to explain a phenomenon comes only later — provided thought does not oblige us to confront a paradox. The poet as *poeta doctus* (the erudite poet) understands how the revelatory power of poetic language can have the advantage over reflective thought.[5] However, a universally binding claim can only be deduced from concepts, as Schiller's essay undertakes to do. Critical thought gives concepts a binding orientation; to this belongs the examination of conditions under which it is possible to legitimate the concepts implied in our questioning, with the evidence as to how they can be verified through perception. Critical thinking must, however, also take care that the receptivity to appearances is not inhibited by the orientation towards concepts.[6]

The analytical circumscription of grace as a phenomenon distinct from what Schiller calls architectonic beauty leads to the first definition of concepts. This explains how, in grace, beauty can be related to man's action in the world of appearances: grace is the "Schönheit der durch Freiheit bewegten Gestalt" (*NA* 20:265; beauty of the physique that freedom sets in motion). But grace becomes binding for humans because beauty attests to a duty: "Schönheit [bekundet] eine *Pflicht* der Erscheinung" (*NA* 20: 264). Schiller calls beauty "eine *frühere* Pflicht, weil der Sinn schon geurteilt hat, ehe der Verstand sein Geschäft beginnt" (*NA* 20:264; I refer to a *former* duty because the senses have already passed judgment before understanding begins its work). How can the senses judge and, through this judgment, make something into a duty? How can the senses, with their judgment, possibly even inhibit understanding? In order to understand this one needs to glance at the structure of beauty, at the "Analytik des Schönen" (*NA* 20:261; Analysis of the Beautiful), to which Schiller expressly and emphatically refers, and at the way it is conceived. Even though Schiller never expressly takes this further, it is nevertheless constantly present in his thought and molds his language of concepts.[7] After his encounter with Kant, Schiller knows that the question, "How is man possible as man?"[8] is linked to the idea of freedom in appearance and to its representation in the beauty of the beautiful and in the grace of the human being. The examination of this link is not our task here.[9] But to understand the definitions in the essay "On Grace and Dignity" the connections that make up this link are needed, both for the method and for the binding nature of the consequences. Since the conception of the Analysis of Beauty is indebted to the encounter with Kant's transcendental critique of reason, so also Kant's method, thought patterns, questions, and conceptual formulations, even where Schiller seeks his own path, are present. They form the frame of reference, not only for the commitments that beauty imposes on humans, but also for those deriving from practical and theoretical reason. In the transcendental critique of reason they all apply to the human being.

Since Kant, transcendental means to us that procedure of self-critical reasoning that uncovers and examines laws that condition human existence and that are present through experience but are not made legitimate by it. Thus, the *Critique of Pure Reason* begins by establishing synthetic propositions *a priori,* and Kant then identifies them as the conditions under which objectivity in understanding is possible — a path on which Kant himself establishes what both understanding and critical reasoning can achieve, and where they meet their insuperable limits. Based on the proposition that man's actions are subjected to *a priori* legislation from practical reason as to the intelligible freedom of his Being as Person, critical reasoning establishes a principle that is independent of understanding's attitude towards nature as appearance, but that causes equally unqualified commitment. The preconditions of the beautiful and the sublime are after all a transcendental result of the *Critique of Judgment,* which, unlike the two other Critiques, does not identify a constitutive principle but does open up for man a broader realm of commitment. The path to a comprehensive circumscription of a transcendental result such as pleasure in beauty is, however, the same as in the *Critique of Pure Reason:* even for the first stocktaking, when beauty is encountered, the "Urteilstafel" (list of judgments in tabular form) offers a register of all possible qualifications of statements that judgment can make formal: about quality, quantity, relation, and modality.[10] If the encounter with beauty is observed in the manifestation of pleasure in an object of beauty in the form of judgment, then the precondition shows itself, here as well, as something astonishing. Beauty becomes without a concept (quality) the object of a universal (quantity) judgment necessarily requiring a positive reaction (modality). As far as the relationships between the results of various forms of judgment are concerned, Kant and Schiller draw different conclusions from yet another astonishing observation. One should consider how further questions about the singularity of the objects of aesthetic judgment are posed, arising from the relation of aesthetic judgments and separated from practical as well as theoretical reasoning. The concrete occasion is provided by the human being himself, appearing, in the realm of his duties, as an object of aesthetic judgment, just as Schiller presents him in "On Grace and Dignity." Human beings can either display grace (beauty of movement) or not, irrespective of any physical (architectonic) beauty they may or may not possess. Grace can be combined with dignity but also, as a result of conflicting commitments, it is possible for dignity alone to be present as an expression of humanity in appearance. And both these qualities can be lost if a human falls prey to animal desires. The concrete occasion combines the possibilities of human appearance with the transcendental question about a possible concept of beauty and finally defines the realm in which man can appear beautiful.

Is the fact that beauty is pleasing, without having or being determined by any concept, enough for us to conclude that there cannot be a concept for beauty and that it cannot be derived from a principle, although in our aesthetic judgment it does lay claim to necessarily universal favor? If such a concept could be found, it would at least have to explain from within itself, from the potential principle of its derivation, why beauty cannot become susceptible to determination through any judgment whatsoever and why it nevertheless imposes a necessary duty on human beings. This condition for the binding nature of concepts and language is perhaps logically-ontologically surprisingly paradoxical.[11] But Schiller does search in this area, and here too he is able to follow Kant's analysis of the relation of aesthetic judgments. Both the result of our behavior towards beauty encountered and the form of moral judgment put forth by practical reason exclude the possibility that the functional nature of the morally good could control pleasure in beauty, in accordance with the principle of practical reason. A judgment that pronounces something beautiful or sublime is aesthetic and not moral. Schiller explains this distinction again, thoroughly and decisively, in his essay "Über das Pathetische" (On the Sublime). What makes the aesthetic judgment binding is not founded on the binding nature of moral judgments of practical reason. Aesthetic judgment, however, is neither immoral nor the existential alternative to moral judgment — as it might be in the case of Kierkegaard or Nietzsche — but a distinct aesthetic commitment — this is valid for Schiller's understanding of grace as well — and thus morally indifferent.[12] How the two relate to each other needs to be established by a transcendental phenomenology of human appearance in the world, with reference to the central question: how is a human possible? Schiller finds himself on this path in his essay "On Grace and Dignity."

This is the main point where persistent reservations about Schiller's philosophy come to the fore: in the end, must not a commitment that follows from the autonomy of beauty found[13] an excessively modest humanism in the face of more extensive challenges from the philosophy of the West or, as a theory of art, turn towards a merely subjective view of aesthetics?[14] However, these reservations do not reach the level of Schiller's inquiry, which is the direction we must pursue. Where is the binding nature of beauty realized? How should we understand objectivity in the relation of the aesthetic judgment to something encountered as beautiful that cannot in any way be controlled by a defining concept? It is impossible to overlook the fact that the bond between aesthetic pleasure and a beautiful object relates to the indeterminable receptivity of human senses. It does not relate to the nervous impulses common to all living creatures, which human sense organs like the eye and ear or the feeling hand transfer. That part of Kant's transcendental finding was also of interest to other eighteenth-century theoreticians.[15] All theories of beauty and art in the eighteenth century, even including Kant's, have in common the view that the enjoyment of beauty always relates to an object: "Wir weilen bei der Betrachtung des Schönen"[16] (We linger at the sight of beauty). This stands in unmistakable contrast to the enjoyment of what pleases, which can only be ascertained as a subjective judgment, orientated towards pleasure experienced by an individual, or to a stimulus.[17] In contrast to fulfilled desire, receptivity to beauty remains bound to the independently lasting presence of the thing that offers itself in various forms of encounter — and brings to light, perhaps in a more original way, how an object reveals itself to humans. The distinction between love and desire that Schiller establishes as the modifications of human receptivity is laid out here. Not only does Schiller part company with Kant on the interpretation of the remarkably stable receptivity of human senses towards an object like beauty, but the paths of all eighteenth-century attempts to define these terms diverge. The distinction between art and knowledge,[18] under discussion since Plato, is contentious. This applies to questions posed by art theory and anthropology in the Enlightenment as a whole and in particular to the sustainability of Schiller's attempt to validate the revelatory power of what is encountered in the sphere of the beautiful and of art as well as the receptivity to beauty that opens up human Being, as opposed to the means of reflection.

Schiller organizes the various approaches to the question concerning the amazing phenomenon of beauty and humans' own receptivity to it in four positions that can be compared with one another. These are the four possibilities of interpreting man's relation to an encounter with beauty, either through his particular sensuous receptivity or through reason: sensuous-subjective; subjective-rational; rational-objective or sensuous-objective. The last characterizes his own answer, the second, Kant's; an example of the first is Edmund Burke, of the third, Gottlieb Alexander Baumgarten. As Schiller says at the beginning of the Kallias-Briefe, addressed to Körner (25 January 1793), each of the first three theories "hat einen Teil der Erfahrung für sich und enthält offenbar einen Teil der Wahrheit; und der Fehler scheint bloß der zu sein, daß man diesen Teil der Schönheit der damit übereinstimmt, für die Schönheit selbst genommen hat" (NA 26:176; is validated by a part of experience and evidently contains a portion of the truth; and the mistake seems simply to lie in taking a particular component of beauty, which corresponds to that, to be beauty itself). If this were examined in detail, this would be the answer to how Schiller was able to combine the enlightenment problems he was familiar with, in a way he himself clearly claims to have done, with Kant's transcendental thought. For this, however, Schiller himself had to see that a transcendental interest is at work in the new inquiry into phenomena and the concept of beauty and art as well as man's own sensuousness: how can the organs of cognitive ability be compatible with the sense for beauty within the conditions of human capabilities? Or, asking from the viewpoint of the phenomena: What element in mankind's appearance can only be seen as an expression of the organic, of physical life as opposed to those movements that command our attention through grace? The analyses of man as a phenomenon in "On Grace and Dignity" focus on this question.

This transcendental interest in the singular independence of beauty first brings into view all objects disclosed in the sphere of human being. The interest is directed towards man's receptivity for such a sphere based on the ability to remain in the presence of whatever senses like the eye and the ear reveal to sight and hearing.[19] The human senses are organs of receptivity and as such they belong to what Schiller teaches us to see as "die höchste aller Schenkungen, als die Schenkung der Menschheit" (*NA* 20:378; the highest of all gifts, the gift of humanity).

> Die Natur selbst ist es, die den Menschen von der Realität zum Scheine emporhebt, indem sie ihn mit zwei Sinnen ausrüstete, die ihn bloß durch den Schein zur Erkenntnis des Wirklichen führen. In dem Auge und dem Ohr ist die andringende Materie schon hinweggewälzt von den Sinnen, und das Objekt entfernt sich von uns, das wir in den tierischen Sinnen unmittelbar berühren. Was wir durch das Auge *sehen,* ist von dem verschieden, was wir *empfinden;* denn der Verstand springt über das Licht hinaus zu den Gegenständen. Der Gegenstand des Takts ist eine Gewalt, die wir erleiden; der Gegenstand des Auges und Ohrs ist eine Form, die wir erzeugen. (*NA* 20:400)

> [It is nature itself that elevates man from reality to appearance by equipping him with two senses that lead him through appearance alone to knowledge of the real. The invasive matter has already been rolled away from the senses, in the eye and the ear, and the object that we touch directly with our animal senses removes itself from us. What we *see* with our eyes is different from what we *feel,* because our understanding leaps over the light to the objects. The object of touch is a force that we experience; the object of the eye and the ear is a form that we create.]

In a way Schiller turns Plato around when he has humans lifted up to the images of the senses in the sphere created from and as appearance.[20] The "einseitige Nötigung der Natur beim Empfinden" (*NA* 20:378; one-sided compulsion nature exercises in sensation) removes something from the things offered to man as objects on this high level. What disappears in this one-sided compulsion for which we, as sensuous beings, are just as receptive, and how is this departure, which, in Schiller's words, pulls us down, experienced? What disappears is our apparent, and yet true, sensuous-objective distance from what we have in view or what the ear retains, for example in the case of the voice of a bird. The removal of this distance, however, hurts the eye if we go too close to the object or if this object itself penetrates our eyes with too bright a light. Plato explains thought-provokingly in his cave image how, at first, the prisoner's eyes hurt when he is released from his bonds and turns — in an opposing direction — towards the source of light and the eternal laws of light production. We "erleiden" (suffer), says Schiller, whose attention to phenomena in both directions is receptive and free, from the "Gegenstand des Takts" (object touched), a painful feeling; we feel the pain of being touched as "eine Gewalt" (a force). But when the ear follows a melody and is responsive to thirds, it feels no pain, and even if it takes exception when the minor third in the cuckoo's song is not a pure one, what presents itself to the human ear as well as its correction by means of the human voice are a far cry from the feeling of pain. Only when loudspeakers assault our ears and the pain prevents us from understanding anything, or when the intensity of a shining light hurts and blinds our eyes do we reach the place where nature as appearance becomes accessible to the concepts of understanding and controllable for its operations in the manner specified by the natural sciences. This is the place where — if we think in Fichte's categories — the I defines itself as being determined by the not-I and guarantees transcendental subjectivity for itself in the act of recognizing its object and its own unity, and, to speak more casually, it is the moment where "that reality" catches up with us again out of the elevated realm founded and reserved for human beings by the original gift of beauty. Does Schiller mean to say that man can only reach knowledge when he is disrupted in his sojourn with the gifts of the senses in the realm of his "absoluten Eigentumsrecht" (NA 20:401; absolute right of possession)?[21] But that would again mean, in an irrelevant debate for Schiller, wanting to decide between art and knowledge, where critical reasoning should in fact separate heterogeneous areas from each other and establish in which heterogeneous commitments man finds himself. If, as grace may show, humans are beholden to the law of beauty for the sphere in which freedom is represented, but have no control over beauty, they remain all the more dependent on knowing the extent to which they can really be certain of themselves. This is so that, by being attentive to all directions, they can preserve and not obstruct the open sphere of receptivity. In any case it is worth remaining attentive to the ontological double meanings of sensuous and of objective, which have their basis in human Being.

Reflection, consciously, independently, and also with curiosity, finds its way from the world of appearance as presented to the human senses, with the aid of the categories of knowledge and the knowable, in the forms of space and time to that place where "[wir] die andringende Materie . . . in den tierischen Sinnen unmittelbaren berühren" (NA 20:400; the penetrating matter comes into direct contact with our senses). This is where nature becomes accessible as appearance by means of the concepts of objective knowledge. The senses, by which "die Natur . . . den Menschen von der Realität zum Scheine emporhebt" (*NA* 20:400; nature raises man from reality to appearance) lead him "durch den Schein zur Erkenntniß des Wirklichen" (*NA* 20:400; through appearance to knowledge of what is real) as well.[22] We are well aware of this and, with reflection, we come to agree on how to isolate that sensitive place with mathematical and scientific precision as the place where we encounter the data of perception. We learn to banish it from the human body as a source, among others, of stimulation to a distance measurable in time and space; to simulate and operate what has become susceptible in our feelings with a technical experiment, turning it into an object of scientific knowledge. We distance ourselves on this path from the light in which man, in the sphere of aesthetic appearances, has the world before him that is revealed to his humanity. We are, however, equally equipped to enter the dark operating rooms[23] in which experience gains self-certainty from experimentation and in which only the inquiring mind, holding to the laws that regulate the whole of nature, provides a reliable and controllable light. There is no way to explain or even reconstruct, on the basis of what knowledge has made accessible or from the Organon or the logical system it uses, what the senses, as active organs in the sphere of human receptivity, reveal as aesthetic appearance or what happens, for example, when the eye feasts on a cherry blossom or the ear on a melody. But this is neither necessary nor sensible.[24] Human receptivity is at all times present and open toward both paths, which are strictly separate, and on one of which the technically dominated world continues to develop as a habitat at our disposal. On both paths Schiller and Kant recognize that humans are bound by laws, insurmountable and inaccessible.

The juxtaposition of the results of a transcendental anthropology, a transcendental theory of knowledge, and a transcendental foundation for a moral doctrine, as well as their cooperation in the conceptual language of receptive, interested, challenged, and committed people requires the diligent attention of a morphologist, keeping in mind man's tendency to lose, among his many activities, his orientation and his open receptivity. The century of European Enlightenment became aware of the physicality peculiar to humans and of the receptive human senses and the disposition they influence and, even in experimentation with models of cognition,[25] it paves the way for inquiries to be taken up by twentieth-century phenomenology. Schiller, as a physician in training with a group of philosophical doctors, had this focus early on.[26] The morphologist within Schiller the doctor, then anthropologist, then artist and historian and art historian, also became a stimulating partner with whom Goethe could discuss his morphological researches, which are indebted to Kant's *Critique of Judgment*. Such morphologically inspired investigations into transcendental findings demand sharp and precise conceptual structure no less than scientific analyses that only concern themselves with whatever can be used as an instrument to formalize ways of control over what can be controlled. This even applies to language itself insofar as it can be presented as a measurable achievement. The morphologist who arrives at this transcendental phenomenology will keep an open sphere in mind where questions about theoretical and practical reason[27] challenge and move human receptivity even in what is hoped for. Two questions remain for the understanding of Schiller's interest. First: what is available to man in the sphere to which he alone has access, where, as in the area of aesthetic appearances, a "right of ownership" (*NA* 20:401) is granted to him alone, and how, to what advantage, and up to which point can he move within it? Second: how can human receptivity be called into play in such heterogeneous ways, without losing the feeling of one's own unity? For the second question one should explore how love, respect, and desire as modes of human receptivity coexist and determine human feeling and can fulfill it but also tear it apart. Let us begin here.

What is human receptivity? The usage of this term seems so obvious that we can easily forget to ask the question. This is surprising, since there is something that is well worth pursuing hidden in the talk of the openness of human receptivity. The receptivity of seeing and hearing obscures the receptivity of the nerves, of which we can also become aware, the receptivity of feeling for the sublime can in turn obscure the receptivity of our knowledge about a physical danger posited by the thing observed, and vice versa. And if the transcendental theory of knowledge forces the comprehension of receptivity from the adoption of the substrate of objective knowing through the spontaneity of understanding, Kant keeps in mind that the path to the accessible object of understanding is tied to the forms of perception, in space and time, that belong to human receptivity. *Receptiveness,* in ascertaining the accessibility of the object of knowledge in the forms of understanding, and *receptivity,* which makes humans open to what unites them and to each other, clearly stand at that transcendental distance from each other at which Schiller regards aesthetic appearance and reality. Anyone wishing information about the usage of the term can find it in the same source Kant and Schiller may have consulted: the article on "Empfangen" in Johann Christoph Adelung's *Grammatisch-kritisches Wörterbuch der Hochdeutschen Mundart:* "Von solchen Veränderungen, die sich aus dem Innern eines Dinges selbst entwickeln, ist nur allein bekommen, niemals aber empfangen üblich"[28] (Of the types of change that develop of themselves from within a thing, only *get* is customary, never *receive*). This noteworthy observation is no longer of interest in Jacob and Wilhelm Grimm's extensive early nineteenth-century work, the *Deutsches Wörterbuch.*[29] How could it escape attention? As the European Enlightenment drew to an end, the new view of freedom as absolute self-existent spontaneity is no longer interested in anything that keeps freedom within the bounds of human receptivity.[30] In looking at Kant's and Schiller's usages it is worth noticing that man, who is receptive to laws that open up the sphere of human Being and intelligible freedom in the responsibility of personhood, possesses neither the right of access nor the disposition to integrate, as a means of control over the self, what, in the objects of his respect and love, presents itself to his receptivity. Blind access and violent integration would be the form in which everything living proceeds, when, for the purposes of self preservation, it assimilates something in order to satisfy a desire. Man cannot escape such bare necessities of living, but even in the fluctuation of nervous tension may not be lost to the unity of consciousness.[31] But this form of unity of apperception does not reveal the unity of human being. Man's receptivity cannot and should not be thought about as an element of the theory of knowledge. Simple receptivity is a possible abstraction for man, but one that allows the conditions under which living is possible to be understood and controlled in the subsumption of what answers to impulses. The receptivity of man himself, however, does not reveal itself in this way. It can be felt and known in the way in which duties imposed by the status of humanity fill his mind with feelings like love and respect when he subjects and submits himself with respect or obedience to what he encounters as laws and appearances in the realm of the human world.[32]

Kant constantly keeps the phenomenality of human receptivity in view. All commitments bestowed on man, which Kant prefers to think about from the perspective of practical reason, apply to this human receptivity that no one can be obliged to possess, because "jeder Mensch [sie] hat"[33] (everyone has it). Everyone has it but not because of their own doing. It is all the more remarkable that there are no studies of this fruitful aspect of the concept, that Rudolf Eisler's *Kant-Lexikon* omits it, and that no article is devoted to it in the comprehensive *Historisches Wörterbuch der Philosophie*.[34] *Empfänglichkeit* is not synonymous with *Rezeptivität*, a term used in the special context of the theory of knowledge. Kant and Schiller still see receptivity as related to human freedom, a meaning which is later lost. The much needed conceptual and historical study of the concept of receptivity in Kant and Schiller cannot be undertaken here. But it has become clear how respect, love, and desire emerge as the three fundamental modifications of human receptivity in Schiller's analysis in "On Grace and Dignity." And if one pursues this thought one understands why Schiller draws attention so emphatically to the danger of warding off receptivity with rational principles.[35] That this is also true for practical reasons with regard to the receptivity to beauty is the one point at which Schiller's explanation of beauty differs from Kant's.[36] For Schiller the openness of the human senses is registered in this receptivity to fulfillment from an encounter, and to lingering with it as a way of experiencing the unity of human Being, without wishing to make this into an act of self-determination.[37] It does not make much sense, in the face of the moral sentiment of respect, to be suspicious of this purely human receptivity for beauty and for man represented with grace and dignity in his freedom, a receptivity that fulfills itself as love, because love is not accompanied by the consciousness of a duty to be obediently fulfilled.[38] Schiller makes one sensitive to the implications of the problem, as he does at the beginning of the essay, by using a mythical image, this time from the Old and New Testaments: why are the children of the house preferred to the servants, since it cannot be because of the obedience that one owes to the Lord and that children freely produce from the spontaneity of their love?

One basic principle of Schiller's analysis of beauty can be explained with reference to this question by a simple thought. Man cannot fully understand what he produces out of pure love, because the mere attempt would give rise to another side of his receptivity, receptivity to obedience.[39] However, when respect for the moral law fills humans with the feeling of the freedom of their personhood, in the responsibility for decisions of conscience, then they know themselves to be free, in their obedience, of everything that would otherwise bind them to the world of appearances. They know themselves only as a member of that spiritual realm, closed to the world of appearances. Precisely this extreme situation, marked by the pathetic and the sublime, in which man is ready to leave the sphere of his existence, with dignity, in the free obligation to uphold the law as his Lord, points to the fact that even behind his connection with this sphere within which he is able to appear, there is an imperative of thought. Reason does not have to provide this itself. Nevertheless reason is beholden to the gift of this sphere. Schiller identifies freedom in appearance as a principal imperative of thought as the concept of beauty. He goes a step further than Kant's *Analytik des Schönen* here, the critical findings of which he does not, however, abandon. His concept designates an idea necessary for pure reason, which establishes the structure of representation of beauty in appearance and at the same time provides the rule for this representation: beauty can only offer itself as an object in aesthetic appearance, in other words, in the sphere whose openness only man is receptive to and under the condition that representation of freedom in appearance refuses every determination that could rationally occur when subsumed into a concept. In the representation of beauty, then, there lies an imperative to which man is receptive and which regulates its commitments to the area to which nature has raised him, by equipping him with particular senses. What is up to man in this receptivity — the question finally to be answered with a view to the analysis of beauty — is achieved in the commitments of "seines absoluten Eigentumsrechts" (his sovereign right of possession) in the sphere of aesthetic appearance (*NA* 20:401). He is entitled and obligated to maintain the purity of the sphere that belongs to beauty alone.

> Dieses menschliche Herrscherrecht übt er aus in der Kunst des Scheins, und je strenger er hier das Mein und Dein voneinander sondert, je sorgfältiger er die Gestalt von dem Wesen trennt, und je mehr Selbständigkeit er derselben zu geben weiß, desto mehr wird er nicht bloß das Reich der Schönheit erweitern, sondern selbst die Grenzen der Wahrheit bewahren; denn er kann den Schein nicht von der Wirklichkeit reinigen, ohne zugleich die Wirklichkeit von dem Schein frei zu machen.
>
> Aber er besitzt dieses souveräne Recht schlechterdings auch nur in der Welt des Scheins, in dem wesenlosen Reich der Einbildungskraft, und nur, solange er sich im Theoretischen gewissenhaft enthält, Existenz davon auszusagen, und solange er im Praktischen darauf Verzicht tut, Existenz dadurch zu erteilen. (*NA* 20:401)

[He exercises this human right of governance in the art of appearance, and the more strictly he differentiates between yours and mine, the more carefully he separates form from substance and the more independence he is able to grant it, the more he can not only extend the sphere of beauty, but also preserve the limits of truth. This is because he cannot purge appearance of all reality without releasing reality from appearance.

However, he holds this free right only in the world of appearance, in the insubstantial realm of imagination, and only insofar as he conscientiously refrains from expressing its existence in theoretical terms, and as long as he refuses to grant it existence in practice.]

If beauty is to be represented in the movements and deeds of man himself, then Schiller's analyses in "On Grace and Dignity" make clear what the strict division of "yours from mine," the careful separation of "form from substance" demand from the "human right of governance" in the "art of appearance."[40] Man is independent in his movements and in what he does. The beauty of grace can, however, only show itself according to its own rule and consequently must come about by "permission of the mind" (*NA* 20:278). Schiller calls this type of being in nature's formations and in art in the "sphere of beauty" sensuous-objective. Where it is possible to "purge appearance of reality" or to keep it pure, the object must thus become evident by its own means in a purer form within beauty, and arouse the human senses that are receptive to it and bind them to itself.[41] Where beauty presents itself as "a fact to our senses"[42] the "free right" of the ruler "in the world of appearances" is at liberty to withstand reflection's advance. What opens up to the receiver as the spontaneity of someone else's freedom then remains closed to such invasion. The extension of the realm of aesthetic appearance elevates man above his mere function in a modern reality governed by the strict laws of method to an aristocratic level where his humanity is represented, and secures him in it, just as beauty itself occurs on an aristocratic level that demands respect.[43] The objects presented as appearances remain accessible to beauty and, in accordance with another standard, also to a reflection that is acquainted with reality. But the movements possible for man in the sphere of beauty and art are not amenable to control, as reason, operating in a heterogeneous reality, requires. Rather, the attempt is to make what we call "reality" "von dem Schein frei" (free from appearance). Sensitivity towards beauty accomplishes this too, as Schiller explains, when it purges reality of appearance. Everyone knows what it means to maintain a pure tone or to play a pure interval, or to say "die Sonne scheint" (the sun shines) and no one would say "die Sonne scheint nur so" (the sun only appears this way). So as not to be blinded by illusion on the path "durch den Schein zur

Erkenntnis des Wirklichen" (through appearance to knowledge of reality) reason needs firmer guidance. This is what Schiller sees as the contribution of Kant's critique of reason.

Translated by Jane V. Curran

Notes

* Translator's note: The German original has the unusual spelling "MenschSein" and later "PersonSein" which will be translated as "being as Person."

[1] There is no basis in Schiller for this way of writing. It indicates that Schiller's question about the unity of man cannot be deduced from the metaphysical concept of being.

[2] At the height of the European Enlightenment, Schiller, watching the progress of the French Revolution and with a glance at Rousseau, whose distinction between a wild man and a Barbarian he knew, asks "woran liegt es, dass wir immer noch Barbaren sind?" (why is it that we are still Barbarians?).

[3] The lines "Was wir als Schönheit hier empfunden, / Wird einst als Wahrheit uns entgegehn" (What we perceive as Beauty here on earth, / Will someday come towards us as the Truth) from the early poem "Die Künstler" ("The Artists") seem to have been revised.

[4] Anyone trying to offer help in reading Schiller's language of concepts soon has the sensation of constructing hurdles where the power of a poet's language seems a steady guide. In this respect a negative reading like Käte Hamburger's can be beneficial in the sense that it incites one to read Schiller's text with care. There is an appeal to start rereading so as to be clear about how much of the European Enlightenment, gathered behind Schiller's thought, with its particular perspective on humans, has been buried in the meantime. On K. Hamburger's arguments see Kenneth Parmelee Wilcox, *Anmut und Wuerde: Die Dialektik der menschlichen Vollendung bei Schiller* (Frankfurt am Main: Peter Lang, 1981), 118. Dialectic as a pattern of thought in Hegel's sense, however, seems to me to be incompatible with Schiller's thinking.

[5] See Karl-Heinz Volkmann-Schluck, *Kunst und Erkenntnis*, ed. Ursula Panzer (Würzburg: Königshausen & Neumann, 2002), 152–89.

[6] For Schiller, as for Goethe, the *Critique of Judgment* is supplemented by the *Critique of Pure Reason*. Schiller confronts this problem at length in the 13th Letter of *On the Aesthetic Education of Man* (*NA* 20:349–50).

[7] Klaus L. Berghahn has written an unsatisfactory commentary that refutes the concepts and their conceptual coherence. See the appendix to *Friedrich Schiller: Kallias*

oder über die Schönheit; Über Anmut und Würde, ed. Klaus L. Berghahn (Stuttgart: Reclam, 1994), 137–73. Berghahn is apparently unaware of the studies by F. Heuer, "Zu Schillers Plan einer transzendentalphilosophischen Analytik des Schönen," *Philosophisches Jahrbuch* 80 (1973), 90–132, and *Darstellung der Freiheit: Schillers transzendentale Frage nach der Kunst* (Cologne: Böhlau, 1970).

[8] See Karl-Heinz Volkmann-Schluck, *Die Kunst und der Mensch: Schillers Briefe über die ästhetische Erziehung des Menschen* (Frankfurt am Main: Klostermann, 1964), 11, 19.

[9] Schiller's theory in the classical period presupposes Kant's transcendental critique of reason in the context of all three Critiques. Cf. F. Heuer, "Zu Schillers Plan einer transzendentalphilosophischen Analytik des Schönen." Schiller is not unprepared for his encounter with Kant; Kant helps him answer questions already posed. Fundamental and indispensable to research on this topic are two studies by Wolfgang Riedel, *Die Anthropologie des jungen Schiller: Zur Ideengeschichte der medizinischen Schriften und der "Philosophischen Briefe"* (Würzburg: Königshausen & Neumann, 1985) and *Jacob Friedrich Abel: Eine Quellenedition zum Philosophieunterricht an der Stuttgarter Karlsschule (1773–1782); Mit Einleitung, Übersetzung, Kommentar und Bibliographie*, ed. Wolfgang Riedel (Würzburg: Königshausen & Neumann, 1995).

[10] Immanuel Kant, *Kritik der reinen Vernunft*, A 67–83, B 92–129; *Prologomena zu einer jeden künftigen Metaphysik*, § 2; *Kritik der praktischen Vernunft*, part I, section 2: "Von dem Begriffe eines Gegenstandes der reinen praktischen Vernunft," *Kritik der Urteilskraft*, §§ 1–22. Anyone uncertain about whether Schiller's acquaintance with Kant's method and language of concepts was sufficiently professional is referred to the letter to Goethe, 19 January 1798, especially *NA* 20:188–91, which provides an incentive to look back at the relevant passages in Kant.

[11] Schiller knows that thought encounters the same difficulty when it takes up the transcendental dimension of anthropological questioning. Thus his callous announcement in the letters *On the Aesthetic Education of Man* is not surprising: "Inwiefern in demselben Wesen zwei so entgegengesetzte Tendenzen zusammen bestehen können, ist eine Aufgabe, die zwar den Metaphysiker, aber nicht den Transzendentalphilosophen in Verlegenheit setzen kann. Dieser gibt sich keineswegs dafür aus, die Möglichkeit der Dinge zu erklären, sondern begnügt sich, die Kenntnisse festzusetzen, aus welchen die Möglichkeit der Erfahrung begriffen wird" (*NA* 20:371; The task of determining how two such different tendencies can be present together in the same being places the metaphysician, but not the transcendental philosopher, in a difficult position. The latter does not pretend to explain the possibility of things, but is content to establish the knowledge from which the possibility of experience is understood). Critical thought knows it is

strong enough to maintain the paradoxical contiguity of heterogeneous necessities, as becomes evident in a morphological-analytical phenomenology of the human being, and to establish the laws within the limits of which human beings should operate if they do not wish to place their capabilities at risk.

[12] The sublime expression of "freedom in appearance" is aesthetic as well. Cf. *NA* 20:213–21.

[13] This is how Heidegger sees it in "Über den Humanismus: Brief an Jean Beaufret," in *Wegmarken* (Frankfurt am Main, 1967), 145–94. Heidegger connects the concept of humanism to metaphysics (see especially 174), for which there is no room in Schiller's thought. In Schiller's inquiry, human being is revealed in open receptivity, from which being, as defined by subjective thought, has shut itself off, with a decision that can be traced back historically to Plato. The morphological glance at this form of thinking, which establishes identity with an indefinite definition of everything excluded from such newfound oneness, is revealing. Troglodytes satisfied with the illusory appearance of shadows, as denounced by Plato in Book VII of the *Republic,* are not worthy of any further attention from the new community, who leave the cave united in the strength of thinking about what obstructs rays of light from the entrance of the cave. What Plato sets in motion in his cave image then becomes comparable with the recent discussion by Jan Assmann in *Die Mosaische Unterscheidung oder der Preis des Monotheismus* (Munich and Vienna: Hanser, 2003).

[14] I have already pointed to the weakness of such a view in *Darstellung der Freiheit,* 98–99, especially note 54. Schiller's concept of receptivity in the aesthetic condition resists systematic control; thought conceived of as absolute subjectivity would locate it in a state of unconditional self-determination. This will be the beginning of the Romantic view of aesthetics, as influenced by Fichte.

[15] One should first ask how, in a new understanding of man, an undeclared motif taken up from the transcendental critique of reason becomes visible and how in it man's own receptivity to the beautiful and the sublime becomes an interesting phenomenon. Werner Strube still adheres to the nineteenth-century style of writing the history of philosophy when he characterizes Edmund Burke's *A Philosophical Enquiry into the Origin of our Ideas of the Sublime and the Beautiful* (1756) as empirical-sensual aesthetics. This hinders the transition to Burke's morphological-anthropological interests at the time that Alexander Baumgarten initiated the field of aesthetics with his similarly motivated question in his *Philosophische Untersuchung über den Ursprung unserer Ideen vom Erhabenen und Schönen,* trans. Friedrich Bassenge, newly introduced and ed. Werner Strube (Hamburg: Meiner, 1989), 1–26. A debate between the various eighteenth-century attempts at a definition of points of view can hardly give the orientation for a barely emerging horizon. Schiller incorporates in his own anthropology and aesthetics, based on Kant's

transcendental critique of reason, the ideas of Henry Home, *Elements of Criticism* (1762) which he knew in translation and found inspiring.

[16] *Kritik der Urteilskraft* § 12.

[17] "Im Grunde haben wir in diesem Fall nicht an der Sache, die uns das Vergnügen macht, sondern bloß an der Empfindung, die sie bewirkt, unser Wohlgefallen. Wir wissen so gar oft nicht, wo der Gegenstand, der uns dieses Vergnügen macht, ist, noch was er ist; wir empfinden und lieben bloß seine Wirkung, ohne uns mit ihm selbst zu beschäftigen" (Johann Georg Sulzer, Article "Schönheit," in *Allgemeine Theorie der schönen Künste* [Leipzig 1774]; orthography modernised by F. H.; Our enjoyment in this case is not of the thing that gives us pleasure but of the feeling it produces. Often we do not even know where or what the object is that gives us this pleasure; we feel and love its effect alone, without having any direct contact with the thing itself).

[18] See the exposition by Karl-Heinz Volkmann-Schluck, *Kunst und Erkenntnis.*

[19] In this point especially both Schiller's and Kant's arguments are indebted to Henry Home.

[20] Martin Heidegger produced a new translation of and commentary on the beginning of the seventh book of the *Politics: Platons Lehre von der Wahrheit.* To become aware of how Schiller reverses the direction of Plato's and Platonism's question see also Heidegger's edited lecture in the Wintersemester 1931/32, *Vom Wesen der Wahrheit: zu Platons Höhlengleichnis und Theätet* in vol. 34 of the Gesamtausgabe (Frankfurt am Main: Klostermann, 1988).

[21] I am leaving it open here as to whether Schiller answers the question about truth in art in contrast to truth in knowledge more thoroughly than Nietzsche does.

[22] The categories, deduced by Kant in the *Critique of Pure Reason* as time schemes, do not reveal forms available to the human senses in the world of appearance; rather, they reveal merely how everything that can be located as appearance in the perception of nature can become the object of rational concepts in the certainty of knowledge. The question and thesis of the *Critique of Pure Reason* also guide Hellmuth Plessner's inquiry about the anthropology and the objectivity of the senses in *Gesammelte Schriften* 3: *Anthropologie der Sinne* (Frankfurt am Main: Suhrkamp, 1980): "Die Einheit der Sinne," see esp. 300–15. Since the work of the phenomenological school, and particularly since Heidegger's existential analysis of being, the conditions for a suitable interpretation of the sensuous have decisively changed; see Ludwig Landgrebe, "Prinzipien der Lehre vom Empfinden," *Zeitschrift für philosophische Forschung* 8 (1954): 195–209. The problem that Schiller had in mind is clearly formulated here, namely, that the "Revision der Ansicht, daß die Sinnesempfindungen letzte Aufbauelemente des Bewußtseins wären" (197; revision of the view that sense perceptions are the final structural elements of consciousness),

necessarily implies "die Aufgabe einer Revision der Kategorien der philosophischen Bewußtseinslehre" (202; the task of revising the categories of the philosophical doctrine of consciousness). See also F. Heuer, "Zu Schillers Plan einer transzendental-philosophischen Analytik des Schönen," 126.

[23] Jan Assmann has drawn attention to the eighteenth-century mystical connotations of becoming certain of the truth. *Das verschleierte Bild zu Sais: Schillers Ballade und ihre griechischen und ägyptischen Hintergründe* (Stuttgart und Leipzig: Teubner, 1999).

[24] The "creations" of human senses in the sphere of aesthetic appearance, the play of colors and contours in natural beauty or in a painting or of the pure tones and intervals in playing or hearing music display a type of testimony ontologically different from objects created from knowledge through categories as time schemes. Schiller's basic rule for what he calls "den Schein von der Wirklichkeit reinigen" (purging appearance from reality) demands that we pay attention to this. Anyone thinking about catharsis in Attic tragedy should not forget how a pure tone or, in dance, the playing of human physical movement arise.

[25] Works such as *L'Homme Machine* (1748) by Julien Offray de la Mettrie or *Traité des Sensations* by Etienne Bonnot de Condillac can be seen as examples of the developing provocative materialist and sensualist positions of a popular philosophical "enlightened" journalism. But then attention is too easily distracted from the impact of a renewed morphological interest in the sensuous spiritual being of man that leads understanding to such ambitious experiments and gives the transcendental dimension to Kant's lectures on *Anthropologie in pragmatischer Hinsicht* (1798).

[26] Wolfgang Riedel, *Die Anthropologie des jungen Schiller,* esp. part 1.

[27] In his "cosmopolitan meaning" Kant brings the "field of philosophy" down to four questions: 1) What can I know? 2) What should I do? 3) What can I hope for? 4) What is man? He gives the responsibility for answering the fourth question to anthropology, with the remark: "Im Grunde könnte man aber alles dieses zur Anthropologie rechnen, weil sich die drei ersten Fragen auf die letzte beziehen" (One could actually reckon all this to belong to anthropology, since the first three questions refer to the last). Immanuel Kant, vol. 3 of *Werke in sechs Bänden,* ed. Wilhelm Weischedel (Darmstadt: Wissenschaftliche Buchgesellschaft, 1983); Immanuel Kant, *Schriften zur Metaphysik und Logik. Immanuel Kants Logik: Ein Handbuch zu Vorlesungen* (Königsberg: Friedrich Nicolovius, 1800), Einleitung, A 25.

[28] Johann Christoph Adelung, *Grammatisch-kritisches Wörterbuch der Hochdeutschen Mundart,* Ausgabe letzter Hand (Leipzig: Breitkopf, 1793–1801).

[29] Leipzig: Hirzel (1854–1954). Reprint Munich: Deutscher Taschenbuch Verlag, 1954.

[30] I hope that Jasmin Mukić will continue the work he began in "Freiheit und Empfänglichkeit: Zur Ästhetik des Schönen bei Schiller." Master's thesis, Philosophical-historical Faculty, Ruprecht-Karls-Universität Heidelberg, 1999/ 2000. 114 pages, typescript.

[31] In the story "Herr und Hund," Thomas Mann observes at a gentlemanly distance as his dog Bauschan chews a mouse into an amorphous pulp and integrates it into his individual dog existence. Gentlemen who, gathered at a finely decorated table, praise the delicious meal and wine, display and recall aesthetic receptivity in taste. It requires not a lack of consciousness but a lack of manners to say "Hunger ist der beste Koch." (Hunger is the best cook.)

[32] To establish it of oneself or even to suggest that it could be established of oneself would be a step towards a self-satisfied humanism and that would lie outside Kant's and Schiller's critical thought.

[33] As "natürliche Gemütsanlagen (praedispositio), durch Pflichtbegriffe affiziert zu werden" (natural dispositions (praedispositio) to be affixed by ideas of duty; Kant, *Die Metaphysik der Sitten. Zweiter Teil. Metaphysische Anfangsgründe der Tugendlehre. Einleitung. XII. Ästhetische Vorbegriffe der Empfänglichkeit des Gemüts für Pflichtbegriffe überhaupt*). See also *Die Religion innerhalb der Grenzen der bloßen Vernunft:* "3. Die Anlage für die Persönlichkeit ist die Empfänglichkeit der Achtung für das moralische Gesetz, als einer für sich hinreichenden Triebfeder der Willkür. Die Empfänglichkeit der bloßen Achtung für das moralische Gesetz in uns wäre das moralische Gefühl, welches für sich noch nicht einen Zweck der Naturanlage ausmacht, sondern nur, sofern es Triebfeder der Willkür ist. Da dieses nun lediglich dadurch möglich wird, daß die freie Willkür es in seine Maxime aufnimmt: so ist Beschaffenheit einer solchen Willkür der gute Charakter; welcher, wie überhaupt jeder Charakter der freien Willkür, etwas ist, das nur erworben werden kann, zu dessen Möglichkeit aber dennoch eine Anlage in unserer Natur vorhanden sein muß, worauf schlechterdings nichts Böses gepfropft werden kann" (The disposition of personality is respect's receptiveness towards the moral law, as a driving force for arbitrariness sufficient unto itself. The receptivity of pure respect for the moral law in us would be moral feeling, which does not constitute a purpose of the natural disposition of itself, but only in so far as it is the driving force of arbitrariness. Since this is only possible because free arbitrariness takes it up into its maxim, the condition of such arbitrariness is good character, and this, like every character of arbitrariness, is something that can only be acquired but for which a predisposition in our nature still has to be present, on which no evil can be forced).

[34] The article "Rezeptivität" in the *Historisches Wörterbuch der Philosophie,* by Thomas Sören Hoffmann, which offers valuable perspectives on the philosophical investigations into the problem since antiquity, concentrates especially on the

relation between receptivity and spontaneity in inquiries in the field of knowledge theory in Kant and later (8:1009–14, especially 1010–11). In Kant's work *De mundi sensibilis atque intelligibilis forma et principiis* (Of the Form and Principles of the Sensible and Intelligible World) from the year 1770, the Latin word "receptivitas" is to be understood as human receptivity. § 3: "Sensualitas est receptivitas subiecti, per quam possibile est, ut status ipsius repraesentativus obiecti alicuius praesentia certo modo afficiatur" (Sensuousness is the receptivity of the subject through which it is possible that its own representative state is affected in a certain way by the presence of any other object). This leaves open the possibility that the receptivity of the knowing subject in the act of understanding is an exception, for Schiller, an abstraction of the receptivity to ideas of duty that, as Kant says, "jeder Mensch hat" (everyone has; Kant, *Metaphysics der Sitten, II, XII*) and that extends also to beauty and the sublime. In § 51.3 of *The Critique of Judgment* Kant uses "Empfänglichkeit für Eindrücke" (receptivity to impressions) synonomously with "Affektibilität" (susceptibility). In *Anthropology from a Pragmatic Point of View* part I, book 1, § 7, the footnote refers to "den große[n] Fehler" (the big mistake) of recognizing "Sinnlichkeit bloß in der Undeutlichkeit der Vorstellungen" (sensuousness only in unclear ideas).

[35] See the 13th of the *Ästhetische Briefe*, particularly footnote 2 (*NA* 20:349–51). If "culture's task" is "erstlich: die Sinnlichkeit gegen die Eingriffe der Freiheit zu verwahren; zweitens: die Persönlichkeit gegen die Macht der Empfindungen sicher zu stellen" (348; first, to protect sensuousness against interference from freedom; second, to secure personality against the power of feeling) then it is necessary to develop receptivity: "Je vielseitiger sich die Empfänglichkeit ausbildet, je beweglicher dieselbe ist, und je mehr Fläche sie den Erscheinungen darbietet, desto mehr Welt ergreift der Mensch, desto mehr Anlagen entwickelt er in sich; je mehr Kraft und Tiefe die Persönlichkeit, je mehr Freiheit die Vernunft gewinnt, desto mehr Welt begreift der Mensch, desto mehr Form schafft er außer sich. Seine Kultur wird also darin bestehen: erstlich: dem empfangenden Vermögen die vielfältigsten Berührungen mit der Welt zu verschaffen und auf seiten des Gefühls die Passivität aufs höchste zu treiben: zweitens: dem bestimmenden Vermögen die höchste Unabhängigkeit von dem empfangenden zu erwerben und auf seiten der Vernunft die Aktivität aufs höchste zu treiben. Wo beide Eigenschaften sich vereinigen, da wird der Mensch mit der höchsten Fülle von Dasein die höchste Selbständigkeit und Freiheit verbinden und, anstatt sich an die Welt zu verlieren, diese vielmehr mit der ganzen Unendlichkeit ihrer Erscheinungen in sich ziehen und der Einheit seiner Vernunft unterwerfen" (349; The more variously human receptivity develops, the more flexible it becomes and the greater the surface it offers for appearances, the more man takes hold of the world and the more talents he develops in himself; the more strength and depth a personality gains and the more freedom reason gains, the more man comprehends the

world, the more form he creates outside himself. His culture will then consist of first: providing the most varied contacts with the world for his receptivity and, on the side of feeling, to force passivity to the limit, second: to achieve the most complete independence of the determining faculty from the receiving faculty, and, on the side of reason, to force activity to the limit. Where the two characteristics are united, man will combine the highest self sufficiency and freedom with the highest fullness of being and, instead of losing himself to the world, will draw it into himself, with the whole infinity of its appearances, and subject it to the unity of his reason).

[36] Schiller's argument can hardly be corrected by referring to Kant. I cannot agree with K. L Berghahn's view that Kant's position in "Die Religion innerhalb der Grenzen der bloßen Vernunft" does away with inconsistencies (Berghahn 148).

[37] This is the dividing line between Kant's thought and — among his followers — Schiller's, as opposed to Fichte's or Hegel's. One has to entice man out of the state of fulfillment he has reached for his senses in the realm of aesthetic appearance, to reclaim the half truth of "sinnlicher Gewissheit" (sense certainty) — as established by Hegel in the *Phenomenology of Spirit* — since the human mind lingers with what it has presented to itself and is not concerned about certainty.

[38] It is also illogical to seek assurance from within Kant's thought for the purity of conviction at the sight of a man acting out of love by means of a moral judgment about appearances. In this case it would require the removal again of the transcendental separation of aesthetic from moral judgment. Despite his recognition of Kant's liberal spirit, Schiller sees a shadow here. "Ich bin sehr verlangend Kants Anthropologie zu lesen, die pathologische Seite die er am Menschen immer herauskehrt und die bei einer Anthropologie vielleicht am Platze seyn mag, verfolgt einen fast in allem was er schreibt, und sie ists, die seiner practischen Philosophie ein so grämliches Ansehen giebt. Daß dieser heitre und jovialische Geist seine Flügel nicht ganz von dem Lebensschmutz hat losmachen können, ja selbst gewiße düstere Eindrücke der Jugend pp nicht ganz verwunden hat ist zu verwundern und zu beklagen. Es ist immer noch etwas in ihm, was einen, wie bei Luthern, an einen Mönch erinnert, der sich zwar sein Kloster geöfnet hat, aber die Spuren desselben nicht ganz vertilgen konnte" (to Goethe, 22 [21] December 1798; *NA* 30:15; I am very desirous of seeing Kant's anthropology. The pathological side of man, which he always turns to the outside and which may be in its place in anthropology, follows one in almost everything he writes and it is that which gives his practical philosophy such a morose outlook. The fact that this cheerful and jovial spirit could not keep his wings completely clear of life's grime and has not even overcome certain gloomy youthful impressions is surprising and reprehensible. There is always something in him that reminds me of a monk, like Luther, who opened up his monastery but could never quite eradicate its traces).

[39] Thus love, as Kant explains, belongs to the "ästhetischen Vorbegriffen der Empfänglichkeit des Gemüts für Pflichtbegriffe" (aesthetic precepts for receptivity of a disposition towards ideas of duty). *Metaphysik der Sitten,* part 2, 12.

[40] Hartmut Reinhardt has demonstrated in a scholarly and stimulating way how fruitfully and precisely these reflections of Schiller's are realized in the poetics of a text such as Goethe's "Märchen" from the contemporary *Unterhaltungen deutscher Ausgewanderten.* "Lizenz zum Spielen: Goethes 'Märchen' in seiner dialogischen Verbinding mit Schillers aesthetischen Schriften," *JbDSG* 47 (2003), 99–122.

[41] Schiller finds more insight into the phenomenon in Baumgarten's than in Kant's explanation. Schiller refers the relevance of Baumgarten's question about the existence of rationality in the objectivity of beauty back to aesthetic theory. See Klaus E. Kähler, "Metaphysik und ästhetisches Weltverhältnis: Der anfängliche Sinn der philosophischen Ästhetik und ihre Krise," in *Denken und Geschichte: Festschrift für Friedrich Gaede,* ed. Hans-Günther Schwarz and Jane V. Curran, 9–19 (Munich: iudicium, 2002). Schiller can do this by thinking about receptivity towards the wealth of objective beauty from the perspective of the transcendental, singular capabilities of the human senses, which are attributable to man and not to the subjectivity of reflection. Thus, at work in Schiller's explanation of man's receptivity for beauty and the sublime is the anthropologically morphological transcendental inquiry of Edmund Burke's *A Philosophical Inquiry into the Origin of Our Ideas of the Sublime and the Beautiful.* Kant's achievement really lies in the transcendental analysis of conceptual determinations that overburden reason and reflection, thus challenging Schiller the phenomenologist and morphologist.

[42] "Kallias" letter to Körner, 23 February 1793 (*NA* 26:210). See F. Heuer, *Darstellung der Freiheit,* 102–9.

[43] "Kallias" letter to Körner 23 February 1793. "In der ästhetischen Welt ist jedes Naturwesen ein freier Bürger, der mit dem Edelsten gleiche Rechte hat, und nicht einmal um des Ganzen willen darf gezwungen werden, sondern zu allem schlechterdings konsentieren muß. In dieser ästhetischen Welt, die eine ganz andere ist als die vollkommenste platonische Republik, fordert auch der Rock, den ich auf dem Leibe trage, Respekt von mir für seine Freiheit, und er verlangt von mir, gleich einem verschämten Bedienten, daß ich niemanden merken lasse, daß er mir dient." (*NA* 26:212; In the aesthetic world each natural being is a free citizen, with the same rights as the noblest of them, and may not, even for the sake of the whole, be coerced, but must be in a position to consent to everything. In this aesthetic world, which is quite different from the most perfect Platonic republic, even the coat I wear on my body claims respect for its freedom and demands from me, as from a bashful servant, that I not allow anyone to notice that it serves me). Schiller is certainly completely conscious of turning away from Platonism.

Works Cited

Adelung, Johann Christoph. *Grammatisch-kritisches Wörterbuch der Hochdeutschen Mundart mit beständiger Vergleichung der übrigen Mundarten, besonders aber der Oberdeutschen.* 1793–1801.

Assmann, Jan. *Die Mosaische Unterscheidung oder der Preis des Monotheismus.* Munich and Vienna: Hanser, 2003.

———. *Das verschleierte Bild zu Sais: Schillers Ballade und ihre griechischen und ägyptischen Hintergründe.* Stuttgart and Leipzig: Teubner, 1999.

Berghahn, Klaus L., ed. *Friedrich Schiller: Kallias oder über die Schönheit; Über Anmut und Würde.* Stuttgart: Reclam, 1994.

Burke, Edmund. *Philosophische Untersuchung über den Ursprung unserer Ideen vom Erhabenen und Schönen.* Translated by Friedrich Bassenge. Newly introduced and edited by Werner Strube. 2nd ed. Hamburg: Meiner, 1989.

Heidegger, Martin. "Über den Humanismus: Brief an Jean Beaufret." In *Wegmarken.* Frankfurt am Main: Klostermann, 1967.

———. *Gesamtausgabe.* Vol. 34: *Vom Wesen der Wahrheit: Zu Platons Höhlengleichnis und Theätet.* Frankfurt am Main: Klostermann, 1988.

Heuer, Fritz. "Zu Schillers Plan einer transzendentalphilosophischen Analytik des Schönen." *Philosophisches Jahrbuch* 80 (1973): 90–132.

———. *Darstellung der Freiheit: Schillers transzendentale Frage nach der Kunst.* Cologne: Böhlau, 1970.

Historisches Wörterbuch der Philosophie. Edited by Joachim Ritter and Karlfried Gründer. Basel: Schwabe, 1971–2001.

Kähler, Klaus E. "Metaphysik und ästhetisches Weltverhältnis: Der anfängliche Sinn der philosophischen Ästhetik und ihre Krise." In *Denken und Geschichte: Festschrift für Friedrich Gaede,* edited by Hans-Günther Schwarz and Jane V. Curran, 9–19. Munich: iudicium, 2002.

Kant, Immanuel. *Gesammelte Schriften.* Vol. 3 (1904): *Kritik der reinen Vernunft,* 2nd ed., 1787. Vol. 4 (1903): *Kritik der reinen Vernunft, 1. Aufl., Prolegomena. Grundlegung zur Metaphysik der Sitten. Metaphysische Anfangsgründe der Naturwissenschaft.* Vol. 5 (1908): *Kritik der praktischen Vernunft. Kritik der Urtheilskraft.* Vol. 6 (1907): *Religion innerhalb der Grenzen der blossen Vernunft. Die Metaphysik der Sitten.* Vol. 7 (1907): *Der Streit der Fakultäten. Anthropologie in pragmatischer Hinsicht.* Berlin: Reimer.

Landgrebe, Ludwig. "Prinzipien der Lehre vom Empfinden." *Zeitschrift für philosophische Forschung* 8 (1954): 195–209.

Plessner, Hellmuth. *Gesammelte Schriften*. Vol. 3: *Anthropologie der Sinne*. Frankfurt am Main: Suhrkamp, 1980.

Reinhardt, Hartmut. "Lizenz zum Spielen: Goethes 'Märchen' in seiner dialogischen Verbindung mit Schillers aesthetischen Schriften." *JbDSG* 47 (2003): 99–122.

Riedel, Wolfgang. *Die Anthropologie des jungen Schiller: Zur Ideengeschichte der medizinischen Schriften und der "Philosophischen Briefe."* Würzburg: Königshausen & Neumann, 1985.

———, ed. *Jacob Friedrich Abel: Eine Quellenedition zum Philosophieunterricht an der Stuttgarter Karlsschule (1773–1782); Mit Einleitung, Übersetzung, Kommentar und Bibliographie*. Würzburg: Königshausen & Neumann, 1995.

Schiller, Friedrich. *Kallias oder über die Schönheit: Über Anmut und Würde*. Edited by Klaus L. Berghahn. Stuttgart: Reclam 1994.

Sulzer, Johann Georg. *Allgemeine Theorie der schönen Künste*. Leipzig: Weidmann, 1774.

Volkmann-Schluck, Karl-Heinz. *Kunst und Erkenntnis*. Edited by Ursula Panzer. Würzburg: Königshausen und Neumann, 2002.

———. *Die Kunst und der Mensch: Schillers Briefe über die ästhetische Erziehung des Menschen*. Frankfurt/Main: Klostermann, 1964.

Wilcox, Kenneth Parmelee. *Anmut und Wuerde: Die Dialektik der menschlichen Vollendung bei Schiller*. Frankfurt am Main: Peter Lang, 1981.

From Romantic Dream to Idyllic Tragedy: Idealism and Realism in Schiller's Dramas, Before and After Kant

Alan Menhennet

IN THE *BRIEFE ÜBER "DON KARLOS,"* Schiller talks of a dream. Prefiguring "On Grace and Dignity,"[1] he speaks of achieving "den vollendetsten Zustand der Menschheit" (*NA* 22:162; humanity in its most perfect state). He calls this dream "romanhaft" (fanciful, far-fetched). He could as easily have said *romantisch,* for in general eighteenth-century usage the words were almost interchangeable. Contact with practical politicians, indeed, is said to have cleansed Posa's idealism of *das Romantische.* Not entirely, though, for when it comes to explaining his treatment of Carlos, the "Bilder romantischer Größe" (*NA* 22:176; images of romantic greatness) he has imbibed from Plutarch, and which make him a (distant) cousin of Karl Moor,[2] are called in aid. Schiller, though himself an arch-idealist, is speaking the language of the *Aufklärung;* in particular that of Wieland, that detached, yet not unsympathetic observer of idealism. Nature, which should govern poetry and thought, is the norm rather than the exception. The extraordinary, let alone the wondrous, falls into the category of *das Romantische* as defined in Wieland's *Hexameron von Rosenhain,* that is, that which is "in Romanen und Komödien häufiger als in der wirklichen Welt"[3] (more frequent in romances and comedies than in the real world). It brings with it the danger of *Schwärmerei,* the substitution of imagined for real truth. Idealism, fuelled by fancy and emotion, is prone to such error at times, and Wieland had already provided a case study in his *Agathon* (1767). Agathon's love for Danae is a "romantische Leidenschaft." Expectation of ideal perfection is so ingrained in his delicate soul that he cannot love without a little "Schwärmerey."[4] But his core belief, that the spiritual is superior to the sensual, is healthy and true. Words like *romantisch* are necessary cautionary signs, but ideals are necessary too, as vehicles for man's higher nature. Like Schiller, Wieland had felt the influence of Shaftesbury.

There is, then, something fanciful in Schiller's project. But fancy can sometimes provide a better soil for the cultivation of true humanity than a vision restricted (like Raimond's in *Die Jungfrau von Orleans*) to "das Natürliche der Dinge"[5] (the natural side of things). In *Don Carlos*, Posa calls his youthful "Traumbild eines neuen Staates" (dream-image of a new state) the product of "schwärmerische Tage," days when the fancy extends reality beyond what prudent wisdom tells us is possible. This particular dream, however, is the vehicle for the ideal of "Menschlichkeit,"[6] that higher human potential that is a "divine flower" that so-called "better reason" must not be allowed to blight. In this case, the voice of enthusiasm is "Begeisterung, die Himmelstochter" (lines 4279–96; Inspiration, the daughter of heaven). Though this is as yet a "Spielwerk," a dream of the imagination, as Schiller says in the *Briefe,* it is "in ihrer [der Menschheit] Natur und ihren Kräften als erreichbar angegeben" (given as achievable in [humanity's] nature and powers). Somewhere, there might arise an enlightened despot with a beautiful soul, ready to extend the purer, gentler humanity already manifest in his own "Gemütszustand" (*NA* 22:164; inner mental and emotional condition), to a whole people. This is certainly a "*subjektive* Möglichkeit" (*subjective* possibility), and even if its realization requires some relaxation of pragmatic realism, it is not illegitimate to posit such an idyllic eventuality. Chance has performed greater wonders before.

The age of Sentimentalism (*Empfindsamkeit*) had its cult of the heroic "beautiful soul," with first Richardson, then Klopstock,[7] providing the best examples. The years of classicism saw a renewal of the idea, with less sentimentality and more sublimity. Even in *Agathon,* where he ironizes the Richardsonian *Tugendheld,* Wieland had used it sympathetically.[8] And in *Oberon* (1780), he celebrated "der menschlichen Natur Erhabenheit" (the sublimity of human nature) in the hermit who teaches Hüon the lesson of self-denial (lines 5388–89), as Goethe did the "great soul" of an Iphigenia whose pure humanity resolves an age-old curse. And we find the terminology of "On Grace and Dignity" prefigured also in *Don Carlos.* The Queen is rightly described by Posa as a "schöne Seele" (line 4307; beautiful soul) and his contrast of her *naïf* with Eboli's calculated virtue (line 2356–57: "Mit sorgenlosem Leichtsinn" [carefree and light-hearted]) recalls the "Leichtigkeit" (ease) with which the beautiful soul fulfills "humankind's most exacting duties" (cf. *NA* 20:287). In the twin heroes of the play, the "rein organisierte, empfängliche Seele" (purely constituted, receptive soul) Posa and the "schön organisierte Jünglingsseele" (beautifully constituted, youthful soul) Carlos,[9] Schiller shows the ideal as a present reality, even if the rationality of Posa's self-sacrifice might be questioned by some.

Schiller confronts these critics in the twelfth *Don Karlos* letter. He admits the *romantisch* and *schwärmerisch* traits in Posa. But he has praise, too, for the non-rational faculties, and points to the fine line between worthy "Enthusiasmus" and dubious "Schwärmerei" (*NA* 22:177). This recalls an essay by Wieland that stresses man's inner capacity for direct contemplation of the good, the beautiful and the divine.[10] *Enthusiasm* is the "Wirkung des unmittelbaren Anschauens des Schönen und Guten, Vollkommenen und Göttlichen in der Natur und in unserm Innersten" (the effect of the direct contemplation, in our inmost soul, of the beautiful and the good, the perfect and divine in nature). *Schwärmerei* is "Krankheit der Seele, eigentliches Seelenfieber" (a sickness, a veritable fever of the soul). One senses the concept of the beautiful soul whose literary equivalent is the idyll, which requires the creation of a reality within which mere *Wirklichkeit* (actuality) is transcended. We shall argue that in the one play in which Schiller crossed that borderline, he entered, as his subtitle indicates, the romantic land conquered for German literature above all by Wieland, and did so with the idyll in mind.

Even in the mid-eighties, we see the yearning for the idyll that appears with full force in Schiller's famous letter to Wilhelm von Humboldt (30 November 1795; *NA* 28). He was not yet so emancipated from what he was later to call the "naturalism" of the *Aufklärung* that he could dispense with cautionary formulations like "dream" and "romantic." But in "On Naïve and Sentimental Poetry" he writes that the "subjective possibility" of the *Briefe* already hints at the "mögliche Realität" (*NA* 20:467; possible reality) of the idyll. In "On Grace and Dignity," the good ship *Schöne Seele* is launched into stormy Kantian waters, but, if at the expense of a few compromises, even contradictions, it manages to stay afloat.

Schiller was both an idealist who believed passionately in harmony, and a dramatist who responded most deeply of all to the tragic, that great rent in the harmony of the universe. This dualism is apparent at the axis of the essay on grace and dignity. Schiller leaves the realm of the beautiful, where, to quote the "Kallias letters," "Pflicht" (duty) has become nature,[11] for that of the sublime, where *Pflicht* subdues *Neigung* (inclination) through the superior authority of the moral will, which appears in the phenomenal world as dignity. The literary form corresponding to the beautiful state is the sentimental idyll ("das Ideal der Schönheit auf das wirkliche Leben angewendet" [*NA* 20:472; the ideal of beauty applied to actual life]), a concept eventually worked out in the treatise on naive and sentimental poetry. The sublime points in the direction of tragedy.

The idea of a contradiction and a battle between reason and senses, will, and desire undoubtedly appealed to the tragedian in Schiller. But his thinking also contains a consistent inner impulse towards reconciliation of the two poles of the dualism through a third concept and a return, in Kerry's words, to "a total and harmonious vision."[12] Beauty and sublimity seem initially to be mutually contradictory. In a state of affection (*Affekt,* the state of being under the influence of emotion), action in accordance with the Law of Reason is possible only through a contradiction with the demands of Nature:

> Und da die Natur ihre Foderungen aus sittlichen Gründen nie zurücknimmt, folglich auf ihrer Seite alles sich gleich bleibt, wie auch der Wille sich in Ansehung ihrer verhalten mag, so ist hier keine Zusammenstimmung zwischen Neigung und Pflicht, zwischen Vernunft und Sinnlichkeit möglich, so kann der Mensch hier nicht mit seiner ganzen harmonisierenden Natur, sondern ausschließungsweise nur mit seiner vernünftigen handeln . . . Die schöne Seele muß sich also im Affekt in eine erhabne verwandeln. (*NA* 20:293–94)

> [And since nature, for ethical reasons, never withdraws her demands, and therefore everything on her side remains the same, no matter how the will behaves in relation to her, so here there is no agreement possible between inclination and duty, between reason and sensuousness; so humans cannot here act with their whole nature in harmony, but only with their reason . . . The beautiful soul, then, must, in emotion, change into a sublime soul.]

This in spite of the fact that in the section on grace he has asserted:

> Eine schöne Seele nennt man es, wenn sich das sittliche Gefühl aller Empfindungen des Menschen endlich bis zu dem Grad versichert hat, daß es dem Affekt die Leitung des Willens ohne Scheu überlassen darf und nie Gefahr läuft, mit den Entscheidungen desselben in Widerspruch zu stehen. Daher sind bei einer schönen Seele die einzelnen Handlungen eigentlich nicht sittlich, sondern der ganze Charakter ist es . . . Die

schöne Seele hat kein andres Verdienst, als daß sie ist. Mit einer Leichtigkeit, als wenn bloß der Instinkt aus ihr handelte, übt sie der Menschheit peinlichste Pflichten aus, und das heldenmütigste Opfer, das sie dem Naturtrieb abgewinnt, fällt wie eine freiwillige Wirkung eben dieses Triebes in die Augen. (*NA* 20:287)

[One refers to a beautiful soul when the ethical sense has at last so taken control of all a person's feelings that it can leave affect to guide the will without hesitation and is never in danger of standing in contradiction of its decisions. For this reason the actions of a beautiful soul are not themselves ethical, but the character as a whole is so . . . The beautiful soul has no other merit besides being. It carries out humankind's most exacting duties with such ease that they might simply be the actions of its inner instinct, and the most heroic sacrifice that it exacts from natural impulse appears to the eye as a free operation of this impulse.]

To justify the assertion that a person whose whole character is moral and who can make painful sacrifices with natural grace must now resist and subdue the natural urge (*NA* 20:297), Schiller has recourse to allegory: The monarch resumes control over his subject. The captain (the moral will) takes back the helm of the ship from an ideal crew that has somehow mutinied (*NA* 20:294). Its harmony destroyed, the beautiful soul has to become heroically sublime. But surely, that very harmony guarantees that while the outcome is painful, the decision is simple.

Schiller does not want to place the "schöne Seele" on a par with ordinary tragic characters. The tragic "schöne Seele" suffers, and does so heroically, but whether its heroism is sublime in the strict sense is unclear, since the question of its inner conflict — if any, indeed — is fudged. Schiller talks not of conflict but of transcendence: "Die schöne Seele geht ins heroische über und erhebt sich zur reinen Intelligenz" (the beautiful soul becomes heroic and elevates itself to pure intelligence). It shifts into heroic mode and — one is tempted to add the biblical word (not used here) that Schiller attaches to the idyllic hero(ine) — "overcomes."

In *Wallenstein,* the main action comes closer to the model of the Nemesis tragedy outlined in the *Agrippina* plan; a tragedy, that is, whose effect depends more on the *form* than on the sympathetic nature (interest) of the central character. But there is, as a kind of inset, an idyllic action featuring two prime examples of the "schöne Seele" who follow the path of duty without a demonstrable victory of will over nature. It is not the will that determines their actions, but the heart, the true location of the idyll, where, without denying human reality *per se,* the ideal can be freed from the restraints of *Wirklichkeit* (reality).[13] Certainly, Schiller is at some pains to indicate "Widerstreit in der Erscheinung" (*NA* 20:298, conflict in the appearance) when Max is placed before a formal choice. But we cannot agree with Reed that Max has to go through a "dark night of the moral conscience."[14] Referred to the tribunal of Love, the dispute resolves itself. Max has said: "Ich weiß das Rechte nicht zu wählen" (line 2281; I cannot decide the right thing to choose). But Thekla speaks for his (and her own) heart: "O das deine hat längst entschieden" (lines 2336–38; Oh, your heart decided long ago). For this is love as defined in "On Grace and Dignity": "das absolut Große selbst, was in der Anmut und Schönheit sich nachgeahmt und in der Sittlichkeit sich befriedigt findet" (*NA* 20:303; absolute greatness itself, that finds itself imitated in grace and beauty and affirmed in the ethical). There is no possibility here of a tragic *conflict* between spirit and sense, for "die Sinnlichkeit . . . [stimmt] in der Anmut und Schönheit mit den Ideen des Geistes zusammen" (*NA* 20:303; sensuousness . . . coincides in grace and beauty with the ideas of intellect). Love here is idealized: it is not the "Genuß oder sinnliche Augenweide" (enjoyment, or a feast for sensual eyes) that Schiller condemns in Bürger's poetry (*NA* 22:253). Max and Thekla are tragic in that they suffer "das Los des Schönen auf der Erde" (the fate of the beautiful on this earth). Whether or not they are sublime in the terms of Schiller's definition is a moot point. For unless we subsume the will in the heart, we cannot be sure that their suffering is an act of the will (by definition a denial of nature) rather than the necessary and natural result of their beauty of soul.

There can be no apotheosis in *Wallenstein.* The idyll is crushed by Fate, the pure form of tragedy, the terrible and magnificent spectacle described with such power in "Über das Erhabene" (*NA* 21:52). With *Maria Stuart,* we come to the question of sublimity achieved through the expiation of guilt. "On Grace and Dignity" does not discuss guilt at length. But it does admit the possibility that even the moral Homer can nod. It is the absolute duty of the will to obey the reason, and if the senses were to override that authority, this would be "ein Verbrechen seines Willens" (*NA* 20:292; a crime of the will) against reason. This implies the need for repentance and atonement, which in turn is a source of sublimity and tragic pleasure. Repentance, and even despair over a criminal act, are "Gemälde der erhabensten Sittlichkeit" (*NA* 20:142–43; pictures of the most sublime morality). The victory of duty over desire, a classic motive of one kind of tragedy, is clearly implicit and becomes explicit in "Über das Pathetische." It can be heroic (self-sacrifice), or expiatory:

> Zum Erhabenen der Handlung wird erfodert, daß das Leiden eines Menschen auf seine moralische Beschaffenheit nicht nur keinen Einfluß habe, sondern vielmehr umgekehrt das Werk seines moralischen Charakters sei. Dies kann auf zweierlei Weise sein. Entweder mittelbar und nach dem Gesetz der Freiheit, wenn er aus Achtung für irgend eine Pflicht das Leiden erwählt . . . Oder unmittelbar und nach dem Gesetz der Notwendigkeit, wenn er eine übertretene Pflicht moralisch büßt. (*NA* 20:212)

> [Sublimity of action requires that a person's suffering should not only not exert any influence on his moral constitution, but rather, and conversely, be the handiwork of his moral character. There are two ways in which this can happen. Either indirectly, and in accordance with the law of freedom, when he chooses suffering out of respect for some duty or other . . . Or directly, and in accordance with the law of necessity, when he does moral penance for a duty he has disregarded.]

After *Wallenstein*, Schiller moved back towards the *Don Carlos* model of moral uplift rather than catharsis. In "Über die tragische Kunst" (On the Art of Tragedy), he nods in the direction of Aristotle and Lessing, and recognizes the paradoxical attraction of "das Traurige, das Schreckliche, das Schauderhafte" (*NA* 20:148; the sad, the terrible, the horrific). But tragic pleasure depends on moral criteria. Catharsis itself is purged from the system. Greek tragedy, judged in the light of the strong dose of purified philosophy that Schiller has imbibed, is found wanting. Its disharmony (necessity or fate) is rejected in favor of "the great harmony" (*NA* 20:157). *Hamartia* (tragic guilt) is no longer a *sine qua non* of tragic pity; indeed, in the various essays that touch on the subject, the majority of the tragic sufferers singled out are essentially heroic (if human) and untainted. The *Warbeck* project was abandoned primarily, as Schiller wrote to Körner (13 May 1801; *NA* 31), because "der Held ein Betrüger ist, und ich möchte auch nicht den kleinsten Knoten im Moralischen zurücklaßen" (the hero is a deceiver, and I would not like to leave behind even the slightest unresolved difficulty in the moral field). This echoes the criticism in "On the Art of Tragedy" that Greek tragedy fails to satisfy reason because, in its final appeal to necessity, "ein unaufgelöster Knoten zurückbleibt" (*NA* 20:157; an unresolved difficulty remains). True, he could still pay lip-service to Aristotle and Lessing, even in 1800: "Der Held einer Tragödie braucht nur soviel moralischen Gehalt als nöthig ist, um Furcht und Mitleid zu erregen" (the hero of a tragedy needs only as much moral content as is necessary to arouse fear and pity). But whereas in the *Agrippina* plan the character who arouses only "die tragische Furcht und das tragische Schrecken" (tragic fear and tragic terror) is preferred to Britannicus, who commands more sympathy, "zuviel von einem stoffartigen Interesse" (*NA* 12:151; too great a material interest), Schiller admits to Körner that he has always warmed more easily to subjects that engage the heart (13 July 1800; *NA* 30). And on 13 May 1801, he tells him: "In meiner jetzigen Klarheit über mich selbst und über die Kunst die ich treibe, hätte ich den Wallenstein nicht gewählt" (with the clear insight into myself and my art that I now possess, I would not have chosen Wallenstein; *NA* 31). By then, of course, he was fully launched into a subject that engaged his heart to the full. But we must return for the moment to the Queen of Scots, and the question of guilt.

Is Mary Stuart an example of "sublimity of action" through expiated guilt? Maria was complicit in the murder of Darnley, and in spite of her sincere repentance — evidence, as we have seen, of "the most sublime morality" — still cannot forgive herself, or feel herself forgiven. In a process that remains obscure, but seems to involve her religious convictions, Schiller contrives an act of expiation by allowing her to link her present undeserved suffering to a past crime. Her love for Bothwell was, in terms of "On Grace and Dignity," not true love, but *Begierde* (desire) of the deepest dye. Her sensual nature was dominant in the deed in a way that still horrifies Kennedy in the recollection:

> Verlassen hatte Euch die zarte Scheu
> Der Menschen; Eure Wangen, sonst der Sitz
> Schamhaft errötender Bescheidenheit,
> Sie glühten nur vom Feuer des Verlangens
> (*Maria Stuart* act 1, scene 4, lines 333–36)

[The tender sense of shame of [true] humanity had abandoned you. Your cheeks, formerly the seat of the delicate blush of modesty, were afire with the glow of unmitigated desire.]

In "On Grace and Dignity," Schiller found this state too awful to contemplate. Whereas Wieland, in *Oberon* (Canto 7, 10–15), portrays the sensuality of Hüon's fall from moral virtue as something human, even (in itself) beautiful, Schiller makes a draconian distinction between *Sinne* and *Seele:* "In einem solchen Falle, wo der Trieb diesen [freien] Lauf selbst nähme, würde der Mensch auch nur Tier sein" (*NA* 20:291–92; In such a case, where the human did not grant free rein to instinct, but where instinct took it anyway, the human would *only* be an animal). He has already given a description of man under the yoke of his physical urges whose lurid rhetoric clashes oddly with the general tone of this essay:

> Das seelestrahlende Auge wird matt oder quillt auch gläsern aus seiner Höhlung hervor, der feine Inkarnat der Wangen verdickt sich zu einer groben Tüncherfarbe . . . die Stimme und der seufzende Atem sind nichts als Hauche, wodurch die beschwerte Brust sich erleichtern will, und die nun bloß ein mechanisches Bedürfnis, keine Seele verraten. (*NA* 20:281)

> [The eye, through which the soul shines, becomes dull, or protrudes, glassy and fixed, from its socket, the fine complexion of the cheeks thickens to a coarse and undifferentiated wash . . . voice and sigh are nothing more than breath through which the laden chest tries to gain relief and which is now evidence simply of an automatic need and not of a soul.][15]

True love is a "Trunkenheit des Geistes" (intoxication with the spirit) whose pure source is man's divine nature, as against "Taumel der Sinnenlust" (*NA* 20:306; the rapture of the senses) or what Kennedy calls "[der] Wahnsinn blinder Liebesglut" (1.4.325; the mad fire of blind passion). In other words, physical desire mired in *Stoff* (matter), a feeling "anspannend für den Sinn, für den Geist hingegen erschlaffend" (*NA* 20:302; that tautens the consciousness but slackens the spirit). Violence is the force that returns to threaten Maria when Mortimer's quiet madness boils over in a flood of sexual desire (3:6), giving her in turn the chance to dissociate herself from it. She has at least the "sittliche Fertigkeit" (moral capacity) that is manifest in grace, but she is not in a state of grace.[16] Only when she sees Leicester for the last time can she say, as the sublime Carlos does,[17] that she has risen above the world of the senses. She is not, nor ever was, a "schöne Seele"; she is a sinner who, like Carlos, is cleansed by a pure fire and becomes sublime.

When Maria reappears, she seems transfigured: "weiß und festlich gekleidet" (dressed festively in white), ready to ascend "auf Engelsflügeln" (on angels' wings) to eternal freedom (5.6.3483–84). One might say that this fifth act shows a predilection, at least, for the idyllic apotheosis: a theoretically suprasensuous sublimity supplemented by religious symbolism.

But the feeling that Schiller is trying to ride up to the heights on a tide of pseudo-religious sentiment, a quasi-mystical Catholicism in which he does not believe, leaves us with a lingering sense of dissatisfaction.

Schiller, then, flirts with transcendence in *Maria Stuart,* but has not yet found the right vehicle for a climactically idyllic and festive finale. His next heroine, Joan of Arc, is a character taken, like Maria, from history, but one whose story is more intrinsically poetic.[18] "Schon der Stoff erhält mich warm," Schiller wrote to Körner (5 January 1801; *NA* 31), "und es fließt auch mehr aus dem Herzen als die vorigen Stücke, wo der Verstand mit dem Stoffe kämpfen mußte" (The subject in itself warms my heart, and in addition, the work flows straight from the heart, more than in the previous plays, where the intellect had to fight with the material). As historical material, it did not give Schiller's imagination completely free rein, nor, in all probability, did he desire it. As he wrote to Goethe (5 January 1798; *NA* 29), he needed the discipline of "[die] objektive Bestimmtheit eines solchen Stoffs" (the objective concreteness of a subject like that), *Wallenstein* in this case. The ideal was for him the true content of poetic literature. True art was, as he said in his review of Bürger's poetry, "idealisierende Kunst" (*NA* 22:253; an idealizing art). "Idealizing" involved inserting "an infinite content,"[19] into the material, but poetry must remain within the bounds of the human,[20] and he found it easier "das Realistische zu idealisieren, als das Ideale zu realisieren" (to idealize the realistic, [rather] than to realize the ideal). Easier, that is, to find a way out of the real-ideal dualism by working from history towards the ideal, than to fashion the ideal into history by inventing an earthly vehicle for it.

The poem "Das Mädchen von Orleans" (The Maid of Orleans), which refers to the play of the same name, shows that, in conscious opposition to Voltaire, he had conceived Joan of Arc as a preeminent example of the "divine in man" and intended that she should shine with a great light. But even a subject that spoke to the heart as much as this one would not serve the purpose unaided. For questions of high philosophy, Schiller found empirical history too unreliable (letter to Goethe, 10 March 1801; *NA* 31). Some of the alterations that he introduced[21] can be classed under the head of the license traditionally allowed to the historical dramatist, but two go beyond that. First, he decided that his heroine should incur a guilt that causes her, as he put it to Goethe (3 April 1801) to be deserted by the gods. This would enable her, by virtue of the *divine* capacity in her *human* nature, to show her "Charakter-Anspruch auf die Prophetenrolle" (her claim to the prophet's role, by virtue of her character). And then he not only rewrote but romanticized history. The supernatural forces that gave Johanna the gift of prophecy once again override the laws of nature. Her chains fall away and the wall of her prison is split in twain. She dashes out to a glorious death on the battlefield — the formal tragedy is the precondition of the idyllic climax — and then rises, bathed in the rosy aureole that Schiller promised her in his poem, to be welcomed by the Virgin into eternal bliss. Both the nominal guilt and the actual apotheosis depend dramatically on what we might call her "wondrous" dimension.

Humboldt, Goethe told Eckermann, had shown him letters in which Schiller "sich . . . mit der Intention plagte, die sentimentale Poesie von der naiven ganz frei zu machen. Aber nun konnte er für jene keinen Boden finden"[22] (sweated and strained to set sentimental poetry completely free from the naïve variety. The trouble was he couldn't find a soil for the former to grow in). From the concept of the "schöne Seele" onwards, Schiller the poet is driven by the logic of his philosophy to seek a basis within nature for the transcendence of the *merely* human. This led him to the concept of a "sentimental idyll" towards which it was the poet's duty to strive, just as it was the role of civilization to lead mankind as a whole to the goal of harmony. In both cases, the outcome is "vollendete Menschheit"[23] (perfected humanity). The object of representation is crucial to the success of the enterprise.[24] But it cannot be a static object. Like grace, ideal harmony is achieved only in movement. Schiller proposes a heroic process, combining the rewards promised in the Bible to "him that overcometh" with a reminiscence of Kant's "What is Enlightenment?"[25] How can this exotic plant grow out of the thin soil of the sensuous world? Since the possibility of the ideal in the world of the senses is an article of faith, the idyll must provide sensuous confirmation (*NA* 20:468; "eine sinnliche Bekräftigung") of this tenet. But far from nourishing this faith, actual experience tends constantly to contradict it.

But the romantic world of the wondrous, once accepted as an aesthetic vehicle, can give concrete form to the abstract idea of the simultaneity of the human and divine. If its manifestations contain spiritual truth, we need not dismiss them as the superstitious nonsense that the dying Talbot thinks has triumphed in Johanna (3.6.2318–30). With his subtitle (*Eine romantische Tragödie*) Schiller claimed the right to enter Wieland's "romantische[s] Land." He never quite came to terms with this "seltsames Mittelding" (curious half-breed) of an author,[26] who respected idealism but was ironically wary of enthusiasm, supported the moral but was by no means ready to dismiss the sensual. But Wieland had argued that the imaginative and emotional impulses that informed what he called man's "instinctartige Neigung zum Wunderbaren" (inclination towards the wondrous that has the character of an instinct) did not necessarily lead to *Schwärmerei,* the substitution of imagined for real truth.[27] *Oberon,* after all, had recently established an example of what Wieland had called the "interweaving of the Wondrous and the Natural," that even the Classical writer could admire, and Schiller had taken from it one of his prime examples of "[die] siegende Macht des sittlichen Gesetzes" (the triumphant might of the moral law). It was surely this work that inspired the passage in "On Naive and Sentimental Poetry" in which he praised Wieland's "Ernst der Empfindung"[28] (seriousness of feeling). The wondrous offered a foundation on which Schiller could construct a sensuous dramatic action that could harbor the super-sensuous. And the "romantisches Gedicht" (poetic romance), the genre in which Wieland had excelled, offered a legitimate path to the land of the wondrous.

In discussing Goethe's projected narrative poem "Die Jagd" (The Hunt), in a letter of 26 June 1797 (*NA* 29), Schiller points out that the poetic romance "darf sich wo nicht des Wunderbaren doch des Seltsamen und Überraschenden mehr bedienen" (has license to make greater use, if not of the wondrous, then certainly of the strange and surprising). Neither author nor reader is expected to believe in the fantasy, but both can find in it a vehicle for what they *can* believe in. There is food for love and a language for the heart[29] in the world of fable, as Max Piccolomini interprets it. The wondrous offers a language in which Schiller can express poetically the transcendent dimension of humanity. He expects his audience to believe, but only within that context, in the intervention of God or the Virgin Mary in human affairs. The revealed religions represent symbolically the higher ideal that is a potential reality within humanity: "die Idee eines Göttlichen" (the idea of a divinity).[30] It is likely that Schiller intended to make symbolic use of the Church in his other romantic plan of 1801, *Die Gräfin von Flandern* (The Countess of Flanders): "Eine höhere Hand ist im Spiele, deren Organ ein Mönch ist. Träume und Visionen" (*NA* 12:293; A higher hand is involved, whose vehicle is a monk. Dreams and visions).

The pattern of trial and triumph that is central to the Hercules theme, and, as we shall argue, to his play *Die Jungfrau von Orleans,* is already present, *expressis verbis,* in *Oberon,* together with the motifs of guilt through sensual indulgence and penance through abstinence. Wieland's poem was a key model for the poetic romance, and some aspects of its action do seem to have lodged themselves in Schiller's memory. His consideration of the highly romantic subject of *The Countess of Flanders* must have brought Wieland to mind. We know that he consulted de Tressan, a writer whose "romantic works"[31] were a prime source for Wieland,[32] and that he envisaged an ending in the festive style of *Oberon:*

> Vereinigung der Liebenden und glückliches Ende. Die Zurückkunft muß ein Freudengenuß, ein Fest sein, es muß zu dem langen Streben und Ausharren ein Verhältnis haben. Oberons Schluß. (*NA* 12:292)

> [The union of the lovers, and a happy ending. The return must be a joyous pleasure, a festive occasion; it must stand in a meaningful relationship to the long period of striving and enduring. The conclusion of *Oberon*.]

We are surely entitled to use Wieland's handling of a romantic story as a pointer to what may have been Schiller's approach to the additional freedom that such an action affords, in particular its heroic moral potential. There are parallels to which we could point, but such things are rarely conclusive in proving influence, which in any case is not our main concern. It is, however, worth reiterating that the apparent punishment visited on Hüon and Amanda is in fact that most romantic motif, a trial that leads to the restoration of the harmonious relation between the human and the wondrous.[33] And then there is the ending that so impressed Schiller, a triumphal, festive, indeed idyllic concluding image of a heroine of quasi-angelic status, bathed in idyllic light, and radiating what amounts to Schillerian grace on all around.

Oberon, then, offered a bridge to the outlook and mentality of Weimar Classicism.[34] The values of Classical *Humanität* could coexist with romance and fairy tale, in a blend that offered more sustenance to the idealist's desire for transcendence than did that supposedly better reason to which we saw Posa refer. This latter is the merely prescriptive and proscriptive rationalism that Schiller and Goethe had attacked in the *Xenien,* and which is represented in *Die Jungfrau von Orleans* by Talbot. Schiller's philosophy, equally rationalist, allows of many more things than are dreamt of in Talbot's. It is fueled by a powerful idealistic faith, but is still more earthbound than the "magic" of the Romantic Movement. As Melitta Gerhard points out, the supernatural in *Die Jungfrau von Orleans* is "totally devoid" of the *frisson* to be found in *Macbeth* and *The Tempest*.[35] Astrology, or the world of romance, could be subsumed in symbolic "play," and its color employed in the interests of a faith that located divinity in humankind. As Caroline von Wolzogen reports, Schiller still believed to the end in the suitability of the romantic as a vehicle for the ideal:

> Zufällig hatte sich ein Blatt des Freimütigen in sein Zimmer verirrt. "Tut es gleich hinaus," sagte er, "daß ich mit Wahrheit sagen kann, ich habe es nie gesehen. Gebt mir Märchen und Rittergeschichten; da liegt der Stoff zu allem Schönen und Großen."[36]

> [By chance, a copy of "The Man of Candor" had strayed into his room. "Throw it straight out," he said, "so that I shall be able to say that I have never seen it. Give me fairy tales and tales of chivalry; that is where you will find the stuff of all that is beautiful and great."]

The idea of the symbolic object cannot be used to strip the wondrous of its quality as a concrete reality within the terms of the dramatic or narrative action. The perceived inhumanity of the conditions imposed by Johanna's mission (the making of widows, to use Karl Guthke's phrase)[37] and the morally questionable nature of a doctrine that sees love as guilt have aroused much criticism and speculation. Gert Sautermeister, for example, argues that Johanna's love for Lionel, the episode in which "Trieb" (urge, impulse) temporarily supplants mission in her mind, is a symbol,[38] one of the "symbolische Behelfe" (symbolic expedients) of which Schiller wrote to Goethe (29 December 1797; *NA* 29), "die . . . die Stelle des Gegenstandes verträten"[39] (which could take the place of the object). Johanna's feeling of guilt is seen as a dawning awareness of a discrepancy between her humanity and the mission that, as Horst Rüdiger has put it, "forces her to deny her nature."[40] This thesis has its attractions, but it is hard to square with the continued authority of the mission, and above all with the wondrous events, and the final apotheosis, of the fifth act. The Black Knight is forewarning her against (and tempting her to avoid) the supreme trial: the renunciation of true love, which she has never known, is now demanded of her in reality. After an initial stumble, she achieves this, so that the formally tragic action of the play creates the conditions for a triumphant and festive ending.

And so, this could be called Schiller's idyllic tragedy. In what amounts to a re-sanctification (*contra* Voltaire) of a theme in which the wondrous is a given ingredient, Schiller sees a *Gegenstand* (subject) that favors the portrayal of harmoniously coexisting sensuous and super-sensuous realities.

Even in "On Grace and Dignity," we find the idea of the magical, for grace is a phenomenon that lies within the sphere of human capacity, but transcends rationally explicable nature. As the expression in the physical world of a beauty that derives from the soul rather than nature,[41] it works "magically."[42] It passes the understanding of nature-bound "ird'sche Klugheit" (earthly cleverness) such as that of Thibaut, Talbot, and even, for a time, the Archbishop himself. As the chosen vessel for God's power and the instrument of His will, Johanna has gifts that transcend humanity. But from the outset, her spirituality can transcend the merely natural *within* her humanity. Raimond cannot define it, but recognizes "was Höh'res" (something higher) in her (line 78).[43] This spiritual and moral capacity works at the heroic level in her response to the trial imposed on her. But it is apparent before that; not, of course, in the superhuman, un-womanly war heroine, but in the woman who is not only "schrecklich" (terrible), but "schön zugleich . . . anzusehn" (956–57; at the same time, beautiful to behold). As early as the prologue, we are told that she has a good influence on all around her (142). This is confirmed by the effect she has on Dunois and La Hire, and above all on Burgund, who describes it as "Zaubers Macht" (1802; the power of a magic charm). There is a difference of degree between her own wondrous deeds and those worked through her by Heaven (2252). But both are emanations of the spirit, which bridges the gap between heaven and earth. The angelic quality that Burgund discerns in her (2014) and that enables her to "do with [him] what she will" (2065) is the voice of "schöne Menschlichkeit" (beautiful humanity), indeed of a "schöne Seele," which manifests itself when she is no longer required to perform as a valkyrie. As Burgund puts it:

> Wie schrecklich war die Jungfrau in der Schlacht,
> Und wie umstrahlt mit Anmut sie der Friede!
>
> (2028–29)

[How terrible the maiden was in battle: and with what grace does peace surround her]

Johanna has to pursue a heroic path that runs parallel to that of the sentimental idyll: leaving the pastoral dream, overcoming difficulties in the trial of life, and rising at last to a Herculean consummation. Schiller himself had, in 1785, made "the vow of Hercules" in undertaking "den edlen Wettlauf zum höchsten Ziele"[44] (the noble race to the highest goal). And so Johanna has to be deserted by her helpers from the realm of the wondrous (with faint but definite echoes of the Passion of Christ),[45] so that her perfected humanity, her *human* divinity may become apparent. She recognizes that the heavenly powers have offered her a choice of paths, not as a punishment, but as something sent upon her, a "Geschick" (3147; destiny), a "Prüfung" (3151; trial), a "Schickung" (3156; an intimation of the divine will). When "heaven has spoken" (3154) and "the Master's will" (3166) is clear, the "conflict in my breast" that is caused by the contrast between "the glistening of [outward] honor and her inner sense of unworthiness" (3171–72), is removed. Her love for Lionel is a source of pain, but not of inner conflict.

Two levels of divinity, the wondrous and the human, are united in Johanna, but only in the final stages do they begin to merge. Without offending against the latter, she can fall in relation to the former, which has to be taken, if not literally, at least seriously. Schiller does try to give it dramatic life. As Storz says, he has done what he can to heighten the legendary aspects of the action, and to alienate it from everyday reality through stylization.[46] He selects his motifs eclectically, but leans towards the image of the Old Testament Jehovah, who exacts revenge from his enemies and demands absolute obedience to his commandments. This is the God who departs from Saul because "thou obeyedst not the voice of the LORD, nor executedst his fierce wrath upon Amalek" (1 Sam. 28:15 and 18). The Amalekites in our play are the English, whose cause, as Johanna says to Burgund (2.10.1770), is as black as that of the French is "lichtweiß" (white as light). The chosen people[47] represent a *political* idyll, "unschuldig, heilig, menschlich gut" (1782–83; innocent, holy, good in their humanity), which gives the battle against the English moral, as well as divine, sanction. The Virgin herself falls into the wrathful Old Testament style when she commands Johanna to "destroy my people's enemies" (1081).[48] So however distasteful to a modern mind the bellicose language and behavior becomes at times, there can be little question of assigning guilt to Johanna in her role as vessel of the supernatural divine power. Her ability to convince Burgund, not just with argument but also with spiritual power that he calls a "himmlische Gewalt" (1803; heavenly power) but which we feel is also human, helps dramatically, if not necessarily in pure logic, to convince us of her innocence in this regard.

Unless God shows her a way out, Johanna is lost in a labyrinth. Her love for Lionel is both a crime and not a crime. She has unwittingly left the wondrous sphere, but has not transgressed the boundary of "beautiful" humanity. Her feelings for Lionel do not even remotely resemble Maria Stuart's passion for Bothwell, in which both "subject" and "object" are sensual. This is not the "Männerliebe" (love for a man) that touches the heart with "sünd'ge[n] Flammen eitler Erdenlust" (411–12; sinful flames of vain earthly pleasure). It is much closer to the love described in "On Grace and Dignity," in which the subject is "moral nature" as opposed to common, merely material and animal nature. Not the triumph of "gemeine Natur" (common nature) over "Menschheit" (*NA* 20:281; humanity), but the "freie Empfindung" (free feeling) that flows "aus dem Sitz der Freiheit, aus unsrer göttlichen Natur" (*NA* 20:303; from the seat of freedom, from our divine nature). Lionel's nobility is the key. His "edle(s) Angesicht" (2576; noble countenance) calls forth her love as an immediate response, and nobility is a sign of the active presence in his being of man's super-sensuous nature. A noble breast is one in which affect can be "uneigennützig" (*NA* 20:285; unselfish). "Nichts ist edel, als was aus der Vernunft quillt; alles, was die Sinnlichkeit für sich hervorbringt, ist gemein"[49] (nothing is noble that does not have its source in reason; all that sensuousness brings forth of itself is common). Lionel does have a body, but we may be assured that it is arrayed in grace. It must surely be this that makes Johanna *see* a man (2580) for the first time. Johanna's response is no doubt *sinnlich* in the sense that it is immediate,[50] but it is the response of a "schöne Seele," in which there is no contradiction between sensuality and morality, to a sensuous phenomenon whose inner driving force is super-sensuous. She remains within the sphere of Schillerian *Humanität*, and so, though there is a feeling of guilt, there can be no question of penance.

As long as she is celebrated as a saint, she has to cope with a "schwere Schuld des Busens" (2541; a heavy burden of guilt in her breast), and is briefly tempted to flee from both fate and mission. Only when Thibaut accuses her of sorcery does she see a way of restoring the communion with her heavenly father. And the thunder that tells her that she is no longer "unbegleitet" (3113; unaccompanied) confirms that she is being put on trial not by man but by God. Her "schwere Schuld" is a flaw in the context of a wondrous life; at the human level, it is a precondition of *heroic* sublimity (*NA* 20:294) through which the "schöne Seele" realizes its divine potential. Rather as, in Schiller's principal poetic portrayal of the idyll-hero, "Das Ideal und das Leben": "dem Heiligen die Schuld sich naht" (stanza 10; what is holy finds itself approached by guilt), guilt comes to her as much from without as from within. She has to overcome, but not, as far as we can see, by virtue of the suppression of the sensuous by the moral, nor by a contrived act of expiation.[51] She suffers as a sensuous being, but there is no real evidence of a division between nature and mind.[52] Of her it can be said (as it could not of Maria) that her whole character is moral. The moral and heroic action does seem, to speak the language of "On Grace and Dignity," to be a "freiwillige Wirkung" (free operation) of a natural impulse (NA 20:287), not a "Brechung der Naturnotwendigkeit" (NA 20:290; breaking [of] the natural necessity).

Since the realization of humanity's divine potential is the final stamp of idyllic authenticity, it comes as no surprise that the action proceeds to an idyllic apotheosis. This motif is not present in "On Grace and Dignity," though the "schöne Seele" is perhaps a kind of epiphany. It would have been exactly illustrated by the marriage of Hercules and Hera, but that project was never realized. Of the dramatic and poetic plans, the subject of Joan of Arc offered the best prospect of a final "Übertritt des Menschen in den Gott" (transition of human into god).[53] The same cast of mind as underlies the Humboldt letter and the theory of the idyll in "On Naive and Sentimental Poetry" is traceable here. In spite of Johanna's natural urge to let the cup pass from her, expiate the sin of having undertaken her mission (2937), and be happy once more "wie im Paradies" (2899; as if in Paradise), the return to Eden is not the Father's will. That would have been the "backward step" of the sentimental pastoral idyll (NA 20:469). She must go forward towards the realization of the sentimental idyll: the "free unification" of inclination and Law, Nature refined upwards "zur höchsten sittlichen Würde" (to the highest level of moral dignity), in fact, "das Ideal der Schönheit, auf das wirkliche Leben angewendet" (NA 20:472; the ideal of beauty applied to the circumstances of actual life). And so Johanna finally becomes in full reality the angel that Burgund has glimpsed in her. "Seht einen Engel scheiden," he says (3508; Look and see an angel departing this life), thinking she is dead. This is of course a paradox: an angel cannot die. But a virtual angel (an angelic potential) was present in the human Johanna, and its full realization inevitably implies her death as a human being. Hence, it is not only history that decrees the formal tragic ending, the death of the heroine. The idyll requires it too. The festive ending, the "Freude" (joy), is not only consonant with but dependent upon the heroine's death. It is hard not to believe that in her final speech Schiller is consciously fulfilling the requirements of the definition in his letter to

Humboldt (the "transition of human into god"). The Virgin appears in the choir of angels, she stretches her arms out to receive Johanna, and an Ascension scene begins:

> Wie wird mir? Leichte Wolken heben mich —
> Der schwere Panzer wird zum Flügelkleide,
> Hinauf — Hinauf — die Erde fliegt zurück . . .

[What is this I feel? Light clouds are lifting me up — the heavy armor is changing into a winged garment — Upwards — upwards — the earth is flying away behind me . . .]

The rest is all harmony, light, and . . . idyllic "Freude."

Notes

[1] The harmony between the sensuous and moral principles that constitutes the "schöne Seele" is "das Siegel der vollendeten Menschheit" (*NA* 20:287; that harmony that seals perfected humanity). When grace is combined with dignity (proof, surely, that grace is inherently moral) then "der Ausdruck der Menschheit [ist] in ihr vollendet" (*NA* 20:300; the expression of humanity is complete in that person).

[2] Moor's "enthousiastische Träume von Größe und Wirksamkeit" (enthusiastic dreams of greatness and active achievement), which make of him an "odd sort of Don Quixote" (*Vorrede, NA* 3:6), are fueled by his reading of Plutarch. See *Die Räuber, ein Schauspiel*, act 1, scene 2. Posa's great heroic gesture of self-sacrifice forms a parallel for a "romanhafter Einfall" (far-fetched idea) of Lycurgus.

[3] Wieland, *Hexameron von Rosenhain*, in *WGS* 1:20, 62.

[4] Wieland, *Geschichte des Agathon* (1767 version), ed. K. Schäfer (Berlin: Akademie, 1961), 258–62.

[5] Cf. *Die Jungfrau von Orleans*, act 5, scene 4.

[6] The heart of the youthful Carlos was one that beat "für Menschlichkeit" (line 166; for [the ideal of] humanity). In the *Briefe*, this youthful ideal is described as truth.

[7] Especially Cidli in Canto 4 of *Der Messias* (The Messiah). Semida speaks of the "Schönheit . . . die deine [Cidli's] Seele voll Unschuld / Über den Staub der Erd' erhöht" (4, 858–59; the beauty that elevates your innocent soul above the dust of this earth). Cf. also Klopstock's praise of Richardson's victorious martyr-heroine in

"Die tote Clarissa" (Clarissa in Death, 1751): "Ruhe dir, und Kronen des Siegs, o Seele, Weil du so schön warst" (May you have rest, and receive crowns of victory, O soul, Since you were so beautiful). Clarissa is seen in the same light by Schiller ("Über den Grund des Vergnügens an tragischen Gegenständen"; *NA* 20:146; On the Reason for the Pleasure Aroused by Tragic Subjects).

[8] The hero loves Danae with both soul and body. But the spirituality of the "Sympathie, welche schöne Seelen in wenigen Augenbliken vertraut miteinander macht" (the spiritual sympathy through which beautiful souls become intimately acquainted in only a few moments) is genuine (Wieland, *Geschichte des Agathon* [1767 version], 405).

[9] *NA* 22:140 (letter 2) and 163 (letter 8). In letter 9, Schiller speaks of "die edle Schönheit dieses Charakters" (*NA* 22:165; the noble beauty of this character).

[10] *Enthusiasmus und Schwärmerei* (1775). See. *WGS* 1:21, 196–97.

[11] Quoted in the note to "On Grace and Dignity" (text *NA* 20:266; note *NA* 21:225).

[12] S. S. Kerry, *Schiller's Writings on Aesthetics* (Manchester: Manchester UP, 1961), 78. An example from "On Grace and Dignity" is the "happy union" between spirit and sensuality effected by taste (*NA* 20:260).

[13] "Über naïve and sentimentalische Dichtung," *NA* 20:489–90: "da er die Menschheit zwar von allen zufälligen Schranken befreyen soll, aber ohne ihren Begriff aufzuheben . . . in seinem Herzen nur trifft er es [das Ideal] an" (since he has to liberate humanity from all incidental limitations, without abrogating the basic concept . . . the heart is the only place where he can find it). Cf. the essay on the Chorus (*NA* 10:9): art must "das Wirkliche ganz verlassen und doch aufs genaueste mit der Natur übereinstimmen" (depart entirely from the world of actuality, and yet remain in the most exact harmony with nature).

[14] T. J. Reed, *The Classical Centre: Goethe and Weimar 1775–1832* (Oxford: Clarendon Press 1986), 144.

[15] The image of the eye that "radiates spirituality" contains an echo of Klopstockian sentimentalism: cf. for example Cidli's "Blick voll Seele" (*Der Messias* 4.1.795; look filled with soul). Schiller finds a parallel in the kind of music he defines as "schmelzend" (melting) and that speaks "to the senses only": "Ein bis ins thierische gehender Ausdruck der Sinnlichkeit erscheint dann gewöhnlich auf allen Gesichtern, die trunknen Augen schwimmen" (*NA* 20:200; What usually happens on these occasions is that a sensuality that extends to an animal state finds expression on the faces of all present; eyes glaze over and swim). For the concept "edel" and its connection with the ideal and the idyll, cf. further the discussion of "Veredlung" (ennoblement) in "Über naïve und sentimentalische Dichtung," *NA* 20:489–90.

[16] *NA* 20:277: moral capacity "muß sich durch Grazie offenbaren" (must reveal itself through grace). The sensuous and moral are in harmony and there is no question of coercion (*NA* 20:279).

[17] "Fürchten Sie keine Wallung mehr von mir . . . Keine sterbliche Begierde Teilt diesen Busen mehr" (lines 5314–19; You need fear no further surges [of desire] . . . No longer does any mortal desire divide this breast).

[18] "Poetisch ist der Stoff in vorzüglichem Grade" (the material is poetic in the highest degree), Schiller said of it (H. Koopman, *Schiller* [Stuttgart: Metzler, 1966], 2:58).

[19] "Über naïve und sentimentalische Dichtung," *NA* 20:469. Cf. "Über Anmut und Würde": "Es ist nicht immer nöthig, daß die Vernunft diese Ideen aus den Erscheinungen herauszieht, sie kann sie auch in dieselben hineinlegen" (*NA* 20:259; It is not always necessary for reason to extract these ideas from the appearances (phenomena), it can also place them into them).

[20] "Das Absolute, aber nur innerhalb der Menschheit, ist seine Aufgabe und seine Sphäre" (*NA* 20:481; The absolute, but only within humanity, is its task and its sphere).

[21] The historical Joan first met the King at Chinon in 1429. The death of Salisbury, which is so prophetically announced in 1.11 as having occurred that very day, had in fact taken place the year before. Bad history, but legitimate romantic drama!

[22] J. P. Eckermann, *Gespräche mit Goethe,* 14 November 1823.

[23] "Über Anmut und Würde," *NA* 20:287.

[24] Since the sentimental poet cannot rival his naive counterpart in "absolute Bestimmtheit der Darstellung" (absolute specificity of representation), he must "gerade in dem Gegenstand [sich] von dem naiven Dichter entfernen, weil er diesem, was derselbe in der Form, vor ihm voraus hat, nur durch den Gegenstand wieder abgewinnen kann" (*NA* 20:468; distance himself from the naive poet precisely in the matter of the object of representation, because in the face of the advantage that the other has over him in matters of form, he can regain parity only through the object).

[25] E.g. Rev. 2:7: "To him that overcometh I will give to eat of the tree of life, which is in the midst of the paradise of God" and *NA* 20:472: "Er führe uns . . . vorwärts zu unsrer Mündigkeit, um uns die höhere Harmonie zu empfinden zu geben, die den Kämpfer belohnet, die den Überwinder beglückt" (Let him lead us forwards into the age of our majority, to give us the experience of the higher harmony that is the reward of him that fights [the good fight], that gladdens him who has overcome).

[26] Letter to Körner, 1 May 1797.

[27] *Über den Hang der Menschen an Magie und Geistererscheinungen zu glauben* (On the Inclination of Man to believe in Magic and the Apparition of Spirits), *WGS* 1:14, 322.

[28] "On the Reason for the Pleasure We Derive from Tragic Subjects" (*NA* 20:140), and "On Naive and Sentimental Poetry" (*NA* 20:447): "Auch in unserm Wieland erkenne ich diesen Ernst der Empfindung . . . nimmer fehlt ihm die Schwungkraft, uns, sobald es gilt, zu dem Höchsten emporzutragen" (In our Wieland too, I recognize that seriousness of feeling . . . he is never lacking in the emotional impetus to raise us up, when the occasion requires, to the highest heights). The "auch" may have as much of the "even" as of the "also" about it, but *Oberon* obviously stood out among Wieland's works for Schiller.

[29] "Eine Sprache braucht das Herz" (*Die Piccolomini,* line 1640; the heart needs a language).

[30] "Über den Gebrauch des Chors in der Tragödie" (*NA* 10:15; On the Use of the Chorus in Tragedy).

[31] Cf. Wieland's footnote to book 4, line 46 of *Klelia und Sinibald* (1783): "Der Zwerg Ardan in Amadis aus Gallien und Fräulein Brangein, die Vertraute der schönen Yselde (Yseult la blonde) sind, nebst den übrigen hier genannten Personen, aus den romantischen Werken des Herrn Grafen von Tressan bekannt genug" (*WGS*1:13, 297; People are pretty well acquainted with the dwarf Ardan in "Amadis of Gaul" and Mademoiselle Brangein, the confidante of fair Yselde (Yseult la Blonde), together with the other personages named here, from the romantic works of the Comte de Tressan).

[32] The entry "Tressan" stands in the margin of no. 6 of the "Entwürfe zu Akt I" (sketches for act 1). Cf. also the reference to "eine Erzählung von Tressan" (a story by Tressan) in the letter to Goethe of 20 March 1801. Wieland utilized de Tressan's *Bibliothèque universelle des romans* as a source on several occasions, including for the story of Hüon of Bordeaux.

[33] Cf. *Oberon,* lines 4206–7: "nur zur Prüfung, nicht zur Strafe" (as a trial only, not as a punishment).

[34] The editors of vol. 21 of the *Nationalausgabe* point to the fact that Wieland's influence has been underestimated, but spoil the effect rather by instituting a contrast with the "philosophy of the graces" as portrayed in *Musarion* (*NA* 21:225). It is *Oberon* that is at issue here.

[35] Melitta Gerhard, *Schiller* (Bern: Francke 1950), 375.

[36] *Schillers Gespräche* (*NA* 42:430). *Der Freimüthige: Ein Unterhaltungsblatt* (The Man of Candor: A Journal of Entertainment), one of whose editors was Kotzebue, was hardly a journal likely to appeal to the high-minded editor of *Die Horen*.

[37] K. S. Guthke, "'Die Jungfrau von Orleans': Sendung und Witwenmachung" in *Schiller Heute,* edited by H-J. Knobloch and H. Koopman, 115–30 (Tübingen: Stauffenburg, 1996).

[38] Cf. Gert Sautermeister, *Idyllik und Dramatik im Werk Friedrich Schillers* (Stuttgart: Kohlhammer, 1971), chapter 2, esp. 60–63.

[39] An object becomes symbolic, for Schiller, by virtue of some attribute that enables the reason to "insert" (hineinlegen) an idea into it (*NA* 20:259). For a fuller discussion, see Sautermeister, 43–63.

[40] H. Rüdiger, "Schiller und das Pastorale," *Euphorion* 53 (1959): 247.

[41] *NA* 20:264: "Die Freiheit regiert also jetzt die Schönheit. Die Natur gab die Schönheit des Baues, die Seele gibt die Schönheit des Spiels" (Freedom now rules beauty. Nature provided beauty of form, the soul provides the beauty of play).

[42] *NA* 20:253: "Der Gürtel des Reizes wirkt also . . . magisch" (The girdle of charm [has] . . . a magical effect). The highest grade of grace is the enchanting (*NA* 20:305).

[43] In the following discussion of "*Die Jungfrau von Orleans,*" the numbers in parentheses refer to lines.

[44] Letter to Körner, quoted by Gerhard, *Schiller,* 81.

[45] The theme of the Father, her refusal to answer accusations against her, her submission to the shame of captivity, her sense of abandonment. Line 3243: "Hast du mich ganz aus deiner Huld verstoßen?" (Have you banished me completely from your gracious favor?).

[46] Gerhard Storz, "Schiller: Die Jungfrau von Orleans," in *Das deutsche Drama,* edited by Benno von Wiese, 326 and 334 (Düsseldorf: Bagel 1968).

[47] God has decided in favor of the French (line 1767).

[48] Cf. Johanna's references to "Rache" (vengeance) in the Montgomery scene (lines 1647–48) and to the "Rachschwert meines Gottes" (line 2257; the avenging sword of my God).

[49] *NA* 20:201. Cf. "Gedanken über den Gebrauch des Gemeinen und Niedrigen in der Kunst" (Thoughts on the Use of the Common and Mean in Art): "Gemein ist alles, was nicht zu dem Geiste spricht, und kein anderes, als sinnliches Interesse erregt" (*NA* 20:241; everything that does not speak to the spirit and that arouses no other interest than the sensuous, is common). Schiller makes a close correlation between grace and nobility in his comments on the genius (the man with God-given talent) in "On Grace and Dignity": "man [kann] erwarten, daß der Stoff sich zur Form veredelt" (*NA* 20:276, n.; we have a right to expect that matter should be ennobled into form).

[50] Cf. *NA* 20:292: "entscheidet er [der Wille] aber unmittelbar, so handelt er sinnlich" (if it decides immediately, it acts sensuously).

[51] There is no mention of penance in the main tragic action. Johanna does bring up the idea of expiation in connection with her imagined pride in abandoning her rustic home and family (lines 2937–38), but this is in a moment of weakness when she seems almost to want to revert to childhood: lines 2926: "Kommt, laßt uns fliehn" (Come, let us flee).

[52] Cf. "Über Anmut und Würde," *NA* 20:262–63.

[53] Schiller to Humboldt, 30 November 1795.

Works Cited

Eckermann, J. P. *Gespräche mit Goethe.*

Gerhard, Melitta. *Schiller.* Bern: Francke, 1950.

Guthke, Karl S. " 'Die Jungfrau von Orleans': Sendung und Witwenmachung." In *Schiller Heute,* edited by H-J. Knobloch and H. Koopman, 115–30. Tübingen: Stauffenburg, 1996.

Kerry, S. S. *Schiller's Writings on Aesthetics.* Manchester: Manchester UP, 1961.

Koopman, Helmut. *Schiller.* Stuttgart: Metzler, 1966.

Reed, T. J. *The Classical Centre: Goethe and Weimar.* Oxford: Clarendon Press, 1986.

Rüdiger, Horst. "Schiller und das Pastorale." *Euphorion* 53 (1959): 229–51.

Sautermeister, Gert. *Idyllik und Dramatik im Werk Friedrich Schillers.* Stuttgart: Kohlhammer, 1971.

Storz, Gerhard. "Schiller: Die Jungfrau von Orleans." In *Das deutsche Drama,* edited by Benno von Wiese. Düsseldorf: Bagel, 1968.

Wieland. *Hexameron von Rosenhain.* In *WGS.*

The Poet as Herald of Grace and Dignity: The Influence of Schiller's Twin Concepts on Stefan George

Christophe Fricker

HAPPINESS MAY BE ALL IN THE MIND, but it is also found in the constitution of people who show forth grace and dignity: "Laß [die Schönheit] die Glückliche sein, du schaust sie, du bist der Beglückte" (let [beauty] be happy; if you see it, you are the happy one), says Schiller in the poem "Das Glück" (Happiness). And a little further on he says about the person listening to a singer inspired by God: "Weil er glücklich ist, kannst du der Selige sein" (both quotations *NA* 1:410; Because he is happy, you can be overjoyed). Schiller's transcendental philosophy is constantly linked with phenomena, what can be seen. Despite all attempts at conceptual clarity, there is no concealing the fact that his thoughts about grace and dignity appeal to the senses. The law of beauty is a point of orientation in a world perceived by the senses. Humans acknowledge a limit to their abilities: they know that they are responsible for the law according to which grace and dignity are manifested, but also that they cannot themselves produce them in accordance with that law.

In what follows I intend to show how Schiller moves from thoughts about individual receptivity to grace and dignity to adopt a broader social and finally historical-philosophical perspective. The role of those endowed with particularly sharp senses will have to be examined. The second stage will show how this dynamic is received in a later period. For this, I will use Stefan George as an example.

Schiller characterizes grace as "Schönheit der Gestalt unter dem Einfluß der Freyheit" (*NA* 20:264, beauty of form under freedom's influence). This contradicts the later statement that grace can appear even where there is no beauty (*NA* 20:288). But the two assumptions are medi-ated by the claim that grace can turn into architectonic beauty when the gestures expressing it become features (*NA* 20:265). Like beauty, grace is objective, a feature of the object itself. The object or, for that matter, a human being is approached for its own sake. This already indicates how an object can structure the reality surrounding it according to its own laws.

Grace is visible in a person's movements. Schiller distinguishes volun-tary and instinctive movements according to their origin. Voluntary move-ments are the result of a decision and are intended to achieve a goal. Yet the way towards this goal does not necessarily determine every single aspect of the movement in question. Thus there is room for "sympathetic" movements which, however, contribute to the achievement of the same goal. In these, personality and character are expressed and grace is exhib-ited. Voluntary movements are "Wirkung des *Entschlusses* und des *Zweckes*" (*NA* 20:268; the effect of the *decision* and the purpose). But the true nature of a person can be told only from the accompanying move-ments. Grace enters by the back door of the will. At the beginning of the essay, Schiller defined architectonic beauty as "*sinnliche[n] Ausdruck eines Vernunftbegriffs*" (*NA* 20:261; the sensuous expression of a rational con-cept). Reason expresses the form of human purpose, but gives nature some elbow room. Schiller comes back to this idea and states analogously that "die Grazie eine *Gunst* sey, die das Sittliche dem Sinnlichen erzeigt" (*NA* 20:278; grace is a favor granted to the sensuous by the ethical). The human mind determines the conditions within which beauty can be brought about by its nature. Through this construction, Schiller attempts to resolve what can appear as a contradiction resulting from an apparent two-fold origin of grace in mind and nature.

From the discussion of actions in a person's mind, Schiller moves on to developing the disposition of those in whom grace appears. He introduces the concept of expressive or mimic movements. What they express is moral attitudes. This visible morality is not necessarily beautiful. It is even unaes-thetic if it suppresses what is natural. But even if one is determined to obey reason, one must pay respect to one's inclinations. If this is the case, grace will appear and it will be both expressive (because it is based in the person's moral attitudes) and beautiful (because it is also based in the sensual). This is followed by the question of how this harmony can be made lasting. How can the beautiful soul be more than just a momentary appearance and permanently trust its inclinations as the source of moral deeds.

Grace appears in voluntary movements where reason maintains its position with regard to nature. Dignity appears when reason tries to control actions grounded solely in nature:

> War es hingegen die Vernunft selbst, die, wie bey einem schönen Charakter der Fall ist, die Neigungen *in Pflicht nahm,* und der Sinnlichkeit das Steuer *nur anvertraute,* so wird sie es in demselben Moment zurücknehmen, als der Trieb seine Vollmacht mißbrauchen will. (*NA* 20:294)

> [If, on the other hand, reason itself, as is the case in a beautiful character, has *taken over* the inclinations and only *entrusted* sensuousness with the helm, it will take it back the moment that instinct tries to abuse its power.]

This immediate action is sublime. It presents itself as suffering and appears as intelligence. Dignity thus means that reason controls both emotions and sympathetic movements. Dignity is the "Ausdruck einer erhabenen Gesinnung" (*NA* 20:289; expression of a superior mentality).

When the realm of morals becomes relevant for the discussion of the concept of dignity, deeds have to be addressed. Schiller develops his ideas about the deeds of the beautiful soul with constant reference to grace and dignity as the poles of a personality. When the person who places obligations does so with grace, he will be loved. If the person placed under an obligation shows dignity, he will be respected. Mistakes are to be criticized with grace and admitted with dignity. Grace can recognize dignity and prove its difference from deliberate exertion. Dignity testifies to grace's moral value by distinguishing it from slackness. Schiller introduces numerous other concepts while connecting the ones outlined so far.

Schiller finally summarizes what the person has achieved in the unity of grace and dignity. The "*Gott* in uns" (*NA* 20:303; the *God* in us) has evolved and is met with love and respect. This last step reiterates that the appearance of grace and dignity is met with amazement. Schiller more precisely defines love and respect and justifies their existence. One views the dominance of reason, appearing as dignity, with respect. To respect another person has a stimulating and absorbing effect on one's own intellect. If reason finds one of its ideas realized in the sensual world, it views it with love. Love is at the same time magnanimous "denn sie empfängt von ihrem Gegenstande nichts, sondern giebt ihm alles, da der reine Geist nur geben, nicht empfangen kann; [und das Selbstsüchtigste] denn es ist immer nur ihr eigenes Selbst, was sie in ihrem Gegenstande sucht und schätzet" (*NA* 20:304; because it receives nothing from its object but gives it everything, since pure intellect can only give, not receive; [and extremely selfish] because it is always only its own self that it seeks and appreciates in its object). The highest form of dignity is majesty. Only what is sacred can be majestic. It forces the observer to look at and into himself. The highest form of grace, on the other hand, is charming.

"On Grace and Dignity" does not concern itself with the question of how beauty becomes relevant for and influential in a society. This question, however, is addressed in the "Letters on the Aesthetic Education of Man." Here, Schiller argues that "der freygebige Augenblick findet ein unempfängliches Geschlecht" (*NA* 20:319; the moment so prodigal of opportunity finds a generation unprepared to receive it; *AEM* 36) and goes past without consequences. During the times of transition to the aesthetic state to come, the nature of men, their sensual impulse, has to be subjected to laws, whereas their moral impulse has to be absorbed by guiding impressions from outside. It is the task of the artist to shape and change his environment by "sie ringsum mit den Symbolen des Vortrefflichen ein[schließen]" (*NA* 20:336; encompass[ing] them about with the symbols of perfection; *AEM* 61). A person's moral impulse, Schiller explains, "ist aufs Unbedingte gerichtet, für ihn giebt es keine Zeit, und die Zukunft wird ihm zur Gegenwart, sobald sie sich aus der Gegenwart nothwendig entwickeln muß" (*NA* 20:335; is directed towards the Absolute. For such an impulse time does not exist, and the future turns into the present from the moment that it is seen to develop with inevitable necessity out of the present; *AEM* 59). When moral striving, bound fast to the senses, is perceived by someone receptive to it, that person must appear to be a seer, since he perceives a segment not only of a personal future but of society's future as well. The seer is not only the one who perceives the appearance of what is not yet available to the senses but also the one who, from the point of view of his insight into the expressive nature of the visible, regards that appearance as not under anyone's control.

Greek antiquity lends itself as an example of a society where mankind's potential has been realized. Schiller contrasts its wholeness with the fragmentation of modernity. Whereas the Greeks' life was "[z]ugleich voll Form und voll Fülle, zugleich philosophirend und bildend, zugleich zart und energisch" (*NA* 20:321; [existed] in fullness of form no less than of content, at once philosophic and creative, sensitive and energetic; *AEM* 35), modern man is "[e]wig nur an ein einzelnes kleines Bruchstück des

Ganzen gefesselt, bildet sich der Mensch selbst nur als Bruchstück aus"
(*NA* 20:323; everlastingly chained to a single little fragment of the whole
[and thus] himself develops into nothing but a fragment; *AEM* 35).

Schiller's explanation of the twin concepts of Grace and Dignity starts
with the "Handlungen" (actions) in a person's mind. The second step
describes how consciousness deals with these actions and how they appear.
Thus Schiller speaks of a person's stance. He then turns to deeds carried
out on the basis of actions reflected upon and voluntarily employed. Lastly
he suggests possible reactions of those observing them.

Receptivity forms the starting point for changes within society. The
problem arises that this receptivity cannot be verbally communicated.
The appearance of beauty is not under anyone's control. One can think of
the laws of beauty but not produce beauty according to these laws. The
beautiful has a universal sensuous appeal but no one can capture this universality conceptually. It is perceived as common sense. In what follows
I shall show, through examples from Stefan George's late poems, how he
emphasizes in his poetry the perceptibility of grace and dignity, and how
he sees and interprets them as prefiguring social renewal but also knows
how long this process will take.

Dirk von Petersdorff has recently shown that George takes up the
eighteenth century's discussion about the autonomy of art at a crucial
moment in his development as a poet: at the beginning of the volume *Der
siebente Ring* (The Seventh Ring). Here George is held to be making the
transition from being an artist only interested in aesthetics to functioning
as a herald of social reform.[1] In the "Time Poem" at the beginning of *Der
siebente Ring* he says that the system of a socially based, regulative, and
integrative art, developed up till now at a distance, aims at becoming the
environment for the coming order, in which the fragmentation of modernity is to be healed. Both Schiller and George see the artist's potential for
piloting the introduction of this new condition as limited: Schiller admits
that contemporary society is unreceptive and George is categorical about
the fact that only very few perceive the appearances that anticipate an ideal
to come. George's friend, the German scholar and poet Friedrich Gundolf, ascribes grace and dignity to George's translations of Dante. Thus he
links the two concepts with a poet celebrated not only as a great innovator
of poetic language but as someone who has a profound influence on history through his poetic innovations.[2] I would like to support Dirk von
Petersdorff's argument by providing textual evidence from George's

poetry. Theoretical writings from the George Circle will be referred to only in passing; George as a person will not be the focus of this essay even though another Gundolf quotation would provide an excellent starting point for this: In his book *George*, Gundolf speaks of "die Anmut und Würde von Georges persönlichem Umgang"[3] (the grace and dignity with which George interacted with others).

In his last volume of poetry, *Das neue Reich*, George twice uses the words "Anmut" and "Hoheit" closely linked with each other. This emphasizes the poet's familiarity with the discussion about grace and dignity.[4] *Das neue Reich* was published in 1928 as volume 9 of the edition of George's collected works. Its motifs and formulations form a complex net of references between the individual poems. The volume consists of a series of hymns, scenes, so-called "Sprüchen" (lines addressed to friends alive and dead), and a number of songs with which the oeuvre ends. I would like to look at the tripartite poem "Hyperion"[5], the second of the hymns, and at the two poems entitled "B.v.St." (*SW* 9:85) from the Sprüche. These short and personal poems are directed towards friends of the poet. Some refer to encounters with people who remain anonymous, others present archetypes (such as "Der Weisheitslehrer" [The Sage]). Against the backdrop of developments of modernity, individuals are presented who embody certain ideals. The Sprüche teach, commemorate, and lead. They form the basis for friendships and sustain them. They are part of the poet's life and work at one and the same time, so they can also be interpreted in the context of the oeuvre's net of references. One of the people addressed is Berthold Schenk Graf von Stauffenberg.[6]

B.V.ST. I

Im sommerlichen glanz der götterstadt
Sannen wir trauernd oft den spuren nach
Des toten königskindes.

Was dient uns schlachtenvorteil scharfsinn kraft!
Im blutgedüngten marschland mutige wehr!
Wenn uns die hoheit stirbt.

Dem frisch-bereicherten bleibt hohl sein saal
Sein garten birgt nie mehr wenn je gefällt
Uralten baumes weihe.

Was dient · sei sie auch mehr als frommer wahn ·
Gleichheit von allen und ihr breitstes glück!
Wenn uns die anmut stirbt.

[In the summery glow of the divine city / We often thought sadly about
the footsteps / Of the king's dead child. // What is the use of advantage
in battle, acuity, power! / Or brave defense in the blood-drenched
marshlands / If dignity recedes from us. // The hall of the recently
blessed remains hollow / His garden no longer protects if ever / The
ancient tree's blessing is felled. // What is the use · Even if more than
pious madness · / Equality for all and universal happiness! / If grace
recedes from us.]

The poem states that military and intellectual achievements are worth-
less where *Hoheit* and *Anmut* are lost. According to Morwitz, the prince
who formerly embodied the two virtues may have been the Bavarian Prince
Luitpold (1901–14), grandchild of Bavaria's last king, Ludwig III.

The terms Anmut and Hoheit are also used in the hymn "Hyperion."[7]
In its first part, the poet leaves his home country to find his cultural origins. He leaves his own people and his friends behind. Even though he
feels close to them, he reproaches them:

Ihr die in sinnen verstrickten
Ihr die in tönen verströmten
Schlaff dann beim werke:
(*SW* 9:12)

[You who are tangled in thoughts / You who are drained into sounds /
Are sluggish then at your work:]

The poet warns these brothers of his not to learn the "Holde gebärde
der freude" (sweet gesture of joy) that pertains to the dancer. It is inappro-
priate for them because they are "schwank" (unstable). If they tried to learn
and imitate the relevant movements the result will seem "roh" (inexpert).
The second part of the poem depicts Greek antiquity as an alternative
world. Hyperion now turns to this land:

Ahnung gesellt mich zu euch
kinder des Inselgebiets
Die ihr in anmut die tat
bilder in hoheit ersannt

Spartas gebändigten mut
Ioniens süsse vermählt.
(*SW* 9:13)

[Presentiment links me to you / Children of the islands / Who ponder deeds in grace / Images in dignity / The tamed pride of Sparta / Joins with Ionian sweetness.]

Having said how he was led into this new and old land, the poet characterizes its inhabitants. Through and within grace and dignity they act and produce works of art. These two concepts are being contrasted with the attitudes of draining and sluggishness that the poet has found in those he had left behind. George names the concepts of grace and dignity in an emphatic way and thus distances himself from the Romantic topos of *je ne sais quoi*. For him it is not impossible to put into words what appears. The relation between the appearance of a new ideal and the renewed possibility of naming it, however, deserves its own study.

Schiller and George coincide in first establishing grace and dignity on a level below the conscious formation of an individual personality. The meaning of Schiller's attribute "magic," namely, the changing of a person but not an identity, is mirrored in George. He rejects "Schlachtenvorteil, Scharfsinn und Kraft" (advantage in battle, acuity, and power), phenomena and features that could very well be seen as positive ones, as long as other factors are not present that cannot be produced or brought about by them but could be their precondition. In "Hyperion" one finds these stages of thought again; the adjective "adligster" (*SW* 9:13, noblest) draws attention to the intensification of something that in the common comprehension is either present or not present but in any case cannot be more or less intensely formed. This demonstrates that George is not referring to the aristocracy of birth. Relating the poem to the Bavarian heir apparent is thus merely incidental. It is, however, interesting that it is part of a poem dedicated to an aristocrat. It shows George's pedagogical talent for addressing anyone in an appropriate language.

It is also important to note that, in the poem, grace and majesty are there for us. They have receded "from us" and thus must have lived "for us" before. This means it is not so essential that men embodying those ideals are alive anywhere in particular but that their existence is perceived and acknowledged. "We" denotes the group of people who perceive and acknowledge. They only constitute a group through these activities.

When individuals are presented in the *Neues Reich,* it is in most cases their posture that is described first, the way they approach and meet the poet. Verbs of movement, "schreiten, kommen, vor etwas treten, gehen" (to stride, to come, to step up to something, to go) help to characterize the first impression of a person's outward appearance. To prove his distance from his countrymen, the poet refers to their inability to move gracefully. In this case he uses the word "hold," a synonym for "anmutig." Those movements are in positive contrast to most others and can serve as an example. They can be understood as a favor granted to the person. The second of the poems about Stauffenberg links his "Gang" (gait) with the fact that he exerts his "herrenrecht" (*SW* 9:85, rights as master). What becomes visible in the movements enables and entitles the person to rule. The politically legitimizing aspect of graceful movement can also be found in Schiller, who uses political examples and concepts (majesty, of course, being the most notable one) as an analogy.

We have reached the realm of actions carried out by a graceful or dignified person. It is again in the second part of "Hyperion" that they are elaborated. The Greeks are graceful and dignified as a people. Graceful and dignified refers not only to some individual members of a people but to the people as a whole. They evoke heroes in dancing; the thinkers are also politicians. Education and art, religion and pleasure unite. In "reigen und rausch" (dancing and intoxication) gods are created. All these actions are performed gracefully and with dignity. Some are also suited to reconciling different areas of human life. Some enable individual human beings to be the origin of what is more than human. The similarity to the concept of Greece as presented in the Aesthetic Letters is obvious.

The constellation of "Tat und Bild" (deed and image) is also used in the first stanza of "Goethes lezte Nacht in Italien" (*SW* 9:7–10; Goethe's Last Night in Italy), the opening hymn of the volume. It depicts a scene typical for the ideas of friendship developed in the *Neues Reich.* Two people "make a vow in front of a an image.[8] The same poem speaks of "gebärden / Attischer würde" (*SW* 9:10; gestures of Attic dignity). Once again in connection with Greece, dignity is presented as a gesture. The word "Gebärde" has evolved from the old "bären," which still survives in the word "gebären" (to give birth). In both cases, something is made visible, an appearance is being brought forward.

The last step is to look at the reactions to movements that display grace and dignity. Both those who have a deeper insight into their meaning and ordinary people seem to see them positively. They are amazed and ascribe the right to rule to the bearer of these movements: "[Wo] / Wir dich bestaunt und gar das volk dich nahm / Für den erstandnen Prinzen" (*SW* 9:85; Where we marveled at you and even the people took you for the resurrected prince).

I shall illustrate the significance of the order of actions, attitudes, deeds, and reactions for the rest of the *Neue Reich* by means of other poems, concentrating particularly on those adjacent to the ones already discussed. I am not, however, implying that Schiller's essay has deliberately been used as a basis for the structure or the diction of the volume. "Hyperion" is followed by the four-part hymn "An die Kinder des Meeres" (*SW* 9:15–20; To the Children of the Sea). Its first three sections present individuals. Once again, George places great emphasis on characteristics of their appearances: he mentions, for example, brow and eye and smile. Among the movements are "sorgloser Gang" (careless gait) and the word "geschmeidig" (lithe/lithely) in an uncommon context, used as an adverb with the verb "stehen" (to stand). In each case, the intense impression of effortlessness and ease is underlined. An epilogue follows the three portraits. At a central position George summarizes the way in which the poet and his friends are attracted by the young men they meet.

> So lebten sie die wir in ehrfurcht nennen
> Von eigner kraft gebändigt hoch und leicht
> Und strahlend wie der leib der Schaumgebornen.
>
> (*SW* 9:19)

[Thus lived those whom we mention in awe / By their own power restrained, high and light / And shining like the body of the one who was born in foam.]

These verses speak of appearances and reactions. The first one speaks of the attitude taken by others towards the three men: one meets them with reverence. The second verse alludes to the powers battling within them but being placed under certain restraints by them. Three adjectives provide further qualifications: "hoch" takes up the noun "Hoheit," whereas "leicht" and "strahlend"[9] intensify the uncoerced and beautiful overall impression. The concluding comparison relates the children to the body of Venus, whom Schiller mentions at the beginning of his essay as the ideal representation of beauty. She is, in his words, "ein beschlossenes, streng abgewogenes

Werk der Notwendigkeit und als solches keiner Varietät, keiner Erweiterung fähig" (*NA* 20:256; a completed, delicately balanced work of necessity and therefore incapable of variation or extension). One notices that not only the three adjectives but the two preceding verses in their entirety are subject to the comparison. Control over the sensual forces by strict laws is also part of the impression of Venus.

The "Sprüche" addressed to Stauffenberg are preceded by the poem "Der Tänzer" (*SW* 9:84; The Dancer).[10] The title announces that it is dedicated to a particular kind of movement. It evokes the image of a group of children. One of them seems to be special and distinguishes himself from the others. This boy "gibt den takt an und den gang" (sets the rhythm and the pace). He has established an orderly system of movements, and interprets them. At the same time, he is the ideal example for their seemingly effortless procession. "Wie leicht sein fuss sich dreht und schnellt und säumt / Wie beugt die hüfte sich gewandt und sacht!" (How easily his foot turns and hastens and tarries / How nimbly and gently he bends at the hip!) Ease and appropriate speed and the impression of experience and diligence convey the image of a perfect personality. The poet sums up his impressions by concluding: "Er ist die ganze jugend wie sie träumt / Er ist die ganze jugend wie sie lacht" (He is the whole of youth as it dreams / He is the whole of youth in its mirth). The young man becomes representative of his generation. He acts for them.[11] The poet is convinced of this special legitimacy because he has observed the posture and movements of the Dancer and their effect on the others. This effect and its recognition by the others are both present in the declaratory "ist" (is) of the last two lines.

Schiller discusses, in a note, the role of the dancing master, acknowledging the "Verdienst um die wahre Grazie" (services to true grace) that he delivers "indem er dem Willen die Herrschaft über seine Werkzeuge verschafft, und die Hindernisse hinwegräumt, welche die *Masse* und *Schwerkraft* dem Spiel der lebendigen Kräfte entgegensetzen" (*NA* 20:269; by granting the will mastery over its tools and by removing the obstacles to the play of lively forces that are set by mass and gravity). He has to make sure that the work of the rule becomes his pupil's nature so that it no longer appears as a rule.[12] George's poem "Der Tänzer" does not explicitly talk about a teacher or leader. In this poem, the ease of the dancer's graceful movements has come about by itself. In turn, the dancer himself becomes the teacher. Through his example and by transmitting the measured movement to the other children, he lets rule become nature in them.

It is decisive that the bodily and transcendental forces shaping a person are brought into a harmonious unity. This unity is to be reached because it is a human being's natural state, and everything else is a deviation from it. To look at body and soul separately can be pointless and confusing. This is also the argument of the poem "Leib und Seele" (Body and Soul) in the final section of the "Sprüche an die Lebenden" (Lines to the Living).

LEIB UND SEELE

Sprach nicht der Weise: Such der seele schönheit
Vor der des leibs? .. ‚Leib · seele sind nur worte
Wechselnder wirklichkeit. Der staat ward faul
Und flach und dreist der bürger. Da erfand
Der Göttliche zu hilf und heil die seele . . .
Unlängst erzähltest du vom früheren freund:
Sein helles aug ward matt · sein mund der blühte
Ward saftlos · enge ward die hohe stirn . . .
Ich weiss nicht ob du leib ob seele maltest.'

(SW 9:86)

[Body and Soul // Did the wise man not say: Seek the soul's beauty / Before you seek the body's? .. 'Body · soul are simply words / Of changing reality. The state became idle, / Its citizens flat and brazen. So the Divine One / Created the soul as a saving measure . . . / Not long ago you mentioned a former friend: / His bright eye grew dim · his mouth that had blossomed / Dried up · his high forehead narrowed . . . / I do not know if you painted body or soul.']

This is not the place to discuss whether "Vernunft" (reason) as used by Schiller is the same as what George calls "Seele" and contrasts with "Leib." It is only important to note that George shows how body and soul themselves are subject to philosophical concepts. Body and soul are names, as are grace and dignity. Poet and thinker, in this case referred to as "Der Göttliche," find them and mark them as their findings.

In eyes, lips and forehead spiritual changes become apparent. This, however, does not reduce the body or parts of it to the role of a mere messenger.[13] In the beginning we reminded ourselves of the necessity of recognizing that we are dealing with very concrete phenomena. Let us now look at individual features of the body that George and Schiller use as examples. They are more than illustrations; they help to make the argument clearer.

According to Schiller, signs of architectonic beauty are "[e]in glückliches Verhältniß der Glieder, fließende Umrisse, ein lieblicher Teint, eine zarte Haut, ein feiner und freyer Wuchs, eine wohlklingende Stimme u. s. f." (*NA* 20:256; well coordinated limbs, flowing outlines, a pleasing complexion, delicate skin, a fine and independent bearing, a mellifluous voice, and so forth). Movements performed gracefully will "leicht, sanft und dennoch belebt seyn. Heiter und frey wird das Auge strahlen, und Empfindung wird in demselben glänzen. Von der Sanftmuth des Herzens wird der Mund eine Grazie erhalten, die keine Verstellung erkünsteln kann. . . . Musik wird die Stimme seyn, und mit dem reinen Strom ihrer Modulationen das Herz bewegen" (*NA* 20:288; become light and gentle, and yet lively. The eye shines bright and clear, and sentiment gleams in it. From the gentle heart, the mouth receives a grace that cannot be produced by dissimulation. . . . The voice will be music and move the heart with the stream of its modulations). In two other places, Schiller adds smiles and glances, and a cheerful brow (*NA* 20:301). He thus lists particular ways in which either the body as a whole or parts of it appear, preferably lips and eyes but also brow and voice.

George, in a different context, calls matter "Kein mindres heiligtum" (no less sacred) when compared to spirit and he explicitly includes the body. Its rank is equal to the spirit's. Spirit and body become one in an appearance and mirror each other. Shared terminology is an indication that Schiller and George attribute similar functions and value to grace and dignity as they describe them. Both authors draw conclusions about a person's character from his or her movements and thus deliberately relate them to morally exemplary actions. Like Schiller, George sees graceful personalities as heralds of their respective vision for society. Individuals are as much in their focus as is society as a whole[14] as well as its outstanding members, beautiful souls. Grace and dignity can become characteristics of a group. This is why Schiller could be seen by the George circle as "der feinste schönheitslehrer"[15] (the finest teacher of beauty). George and Wolfskehl, in their introduction to the third volume of their anthology *Deutsche Dichtung* (German Poetry), entitled *Das Jahrhundert Goethes* (Goethe's Century), put a stronger emphasis on Schiller's ideas about an aesthetic education than on his poetry. They admit that the ambition of Schiller's program makes it clear that he is a stranger among his own people and will remain a stranger for a long time.[16] George and Schiller know that the aesthetic state will not come about overnight.

Notes

This essay is based on numerous conversations with Dr Fritz Heuer, to whom I am extremely grateful. My work on this project has been generously supported by the Killam Fund. I am grateful to its trustees.

[1] Dirk von Petersdorff, "Wie viel Freiheit braucht die Dichtung? 'Das Zeitgedicht' im 'Siebenten Ring,'" *George-Jb.* 5 (2004/05): 45–62.

[2] Friedrich Gundolf, "Dante," *Castrum Peregrini* 91 (1970): 30–39.

[3] Friedrich Gundolf, *George* (Berlin: Bondi, 1920), 256.

[4] See also H. Stefan Schultz, "Über das Verhältnis Stefan Georges zu Schiller," in *Studien zur Dichtung Stefan Georges* (Heidelberg: Lothar Stiehm, 1967), 68–89.

[5] Stefan George, *Sämtliche Werke*, 9:11–14. Subsequent references to this work are cited in the text using the abbreviation *SW* and the volume and page number.

[6] Among the biographical literature about Berthold Stauffenberg, two works pay particular respect to the three brothers' connection to Stefan George: Peter Hoffmann, *Claus Schenk Graf von Stauffenberg und seine Brüder* (Stuttgart: DVA, 1992); and Michael Baigent, *Secret Germany: Claus von Stauffenberg and the Mystical Crusade against Hitler* (London: Penguin 1995).

[7] In recent years, a number of authors have dealt with the relationship between Stefan George and Hölderlin. The most comprehensive study has been undertaken by Henning Bothe, *"Ein Zeichen sind wir, deutungslos": Die Rezeption Hölderlins von ihren Anfängen bis zu Stefan George* (Stuttgart: Metzler, 1992). Alexander Losse examines "Hyperion" in *Castrum Peregrini* 250 (2001): 95–102. Ute Oelmann stresses the far-reaching importance of the discovery of Hölderlins hymns for George's last work. See her commentary to the *Neues Reich* (*SW* 9:116–17).

[8] See *SW* 9:8, lines 5–7.

[9] The question in how far the appearance of beauty is a "scheinen" in the two senses of the German word was discussed by Emil Staiger and Martin Heidegger on the occasion of Staiger's interpretation of "An eine Lampe" by Mörike. See Emil Staiger, *Die Kunst der Interpretation: Studien zur deutschen Literaturgeschichte* (Zürich: Atlantis, 1955), 34–49.

[10] The Sprüche to B.v.St. are followed by a caesura. Thus only the preceding poem is discussed here.

[11] Analogous observations can be made with respect to other archetypes in the *Neues Reich,* for example the "Sühner."

[12] Gabriele Brandstetter finds the basis for Schiller's remarks about ballet in the discussion about a reform of dance started by the French master Noverre. See her article " 'Die Bilderschrift der Empfindungen': Jean-Georges Noverres *Lettres sur la Danse, et sur les Ballets* und Friedrich Schillers Abhandlung *Über Anmut und Würde,*" in *Schiller und die höfische Welt,* ed. by Achim Aurnhammer, Klaus Manger, and Friedrich Strack, 77–93 (Tübingen: Niemeyer, 1990). Brandstetter also refers to Schiller's poem "Der Tanz."

[13] On the referentiality of grace, see Janina Knab, *Ästhetik der Anmut: Studien zur "Schönheit der Bewegung" im 18. Jahrhundert* (Frankfurt am Main: Peter Lang, 1996).

[14] The commonalities between members of this group are part of the poem "Geheimes Deutschland" (*SW* 9:45–49), which does not speak about the potential deeds of this group. Cf. Kurt Hildebrandt, *Das Werk Stefan Georges* (Hamburg: Hauswedell, 1960), 416–21. It is noteworthy that from the space George grants different people in his poetry one cannot infer their respective importance for the poet in real life. It would be interesting to base a sociological account of George's Circle merely on the poetry.

[15] *Deutsche Dichtung, vol. 3: Das Jahrhundert Goethes,* ed. and with an introduction by Stefan George and Karl Wolfskehl (1902; repr., Stuttgart: Klett-Cotta, 1995), 6. Other works from within the George circle dealing with Schiller are the respective chapter in Max Kommerell, *Der Dichter als Führer in der deutschen Klassik,* 2nd ed. (Frankfurt am Main: Klostermann, 1940); and Rudolf Fahrner's dissertation, *Hölderlins Begegnung mit Goethe und Schiller* (Marburg: Elwert, 1925). Kurt Hildebrandt, in his book *Leibniz und das Reich der Gnade* (Den Haag: Nijhoff, 1953), discusses "Über Anmut und Würde" with respect to Leibniz and Kant. He sees the essay entirely under the influence of the latter. According to Hildebrandt, Schiller had the opporunity to mediate between the two but did not do so. Hildebrandt feels that this was a mistake "in dieser Epoche der übersteigerten Ichheit die titanische Hybris" (424; in this era of excessive egotism and titanic hubris). With reference to the "Ästhetische Briefe," Hildebrandt accuses Schiller of not being clear about the role of beauty at all: "Wechselnd herrscht die Idee der moralischen Vollendung als der Wahrheit, für die die schöne Erscheinung nur Gleichnis, Vorbereitung, eben nur Sinnenwelt ist, und die Idee des Schönen, die Sinnenwelt und Sinnlichkeit vereinigt, in ihrer Erscheinung die Vergegenwärtigung, die Vollendung, die wirkliche Wahrheit" (426–27; The idea of moral perfection as truth for which beautiful appearance is only an image or preparation, is in fact only the world of the senses, alternates with the idea of beauty [as truth] that unites the world of the senses with sensuousness and which is in its appearance realization, perfection, real truth).

[16] George and Wolfskehl, *Deutsche Dichtung, vol. 3: Das Jahrhundert Goethes,* 7.

Works Cited

Baigent, Michael. *Secret Germany: Claus von Stauffenberg and the Mystical Crusade against Hitler.* London: Penguin, 1995.

Bothe, Henning. *"Ein Zeichen sind wir, deutungslos": Die Rezeption Hölderlins von ihren Anfängen bis zu Stefan George.* Stuttgart: Metzler, 1992.

Brandstetter, Gabriele. " 'Die Bilderschrift der Empfindungen': Jean-Georges Noverres *Lettres sur la Danse, et sur les Ballets* und Friedrich Schillers Abhandlung *Über Anmut und Würde.*" In *Schiller und die höfische Welt,* ed. Achim Aurnhammer, Klaus Manger, and Friedrich Strack, 77–93. Tübingen: Niemeyer, 1990.

Fahrner, Rudolf. *Hölderlins Begegnung mit Goethe und Schiller.* Marburg: Elwert, 1925.

George, Stefan. *Sämtliche Werke.* Stuttgart: Klett-Cotta, 1982–.

George, Stefan and Karl Wolfskehl, eds. *Deutsche Dichtung: Band 3: Das Jahrhundert Goethes.* 1902; repr., Stuttgart: Klett-Cotta, 1995.

Gundolf, Friedrich. *George.* Berlin: Bondi, 1920.

———. "Dante." *Castrum Peregrini* 91 (1970): 30–39.

Hildebrandt, Kurt. *Das Werk Stefan Georges.* Hamburg: Hauswedell, 1960.

———. *Leibniz und das Reich der Gnade.* Den Haag: Nijhoff, 1953.

Hoffmann, Peter. *Claus Schenk Graf von Stauffenberg und seine Brüder.* Stuttgart: DVA, 1992.

Knab, Janina. *Ästhetik der Anmut: Studien zur "Schönheit der Bewegung" im 18. Jahrhundert.* Frankfurt am Main: Peter Lang, 1996.

Kommerell, Max. *Der Dichter als Führer in der deutschen Klassik.* Frankfurt am Main: Klostermann, 1940.

Losse, Alexander. " 'Hyperion.' " *Castrum Peregrini* 250 (2001): 95–102.

Petersdorff, Dirk von. "Wie viel Freiheit braucht die Dichtung? 'Das Zeitgedicht' im 'Siebenten Ring.' " *George-Jb.* 5 (2004/05): 45–62.

Schultz, H. Stefan. "Über das Verhältnis Stefan Georges zu Schiller." In *Studien zur Dichtung Stefan Georges.* Heidelberg: Lothar Stiehm, 1967, 68–89.

Staiger, Emil. *Die Kunst der Interpretation: Studien zur deutschen Literaturgeschichte.* Zürich: Atlantis, 1955.

The Text

On Grace and Dignity[1]

Friedrich Schiller
Translated by Jane V. Curran

GREEK FABLE PORTRAYS the goddess of beauty wearing a girdle[2] that has the power to impart *grace* and love to the wearer. She is the divinity who has the *Graces*[3] for companions.

The Greeks still *maintained a distinction,* then, between grace, or the Graces and beauty, since they attached attributes to them that do not apply

---

[1] N.B. Use of the preposition "über" to introduce the topic is a common choice for Schiller (see Introduction). It designates the work as belonging to the essay genre. This distinguishes it from the stricter discipline of a treatise and suggests a looser, more dialectical structure punctuated with rhetorical devices. The concepts of grace and dignity derive from the ancient rhetorical terms "venustas" and "gravitas."

Bold type page numbers in brackets of the form [**NA 36**] indicate the beginning of each page of the essay as printed in volume 20 of the Schiller *Nationalausgabe.* The same page notations are found in the reprinting of Schiller's original essay, based on the version of the *Nationalausgabe,* that follows this translation.

There are two kinds of footnotes in the essay: numbered notes such as the present one, which are offered by the present translator for additional information, and asterisked notes, which translate the notes Schiller included with the original essay.

[2] Quite apart from its divine or magical qualities, the girdle enhances the outline of the female form.

[3] Italicized words correspond to those printed in Schiller's original in *Sperrdruck,* a typesetting technique that sets extra space between a word's letters, by convention imparting emphasis.

to the goddess of beauty. All grace is beautiful, since the girdle of charm is *a possession* of the goddess of Cnidus; but not all beauty is graceful, because Venus remains as she is, even without the girdle.

According to this allegory, *only* the goddess of beauty wears or bestows the girdle of charm.[4] *Juno*, glorious goddess of heaven, first has to *procure* the girdle from Venus before she can cast her spell over Jupiter on Mount Ida. Even royalty adorned with a certain degree of beauty (undeniable in the case of Jupiter's wife) is not certain to please without the presence of grace. The noble queen of the gods does not expect to win Jupiter's heart simply on the strength of her own charms, but by means of Venus's girdle.

The goddess of beauty, however, is able to relinquish her girdle and *transfer* its power to what is less beautiful. Thus, grace is not the *exclusive* prerogative of beauty; rather, it can pass over to what is less beautiful or even to what is not beautiful, but it can only be passed from the hands of the beautiful.

The same Greeks advised those who, though possessed of every spiritual gift, lack a graceful and pleasing appearance, to sacrifice to the Graces. These goddesses were presented as the companions of the fair sex but could also become well-disposed towards a man and be indispensable to him if he wished to make himself pleasing.

What is this grace then, that associates preferably, but not exclusively, with the beautiful? [**NA 252**] That originates with the beautiful but reveals the effects of the beautiful to what is not beautiful as well? *Without which* beauty can exist but *through which* alone attraction can be instilled?

Early on, the Greeks made a distinction with a subtlety of feeling that reason could not yet *elucidate*. Feeling, striving for expression, borrowed images from imagination, since understanding had no concepts to offer yet. This myth is therefore worthy of the philosopher's respect, since in any case he has to be satisfied with finding concepts to fit the perceptions in

---

[4] The myth used here appears as well in the entry "Reiz" in Sulzer's *Allgemeine Theorie der schönen Künste*, a work Schiller seems to have consulted. Schiller's poems "Die Götter Griechenlands" and "Die Künstler" also refer to the same myth. Kant mentions the pleasing effect on the reader of Homer's account of the myth. (*Beobachtungen über das Gefühl des Schönen und Erhabenen* [1764; *Werke II*, ed. Otto Buek (Hildesheim: Gerstenberg, 1973), 243–86]).

which pure natural sense puts forth its discoveries, in other words, with explaining the figurative language of sensations.

If one removes the allegorical cloak from the Greeks' conception, it seems to have no other sense than the following:

Grace is a *movable* beauty, a beauty that can appear in a subject by chance and disappear in the same way. In this it distinguishes itself from *static* beauty, which is necessarily granted along with the subject itself. Venus can remove her girdle and give it to Juno for a moment; her beauty could only be given in conjunction with her person. Without her girdle she is no longer the charming Venus; without beauty she is no longer Venus.

The girdle, as the symbol of movable beauty, has the particular feature that it lends the objective characteristic of grace to the person wearing it and is therefore different from any other adornment that does not change the actual person but only changes the subjective impression of that person in another person's conception. The clear sense of the Greek myth is that grace is transformed into a characteristic of the person and that the wearer of the girdle truly *is* lovable, rather than merely *seeming* to be.

A girdle, which is nothing more than a randomly chosen external ornament, seems not to be the most suitable image for the *personal* characteristic of grace; however, a personal characteristic that is also understood as separable from the subject could not be represented in any other way than by a randomly chosen decoration [*NA* 253] that can be separated from the person without consequences to the person.

The girdle of charm thus does not have a *natural* effect, since in that case it would not be able to change anything in the actual person, but a *magical* effect, that is to say, its power extends beyond all natural circumstances. This knowledge (which is of course only provisional) should solve the contradiction into which representation always and inevitably falls when it tries to express in natural terms something that lies outside nature in the realm of freedom.

If the girdle of charm expresses an objective characteristic that can be separated from the subject without changing anything in the nature of that subject then it designates none other than the beauty of movement, since movement is the only change an object can undergo without altering its identity.

Beauty of movement is a concept that satisfies both demands contained in the myth mentioned at the outset. *First,* it is objective and applies to the object itself, not simply to the way in which we perceive it. *Second,* it is something accidental to it, and the object remains even if we remove the characteristic in our imagination.

The girdle of charm does not lose its magical power, not even in relation to the less beautiful or even the non-beautiful. This means that even the less beautiful and the non-beautiful can move in a *beautiful way*.

Grace, according to the myth, is something *accidental* in the subject; thus, only accidental movements can have this characteristic. In an ideal of beauty all *necessary* movements must be beautiful because, as necessary, they belong to the nature of the ideal. The beauty of these movements is already *present* in the concept of Venus; beauty in the accidental, on the other hand, is an *extension* of this concept. There can be grace in a voice, but no grace in the act of drawing breath.

But is all beauty in accidental movement to be called grace? [*NA 254*]

One hardly needs to be reminded that the Greek myth restricts grace and the graces to humans and it even goes so far as to restrict physical beauty of form within the confines of the human race, among whom, as is well known, the Greeks included their gods. However, if grace is a prerogative of human development, then none of those movements that humans have in common with merely natural beings can lay claim to it. If curls on a beautiful head could move gracefully, there would be no reason that the branches of trees, the ripples of a stream, ears of corn or the limbs of an animal could not do the same. But the goddess of Cnidus only represents the human race and her meaning for them ceases at the point where they become merely objects of nature and of the senses. [the soul's]

Grace, then, can only be attributed to arbitrary movements and only to those that are an expression of *moral* sentiments. Movements that have no other source than sensuality, despite their arbitrariness, still only belong to nature, which cannot of its own accord ever arrive at grace. If desire or instinct could be expressed as grace, then grace would no longer be capable or worthy of human expression.

And yet for the Greeks only *human beings* can contain all beauty and perfection. For them, the senses can never be revealed without the soul, and for their sense of what defines the human, it is also impossible to *isolate* raw animal instinct from intelligence. Just as they immediately give a bodily form to each idea, even the most spiritual ones, so the Greeks demand of each instinctive action in humans that it also present a moral purpose. For the Greeks, nature is never *simply* nature, and that is why they are not ashamed to honor it. For them, reason is never *simply* reason, and that is why they do not tremble to stand beside it. Nature and morality, matter and spirit, earth and heaven flow beautifully together in their poetry. [*NA* 255] They bring the freedom that resides only on Olympus into the realm of the senses as well so that we must let it pass when they introduce sensuality onto Olympus.

The subtle sense that the Greeks have of the material as always being accompanied by the spiritual does not admit of any arbitrary movement in human beings that belongs to sensuality alone and is not, at the same time, an expression of the morally sensitive spirit. Therefore, for the Greeks, grace is nothing other than this type of beautiful expression of the soul in arbitrary movement. Wherever there is grace, then, the soul is the moving principle and the foundations of beauty in movement are found in it. The mythical image is thus resolved into the following idea: "Grace is a beauty not granted by nature, but brought forth by the subject itself."

Up until now I have restricted myself to developing the concept of grace out of the Greek fable, I hope without forcing its meaning. Now I permit myself to explore the path of philosophical inquiry and whether, as in so many other cases, it is true here too that reason engaged in philosophy can boast of few discoveries that sense had not already *anticipated* and that poetry had not already *revealed*.

Venus, without the girdle and without the graces, represents for us ideal beauty, just as it comes from the hand *of nature*, and, *without the involvement of a sensitive mind,* is produced by fashioning forces. The fable is right to adopt a divine representative for this particular beauty because natural instinct already differentiates it very clearly from the kind that owes its origin to a sensitive mind.

I permit myself to name this beauty, which comes directly from nature and is formed by the rule of necessity, beauty of design (*architectonic beauty*) as opposed to beauty that conforms to the conditions of freedom. And so I designate with this name that part of human beauty [*NA* 256] that is not simply *formed* from natural forces (which is true of every appearance) but that is *also only determined by natural forces.*

Well-coordinated limbs, flowing outlines, a pleasing complexion, delicate skin, a fine and independent bearing, a mellifluous voice, and so forth, are the advantages one owes simply to nature and good fortune. *Nature* grants and develops the appropriate disposition and *fortune* protects nature's constructions from invasion by alien forces.

Venus rises *in perfect form* from the foam of the sea. She is perfect because she is a completed, delicately balanced work of necessity and therefore incapable of variation or extension. Since she is nothing other than a beautiful exposition of the purposes nature has in mind for mankind and therefore each of her characteristics is completely determined by the concept that lies at its base, she can be judged to be fully present as regards her disposition, even though this only develops over time.

The architectonic beauty of human form needs to be distinguished from the technical perfection of the same. The latter is to be understood as *the system of purposes* as they unite amongst themselves to form the highest final end; the former, however, is simply *a characteristic of the representation* of these purposes as appearance, revealed to the powers of observation. When one speaks of beauty, then, neither the material worth of these purposes nor the formal artistry of their combination is taken into consideration. The powers of observation are restricted to the type of appearance and pay no attention at all to the logical structure of the object. Although the architectonic beauty of human form is determined by the concept that lies at its base and by the purposes that nature intends for it, aesthetic judgment still *isolates* it from these purposes [*NA 257*] and nothing enters into the image of beauty except what directly and peculiarly belongs to the appearance.

One cannot claim, either, that the dignity of humanity *increases* the beauty of human design. Our judgment of the latter can be influenced by our view of the former, but then it ceases to be an aesthetic judgment. The technical aspect of human design is an expression of destiny and should therefore fill us with awe. But this technical aspect is not presented to the *senses*, but rather to the *understanding*. It can only be *thought*; it cannot *appear*. Architectonic beauty on the other hand can never be an expression of purpose because it is directed towards a quite different faculty from the one that decides about purpose.

If human beings are granted beauty, in preference to all the other technical constructions of nature, this is only true insofar as humans can demonstrate this advantage in their *outward appearance*, without having to insist on their human nature. This could only be done by means of a concept, so that the understanding, rather than the sense, would be the judge of beauty, and this results in a contradiction. If humans wish to assert their right to the award of beauty, they cannot draw attention to the dignity of their moral purpose nor can their superior intelligence count in their favor. In this regard the human is nothing but an object in space, nothing but an appearance among other appearances. His standing in the world of ideas is not respected in the world of the senses, and if he claims the highest rank there, he can only do so on the basis of what is *natural* to him.

However, this nature itself, as we know, is determined by the idea of his human nature and so, indirectly, his architectonic beauty is too. If humans distinguish themselves by superior beauty from all other sentient beings around them, they undeniably owe this to their human purpose, which holds the reason for distinguishing humans from other sentient beings in any case. But human form is not beautiful because [*NA* 258] it is an expression of this higher purpose; if it were, then the form would cease to be beautiful as soon as it expressed a lower purpose and the opposite of this form could also be beautiful, so long as one supposed it to express a higher purpose. If, however, one could completely forget what a human countenance expressed, could attribute the raw instinct of a tiger to it, without changing its appearance, then the eyes would assess it in exactly the same way and the senses would declare the tiger to be the Creator's finest achievement.

The purpose of humans as intelligent beings only contributes to the beauty of their form to the extent that its representation, that is, its expression as appearance, *corresponds* at the same time to the conditions under which beauty is created in the world of the senses. For beauty itself must always remain as a free natural effect, and reason's idea, which determined the design of human form, can never *distribute* beauty, only *sanction* it.

One could protest that absolutely everything that presents itself as appearance is effected by the forces of nature so that this cannot be an exclusive feature of the beautiful. It is true that all technical formations are produced by nature, but they are not technical by nature, at least they are not judged to be so. They are only technical through understanding and their technical perfection thus also already exists in the understanding before it passes over into the world of sense and becomes appearance. Beauty, on the other hand, has the peculiar characteristic that it is not simply represented in the world of the senses but also arises in that world, that it is not only expressed but also created by nature. It is nothing but a characteristic of the sensuous, and the artist who aims at beauty can only achieve it insofar as he maintains the appearance of nature's having formed it.

To judge the technical aspects of the human form one has to have recourse to a conception of the purposes for which it is intended; [*NA* 259] this is completely unnecessary for judging its beauty. The senses are a fully competent judge in this matter and it could not be so if the world of the senses (which is their only object) did not contain all the conditions of beauty and was thus not completely adequate to its creation. The beauty of a human being is naturally based in the concept of humanity in an *indirect* way, because one's whole sensuous nature is based in this concept; but because the senses, as is known, only associate *directly*, it is just as if beauty were a completely independent effect of nature.

According to what has been said so far, it should seem that beauty is of no interest to reason because it only arises in the world of the senses and only presents itself to the sensuous faculties. Since, if we separate off from its concept, as foreign, whatever *conception of perfection* our judgment of beauty necessarily brings to bear, there appears to be nothing left to make it the *object of pleasure for reason*. Nevertheless, it is just as evident that beauty appeals to reason as it is clear that it does not reside with any characteristic of the object which could only be discovered by reason.

In order to solve this apparent contradiction, one has to remember that there are two ways for appearances to become objects of reason and to express ideas. It is not always necessary for reason to *extract* these ideas from the appearances; it can also *place* them into them. In both cases, the appearance will be adequate to the concept of reason, with the one difference that in the first case, reason objectively finds it present and only, as it were, receives it from the object because the concept has to be applied in order to explain the composition and often even the possibility of the object. In the second case, on the other hand, reason itself turns something that is given as appearance, independent from its concept, into an expression of that concept and thus treats something purely sensuous as more than sensuous. [*NA* 260] In the first case, then, the idea is objectively necessary to the object; in the second case its link to the object is at the most subjectively necessary. I do not need to mention that by the first I mean perfection and the second, beauty.

Since then in the second case it is a pure matter of chance for the sensuous object as to whether there is reason present to link the conception of this object with one of reason's ideas, with the consequence that the objective composition of the object has to be seen as fully independent of this idea, it is right to restrict the beautiful, *objectively*, to purely natural circumstances, and to declare it nothing but an effect in the world of sense. But because — on the other hand — reason makes transcendental use of this effect from the purely sensuous world, and in giving it a higher meaning puts its stamp on it, so to speak, therefore it is equally right to place the beautiful *subjectively* into the intelligible world. Beauty is therefore to be seen as the citizen of two worlds, one *by birth,* the other *through adoption.* It receives its existence in the sensuous world and *achieves* citizenship in the world of reason. This explains why taste, as a faculty of judgment for beauty, steps in between spirit and sensuality and binds these two mutually disdainful natures into a happy union — just as it gains the respect of reason for the *material* and inclines sense towards the *rational* — as it ennobles opinions and elevates them to ideas, and even transforms the sensuous world, in a certain way, into a realm of freedom.

However, if it is accidental — with regard to the object itself — whether reason binds one of its ideas with the conception of the object, nevertheless, it is necessary — for the subject perceiving — to link such an idea to such a conception. This idea, and the sensuous characteristic in the object that corresponds to it, must stand in a relation to one another such that reason, by its own invariable laws, is compelled to undertake this act. The reason for associating a particular idea only and exclusively with one *particular* type of appearance lies in reason itself, [**NA 261**] and the reason for giving rise to *this* idea and no other lies in the object itself. What sort of idea this is, that draws reason into the beautiful, and through which objective characteristic the beautiful object is capable of serving this idea as a symbol — these questions are too important to be answered here in a cursory way. I shall save their discussion for an analysis of the beautiful.

The architectonic beauty of humans is thus, in the way I have mentioned, the *sensuous expression of a rational concept,* but it is this in no other sense and with no greater right than any other beautiful natural form. With respect to *degree* it exceeds all other beauties, but with respect to *kind* it stands alongside all others because it too reveals nothing of its subject except what is sensuous and only receives a meaning above the senses in its conception*). The fact that the representation of purposes is more beauti-

---

* Since — to repeat — through *sight alone,* everything *objective* about beauty is given. But because what gives humans the advantage over all other sensual beings does not *appear* to the sight alone, a characteristic that already reveals itself to sight cannot make this advantage visible. Its higher calling, the only basis for this advantage, will thus not be expressed by this beauty, and the idea of this calling can therefore never be a part of the beauty or be included in aesthetic judgment. The thought itself, whose expression is human formation, is not revealed to the senses,

ful in humans than in other organic forms should be seen as a *favor* that reason, as the lawgiver of human design, grants to nature, which puts those laws into practice. Reason is strict about its principles in relation to the design of humans, but luckily its demands *correspond* to the needs of nature, [**NA 262**] with the result that that it carries out reason's requirements simply by acting according to their inclination.

However, this is true only of the *architectonic* beauty of humans, where the necessity of nature is supported by the necessity of the teleological basis that determines it. Only here could beauty be *assessed* in relation to the design of the form, but this does not happen when the necessity is one-sided and the suprasensual cause, which determines the appearance, changes at random. *Only* nature takes care of the architectonic beauty of humans because already here, in the first construction, understanding *transferred* to it, once and for all, everything that humans *need* in order to fulfill their purpose. Nature therefore has no need to fear any changes in her *organic* industry.

A human being, however, is a *person,* a being, that can in *itself* be the cause and even the absolutely final cause of its condition and which can change in accordance with reasons which it draws from itself. Its type of appearance is dependent upon the types of feeling and willing, that is to say, upon the conditions that it freely determines by itself, not those determined in accordance with the necessities of nature.

If human beings were simply creatures of the senses, nature would establish the *laws* and determine the *instances* in which they could be invoked. However, she shares the control with freedom, and although her laws exist, it is the mind that decides about the instances.

The realm of the mind extends *as far as nature is alive* and only ends where organic life loses itself in formless mass and the animal powers cease. As we know, all movable powers in humans are bound together, so that one can see how the mind — even when it is merely considered as the principle of arbitrary movement — can extend its effects throughout the whole

---

only its effects in the realm of appearance. The mere senses do not raise themselves up to the suprasensual cause of these effects any more than (if I may be permitted this example) the simply sensual man ascends to the idea of the highest origin of the world when he satisfies his desires.

system. Its influence is not only experienced by the instruments of the will, [*NA* 263] but also, at least indirectly, by those instruments over which the will does not have direct authority. The mind does not only determine them intentionally, when it acts, but also unintentionally, when it simply receives.

As is clear from the above, nature on its own can only bring about the beauty of those appearances that it is free to determine in accordance with the law of necessity. But with *arbitrariness, chance* enters into its creation, and although the changes it underwent under the rule of freedom are effected *in accordance with* no laws but its own, nevertheless, they no longer emerge *from* these laws. Since it is now up to the mind to make use of its tools, nature cannot command the part of beauty that depends on that use, and is therefore also not responsible for it.

Thus humans would be in danger of *sinking,* as appearances, at just that point where, by making use of their freedom, they raise themselves to the level of the pure intelligences, and of losing in terms of taste what they had gained from the tribunal of reason. The destiny *fulfilled* by their actions would cost them the advantage approved by the destiny but *only intimated* in their form. And even though this advantage is only a sensuous one, we still find that reason has granted it a higher significance. Nature, which loves harmony, is not guilty of such a base contradiction, and whatever is harmonious in the sphere of reason will not be revealed as discordant in the world of the senses.

If the person, or free principle, in humans undertakes to determine the play of appearances and, by its intervention, removes from nature the power to preserve the beauty of its work, then it is stepping into nature's place and taking over (if I may use this expression) its rights and part of its duties. When the mind includes in its own course the sensuous that it controls, and makes the sensuous dependent on its own conditions, then in a way it is turning itself into appearance and declaring itself subject to the law imposed on all appearances. [*NA* 264] It undertakes for its own sake the obligation to allow nature, which depends on it, to remain nature, even while in its service, and not to *contradict* its former duties. I refer to beauty in appearances as a *duty* because the demand for it in the subject is found in reason itself and is therefore universal and necessary. I refer to a *former* duty, because the senses have already passed judgment before understanding begins its work.

Freedom now rules beauty. Nature provided beauty of form; the soul provides the beauty of play. Now we also know what grace is. Grace is beauty of form under freedom's influence, the beauty of those appearances that the person determines. Architectonic beauty honors the creator of nature, grace honors those who possess it. The former is a *talent*, the latter, *personal* merit.

Grace can only apply to *movement* because a change of disposition is only revealed as movement in the sphere of the senses. However, this does not preclude the display of grace in rigid and restful features. The rigid features were originally nothing other than movements that through frequent repetition became habitual and left lasting traces.*[5] [*NA 265*]

However, not all movements in humans are capable of grace. Grace is always only beauty of the physique that *freedom sets in motion*, and movements that *simply belong to nature* are not worthy of the name. While it is true that a lively mind takes hold of almost all movements of its body, when the chain by means of which a beautiful feature joins onto a moral sense is very long, it becomes a characteristic of form and can hardly count

---

* This is why Home assumes too *narrow* a meaning for the idea of grace when he says, "that when the most graceful person is *at rest*, neither moving nor speaking, we lose sight of the characteristic of grace, just as color is lost in the darkness" (*Elements of Criticism* 2:39). No, we do not lose sight of it so long as we perceive the features of the sleeping person, which have been formed by a benign and gentle intellect. Precisely the most valued part of grace remains, the part which transferred itself from *gestures* to *features* and thus revealed the *skill* of disposition in fine sentiments. But where the *editor* of *Home's* works thinks he could set his author straight with the observation (cf. above, p. 459) "that grace is not simply restricted to voluntary movements, that a sleeping person does not cease to have charm" — and why? "because only in this state are the instinctive, gentle and for this very reason so much the more graceful movements properly visible," there he empties the concept of grace absolutely, whereas Home had merely restricted it too much. Instinctive movements in sleep, if they are not mechanical repetitions of voluntary ones, can never be graceful and they can certainly not be more so, and if a sleeping person is charming, it is certainly not on account of movements, but because of the features produced by previous movements.

[5] Schiller refers in his note to Henry Home, Lord Kames, whose *Elements of Criticism* were first published in 1762. Schiller consulted the third German edition of 1790–93, with commentary by Georg Gottlieb Schatz. For a recent edition see "Elements of Criticism," in *Collected Works of Henry Home, Lord Kames,* vol. 1, introduced by John Vladimir Price (London: Routledge/Thoemmes, 1993).

as grace any longer. Finally, mind even *constructs* itself a body and the *form* itself must join the *play,* so that grace often eventually turns into architectonic beauty.

Just as a hostile, unsettled spirit destroys even the most noble beauty of form to the point that, when it is in the unworthy hands of freedom, one can no longer recognize nature's finest achievement, so one sees from time to time a serene and harmonious disposition coming to the aid of the technical when it is obstructed, setting nature free and, with divine glory, *releasing* the bonds that cramp and constrict. The plastic nature of humans has within it an endless number of devices that compensate for its imperfections and correct its faults whenever the moral intellect wishes to support its formative work or sometimes when it simply does not want to disturb this process.

Since the *static movements* (gestures transformed into features) are not excluded from grace, it could appear that even the beauty of *apparent* or *imitated movements* (flickering or weaving lines) can likewise be added, just as Mendels[s]ohn actually claims.*[6] But the concept of grace [*NA 266*] would thus be extended to the concept of beauty in general, since *all beauty* is ultimately a characteristic of true or apparent (objective or subjective) movement, as I hope to demonstrate in an analysis of the beautiful. Only those movements that also correspond to a sentiment can display grace.

The person — it is clear what I mean by this — prescribes the body's movements either through the will, when it wants to realize an anticipated effect in the world of sense, and in this case, the movements are called *voluntary* or intentional, or they can occur without the person's willing, following a law of necessity — but at the behest of a sentiment; these I call *sympathetic* movements. Although the latter are instinctive and based in sentiment, one ought not to confuse them with those determined by feelings and natural instinct, since natural instinct is not a free principle, and what it brings about is not an action by the person. By the sympathetic

---

* Mendelssohn, *Philosophische Schriften* (Berlin: Voss, 1761), 1:90.

[6] Schiller is referring to the essay "Über die Empfindungen" (On the Sentiments). Mendelssohn's understanding of grace can be found in "Betrachtungen über das Erhabene und Naïve" (Observations on the Sublime and the Naïve). For a recent English edition see Moses Mendelssohn, *Philosophical Writings,* ed. Daniel O. Dahlstrom (Cambridge: Cambridge, UP 1997).

movements, I mean only those that accompany moral sentiment or moral attitude.

The question arises, then: which of these two types of movement, both grounded in the person, is capable of grace?

The things that one must necessarily separate in philosophy are not consequently always separated in reality as well. Thus one seldom finds intentional movements without sympathetic ones, because they originate in the will, and it determines according to moral sentiments, from which the sympathetic movements arise. When people speak, we see their gaze, their facial features, their hands, often even their whole body *speaking at the same time* and the *mimetic* part of the conversation is frequently considered the most eloquent. But even an intentional movement has to be considered a sympathetic one as well, as soon as an instinctive element joins in with what is intentional. [*NA 267*]

The way in which an intentional movement is performed is not so precisely determined by its end as to prevent there being several ways of doing it. Whatever is left undetermined by either will or purpose can be sympathetically determined by the emotional state of the person and serve as the expression of that state. In stretching out my arm to receive an object, I am fulfilling a purpose, and the movement I make is prescribed by the intended goal. But the path my arm takes to reach the object and the extent to which the rest of my body follows — how fast or slowly, and how much or how little effort I put into the movement, these exact calculations are not my concern at the moment, but are left up to my natural element. But whatever is not simply determined by a purpose must still be decided somehow and this is where my sensibility can be decisive, providing the *tone* that determines the manner of the movement. The part that the sensibility contributes to an intentional movement, then, is the instinctive part, and it is there that one must seek grace.

If an *intentional* movement is not combined with a sympathetic one, or, to say much the same thing, if it is not mixed with something *instinctive* that has its origin in the moral sensibility of the person, it can *never* display *grace,* since it requires a certain disposition as cause. Intentional movement *results* from an act of the disposition that has already occurred when the movement begins.

Sympathetic movement, on the other hand, *accompanies* the act of the disposition and the emotional state that enables the act to occur, and it must therefore be considered to be *parallel* with them.

It is already clear from this that the first type, which does not directly flow from the character of the person, cannot be a representation of the character. [*NA 268*] This is because, between the character and the movement itself comes the *decision*, which, when considered on its own terms, is something completely neutral; movement is the effect of the *decision* and the purpose but not of the person and the character.

Intentional movement is coincidentally linked with the prerequisite character, whereas the accompanying movement, by contrast, is necessarily tied to it. The former relates to the disposition just as conventional script relates to the thought it expresses; the sympathetic or accompanying movement, on the other hand, relates in the way that cries of passion are associated with the passion itself. Intentional movement is therefore not a representation of the mind on account of its *nature,* but simply as a result of *custom.* Thus we cannot really say, either, that the *mind* reveals itself in an intentional movement because that movement only expresses the *matter of the will* (the purpose) not *the form of the will* (the character). Only the accompanying movement can instruct us about that.*

Therefore, one can deduce from a person's words how he would *like to be viewed,* but what he *really* is must be guessed from the mimic gestures accompanying the speech, in other words, from the *uncontained* movements. However, when one experiences someone who can *contain* his facial features as well, from that moment on, one no longer trusts that face or takes its features to be an expression of his attitude.

[*NA 269*] Now a person could, through artifice and work, be capable of bringing these accompanying movements under the control of his will and, like an accomplished magician, have any form he pleased fall onto the mirror that reflects his soul in mime. But everything about such a person is a lie, his whole nature consumed with art. Grace must always be natural, in

---

* When an incident occurs in front of a large group, it can happen that each person present has a different opinion of the character of the person involved in the action. This is how coincidental the connection can be between intentional movements and their moral causes. But if someone in this group unexpectedly caught sight of a dear friend or a detested enemy, the unambiguous facial expression would rapidly and clearly expose the feelings in his heart, and the judgment of the whole group as to his current state of emotion would probably be unanimous, since here the expression is bound by natural necessity to its cause in the emotions.

other words, instinctive (or it must at least appear to be so) and the subject must not appear to be *conscious of possessing grace*.

From this we learn, in passing, what to think about *imitated* or *trained* instances of grace (which I should like to call grace in the theater or the grace of the dance master). It is a worthy counterpart to the *beauty* produced at the dressing table from rouge and white lead, hairpieces, bust enhancements, and whalebone corsets. It relates to true grace in approximately the same way that *cosmetic beauty* relates to *architectonic* beauty.*[7]

---

* By this juxtaposition I am neither detracting from the dancing master's services to true grace nor denying the actor his right to claim it. Undeniably, the dancing master comes to the aid of true grace by granting the will mastery over its tools and by removing the obstacles to the play of lively forces that are set by *mass* and *gravity*. He can do this only in accordance with *rules* that maintain the body in a beneficial discipline and, as long inertia resists, may be and appear *stiff*, that is to say, *forced*. When he dismisses his pupil from school, the rule must already have accomplished its task in him, and does not *need to accompany* him into the world: the work of the rule must enter nature.

The disdain with which I speak of grace in the theatre only applies to *imitated* grace and I have no hesitation in rejecting this type, both on the stage and in life. I admit that I do not care for actors who have labored to produce *grace* at the dressing table, regardless of how successful their imitation may be. We make the following demands of actors: 1) *truth* of presentation, and 2) *beauty* of presentation. Now, I claim *with regard to the truth of presentation,* that the actor must produce everything by means of art, and nothing by nature, because otherwise he is not an artist, and I will admire how masterfully he plays the raging Guelfo if I hear that he is a person of gentle character. On the other hand, I claim *in relation to the grace of representation* that he must owe nothing to art and that here everything in him must be a voluntary work of nature. If I recognize in the truth of his performance that this character is not natural to him, I will only hold him even higher in my estimation; if I recognize in the beauty of his performance that these graceful movements are not natural to him, I will not be able to withhold my anger against the *man* for calling on the *artist* for help. The cause is that the essence of grace disappears with its naturalness and that grace is a demand we feel justified in making of a mere person. What would I now reply to the mime artist who wanted to know how to come by grace, since he is not permitted to *acquire* it? In my view, he should first ensure that his own humanity is brought to the fore, and then represent it on the stage (if that is his profession).

Both can have precisely the same effect on [*NA 270*] untrained senses as the original that they are imitating, and with a high degree of artistry they can also sometimes deceive the expert. But in the end, some movement will appear forced and the intention will become clear, and then the inevitable consequence is indifference or even disdain and disgust. As soon as we notice that the architectonic beauty is *artificial,* we see the same measure of humanity (as appearance) disappear as was added from a foreign nature — and how should we, who do not even gladly excuse the dismissal of an accidental advantage, regard an exchange with pleasure or mere indifference, when a part of humanity is given up for a baser nature? How should we, even if we can excuse the effect, not have disdain for the deception? As soon as we notice that the *grace* is artificial, our hearts close, and our souls, which surged upwards, now flee backwards. Suddenly, we see that mind has become matter and heavenly Juno has become a cloud.

Although grace must be or appear to be instinctive, we still only look for it in movements that depend on the will, [*NA 271*] to a greater or lesser extent. One does attribute grace to a certain language of gesture, and one speaks of a graceful smile and an attractive blush, both of which are sympathetic movements, decided upon not by the will but by the emotions. Even if one does not hold that these are under our control or that one can still doubt whether the will actually belongs to grace, still, in most cases by far, where grace is revealed, it is through willed movement. It is true that we attribute grace to certain gestures and speak of a graceful smile or a charming blush, both of which are sympathetic movements, about which the character rather than the will decides. Even if one does not count the fact that the first is definitely within our power and that in the case of the second, one could question whether it really does belong to grace, still, by far the greatest number of cases in which grace reveals itself come from the area of instinctive movements. We expect grace from speech and song, from instinctive movements of the eyes and mouth, from the movements of hands and arms whenever freely undertaken, from the

---

[7] In his footnote, Schiller makes a reference to a hero who sums up the drama of the Sturm und Drang (Storm and Stress) period: Guelfo, the main character of Friedrich Maximilian Klinger's play, *Die Zwillinge,* 1776 (*The Brothers*).

gait, posture, and stance, from the whole bearing of a person, insofar as it is under his control. As will become clear later on, we expect something very different from grace in a person's movements if a natural urge or an overbearing emotion *alone* produces them and they are thus sensuous in origin. Such movements belong to *nature* and not to the *person;* all grace, however, must stem from the person alone.

If, then, grace is a characteristic we expect from intentional movements, and if, on the other hand everything intentional must be banned from grace itself, then we will have to look for grace in what happens unintentionally when intentional movements are carried out, and also corresponds to a moral cause.

In this, only the category of movements is described among which grace can be sought. A movement can have all these characteristics without being graceful. It is simply *expressive* (mimic).

Expressive (in the broadest sense) is what I call every appearance in the body that is accompanied by an expression of temperament. In this sense, then, all sympathetic movements are expressive, even those that simply serve to accompany affections of sensuality.

Even animal forms are expressive, when their inner disposition is displayed externally. But there it is an expression of *nature,* never of *freedom.* [*NA* 272] In the permanent form and in the set architectonic features of an animal, nature makes its *purpose* known and in the mimic features, an aroused or satisfied *need.* The cycle of necessity applies to the animal as to the plant, without being interrupted by a *person.* The individuality of its existence is only an individual image of a general concept of nature; the particularity of its present situation is simply an example of nature's purpose, carried out under certain natural conditions.

Only human form is expressive in the *narrower* sense of the term, and only in those appearances that accompany and serve to express its moral attitude.

Only in *these* appearances: since in all others the human being stands on the same level as the other sensuous beings. In his permanent form and in his architectonic features it is only *nature* displaying its plan, as is the case with animals and other organic beings. Nature's plan can of course extend much further in the human than in the other beings, and the combined methods of achieving it are more elaborate and intricate, but it is all on account of *nature,* and the human being cannot take any credit.

In animals and plants, nature not only determines the purpose; *she alone carries it out*. In humans, however, she only determines the purpose, and leaves them to fulfill it *themselves*. It is this alone that makes them humans.

The human being, alone among all known beings, has, as person, the prerogative of delving with his will into the cycle of necessity, which is unbreakable for merely natural beings, and of initiating a fresh series of appearances in himself. The act by means of which he brings this about is mostly called an *action* and those of his accomplishments that flow from such an action are, by contrast, called his *deeds*. A human being, then, can only prove himself a person by his deeds.

The constitution of an animal does not only express the concept of its purpose, but also the relationship of its present condition to this purpose. [*NA 273*] Now since, in an animal, nature not only gives but also fulfills the purpose, the constitution of an animal can never express anything other than the work of nature.

Since nature *gives* purpose to human beings but *places* the fulfillment of that purpose *in their will,* the present relationship of their condition to their purpose cannot be a work of nature, but must be their own work. The expression of this relationship in their constitution thus does not belong to nature but to themselves, that is, it is a personal expression. If we discover from the architectonic part of their constitution what *nature* plans for them, then we discover from the mimic part what *they themselves have done* to fulfill this plan.

We are thus not satisfied when a human form presents to our eyes the universal concept of humanity or perhaps the degree to which *nature* has fulfilled it in this individual, since that would be something it had in common with every technical constitution. We expect that form also to reveal to us the extent to which, in its freedom, it cooperated with nature, i.e. displays character. In the former case one can easily see that nature *planned* for a human being, but only in the second case does it emerge whether it *actually* became one.

The constitution of a human being is therefore only *his* in so far as it is mimic; but *in so far as it is mimic,* it is his. Since, if the greatest number of these mimic characteristics or even all of them were simply an expression of the senses and could already adhere in him as animal, then he would still have been determined, and capable of restricting his sensuality through his freedom. The presence of such characteristics thus proves that this capability has not been exercised, and that the purpose has not been fulfilled; it is just as certain that it is expressive of a moral, as the omission of an action required by duty is constitutive of an action.

One has to distinguish the expressive characteristics, which are always an expression of the soul, from the dumb characteristics, which only plastic nature, in [*NA* 274] operating independently of any influence from the soul, imprints on the human form. I call these characteristics *dumb* because, as indecipherable codes of nature, they are silent about character. They only show the characteristics of nature in the species and are often sufficient in themselves to differentiate the *individual,* but they can never reveal anything about the *person.* For the physiognomist, these dumb characteristics are not lacking in significance at all, because the physiognomist does not simply want to know what the human being has made of himself, but also what nature has done for and against him.

It is not so easy to draw a line where the dumb characteristics end and the expressive ones begin. The power of formation, operating consistently, and lawless emotion, are in constant strife over their territory, and what *nature* built up, with tireless, silent activity, is often pulled down again by *freedom,* like a swelling river bursting its banks. An active spirit gains influence over *all physical movement* and finally comes indirectly to the point of changing even the set forms of nature, which are not accessible to the will, through the power of sympathetic play. In such a human being everything comes down to character, as we discover in some faces that have been *molded* by a long life, extraordinary fortunes, and an active mind. Among such forms, only the *generic* belongs to plastic nature; the whole *individuality* of the constitution belongs to the person. Thus one is very right in saying that in such a form, everything is soul.

On the other hand, those pupils shaped by the *rule* (which is able to lay sensuality to rest, but cannot rouse humanity) do not, by their flat and inexpressive constitution, show us anything beyond the hand of nature. The inactive soul is a modest guest in the body and a peaceful, quiet neighbor of the self-reliant formative power. No strenuous thought, no passion intrudes into the calm tempo of physical life; the *design* will never be jeopardized by *play,* neither will vegetation be disturbed by freedom. Since the deep calm of the mind does not cause any notable depletion of strength, the output will never exceed the input; [*NA* 275] instead, the animal economy will have a surplus. The mind, for a small wage of happiness, carries out the punctual administration of nature and can pride itself on keeping *the books* in order. What organization can always accomplish will be accomplished, and the businesses of feeding and procreation will flourish. Such a harmonious agreement between natural necessity and freedom cannot be anything but advantageous for architectonic beauty and it is also here that it can be observed in all its purity. However, the universal powers of nature, as we know, are waging eternal war on the particular ones, or the organic ones, and the most elaborate technique will eventually succumb to *cohesion* and *gravity*. For this reason, the beauty of physique as a *purely natural product* has its particular period of blossoming, ripening, and decaying, which play can accelerate, but never delay; and the customary end is that *mass* gradually takes control over *form*, and the living impulse for formation preserves its grave in the material that has been *amassed*.*

---

* For this reason, one often finds that such physical beauty already becomes noticeably coarse because of obesity in middle age and that, in place of the barely perceptible lines in the skin, furrows set in and sausage-shaped folds, so that the *weight*, unobserved, gains influence over the form, and the charming and varied play of beautiful lines over the surface is lost in a steadily swelling cushion of fat. Nature takes away what it had given.

Incidentally, I notice that something similar occasionally happens with *genius* which, in its origins and in its effect, has in any case much in common with architectonic beauty. Like architectonic beauty, it is simply *a product of nature,* and in the mistaken human mentality that esteems most highly precisely those things that cannot be imitated in accordance with any rules and those that cannot be achieved through merit, beauty is more admired than charm, and genius is more admired than the acquired powers of the intellect. Both these *favorites of nature,* with all their bad habits (on account of which they not infrequently deserve to be an object of scorn) are regarded as a kind of hereditary nobility or higher caste, because their advantages are dependent on nature and thus lie beyond selection.

But just as happens with architectonic beauty when it does not concern itself soon enough with attracting support from and a representative for *grace,* the same is true of genius when it fails to reinforce itself with principles, taste, and learning. If its only equipment is a vivid and luxuriant imagination (and nature can certainly not dispense anything other than sensual advantages) then it might soon think about securing this ambiguous gift by the only procedure whereby the gifts of nature can become possessions of the mind; I mean by imparting form to matter, since mind cannot call anything its own except what is form. The overgrown, overwhelming

[*NA* **276**] However, although no *single* silent feature expresses the mind, this kind of silent development is indeed characteristic *as a whole;* for the same reason as is also true of a sensually expressive development. That is, the mind should be active and morally sympathetic; in this way it shows itself to be at fault if its form displays no such traces. Although the pure and beautiful expression of its purpose, in the architecture of its form, fills us with benevolence and respect for supreme reason, its origin, these two sentiments will only remain separate for as long as this expression is, for us, simply a product of nature. If we think of it [*NA* **277**] as a moral person, we are justified in expecting an expression of the same in his physique and if this expectation is thwarted, contempt inevitably follows. Simple organic creatures are worthy of our respect as *creatures,* but human beings can only be so as *creators,* (that is, as originators of their condition). They should not simply reflect the beams of a foreign reason, as other sensuous beings do, even if it were divine reason; rather they should glow with their own light, like a sun.

Thus, an expressive formation is demanded of human beings as soon as one is conscious of their ethical purpose; but it must also be a creation that speaks to their advantage; that is to say, one that expresses a type of sentiment suited to their purpose, a moral practice. Reason demands this of human formation.

Human beings, as appearance, are also an object of the senses. Where the *moral* feeling finds satisfaction, the *aesthetic* feeling does not wish to be

---

power of nature, unrestrained by any corresponding power of reason, will outgrow the freedom of understanding and choke it, just as, in architectonic beauty, mass ultimately suppresses form.

I think that experience provides plenty of instances of this, especially in poetic spirits who are famous before reaching maturity and, as is often the case with beauty, whose entire talent is their *youth.* But when that brief springtime has passed, and one looks for the expected fruits, these are often spongy and misshapen creations, produced by a misguided, blind impulse towards form. Precisely where one expects matter to have been refined into form and creative mind to have set down ideas in perceptible form, they have fallen prey to matter, like every other product of nature, and the promising meteors appear as common lights — or even as something less. This is because the poetic imagination occasionally sinks back completely into the matter out of which it developed and does not disdain to serve nature with another, *more solid* product, if it can no longer manage a poetic creation.

reduced, and the correspondence with an idea may not sacrifice any of the appearance. Thus, however rigorously reason demands an ethical expression, the eye demands beauty just as persistently. Since both these demands are made of the same object, although they come from different courts of judgment, satisfaction for both must be found in the same source. The frame of mind in which a human being is most able to fulfill his moral purpose must permit the type of expression that is also most advantageous for him as simple appearance. In other words: moral capacity must reveal itself through grace.

It is here that the greatest difficulty arises. The very concept of morally expressive movements requires that they have a moral origin that lies beyond the world of the senses; equally, the concept of beauty requires it to have no other origin than a sensuous one and that it be, or at least appear to be, a completely free result of nature. But when the final cause of morally expressive movements necessarily lies *outside* the world of the senses and the final cause of beauty [*NA 278*] equally necessarily lies *within* it, then *grace*, which should unite the two, stands in evident contradiction.

In order to remove this, one will have to assume, then, "that the moral origin in the disposition, which is the basis of grace, necessarily produces, in the sensuality dependent upon it, precisely that state that contains the *natural conditions* for beauty in itself." This is because the beautiful, as is clear from everything sensuous, establishes certain conditions and, as it is beautiful, these are merely sensuous conditions. Now in that the mind (in accordance with a law that we cannot fathom), because of the state in which it finds itself, prescribes the state of the nature that accompanies it and in that the state of moral practice is precisely that through which the sensuous conditions of beauty are brought to fulfillment, the mind makes the beautiful *possible* and that alone is *its* action. The fact that beauty *actually* arises from it is a consequence of those sensuous conditions, that is to say, a *free effect of nature*. But because in *intentional* movements, where it is treated as the means of carrying out an aim, nature cannot really be called free, and because in *instinctive* movements that express morality it cannot be called free either, the freedom with which nature expresses itself, despite its dependence on the will, is by *permission* of the mind. One could say, then, that grace is a *favor* granted to the sensuous by the ethical, just as architectonic beauty can be regarded as nature *consenting* to a technical form.

With permission, I shall illustrate this with an image. When a monarchic state is run in such a way that, although everything proceeds in accordance with the will of one person, the individual citizen can still persuade himself that he is living according to his own lights and simply following his inclinations, one calls this a liberal government. However, one would be very hesitant to give it this name if *either* the ruler imposed his will against the citizen's inclinations or the citizen imposed his inclinations against the will [*NA* 279] of the ruler; since, in the first instance, the government would not be *liberal*, and in the second it would not be a *government*.

It is not difficult to apply this to the human constitution under the regime of the mind. When the mind expresses itself in the sensuous nature that depends on it in such a way that nature faithfully carries out the will of the mind and expresses its sentiments clearly, without contravening the demands that the senses make upon them as upon appearances, then there will arise what we call grace. However, one would be equally far from calling it grace if either the mind were to reveal itself forcibly in the sensuous or if the expression of the mind were missing from the free effect of the sensuous. For in the first case there would be no beauty present and in the second it would not be the beauty of play.

Thus it is always only the suprasensuous cause in the disposition that makes grace expressive and always a merely sensuous cause in nature that alone makes it beautiful. One cannot say that the mind *produces* beauty any more than one can say, in the example given, that the ruler *brings* freedom *about;* one can *allow* a person freedom but not *give* it.

But just as the reason for a people feeling free under the yoke of someone else's will lies for the most part in the attitude of the ruler, and a conflicting mentality on his part would not be very conducive to freedom, so we also have to look for the beauty of free movements in the ethical constitution of the mind that dictates to them. And now the question arises as to what kind of *personal constitution* allows greater freedom to the sensuous instruments of will and what kinds of moral sentiments are most compatible with beauty as expressed?

This much is clear: that neither the will, in deliberate movement, nor affect, in sympathetic movement, ought to use *force* against the nature dependent upon it, if it is expected to respond with beauty. [*NA* 280] The general feeling alone among humans makes *ease* into the main characteristic of grace, and where effort is required, ease can never be the outcome. It is also clear that, on the other hand, nature ought never to use force against the mind if a beautiful, moral expression is to occur, for wherever nature *reigns* alone, humanity disappears.

One can think of three ways altogether in which a human can relate to himself, that is, in which the sensuous part can relate to the rational. Among these we must look for the one that best suits him in appearance and that appears as beauty.

Humans either suppress the demands of their sensuous nature in order to have a proper relation to the higher demands of their rational nature; or they reverse this and subjugate the rational part of their being to the sensuous, and thus respond only to the prod that natural necessity uses to mobilize them as well as other appearances; or the impulses of the sensuous settle into harmony with the rules of the rational and human beings are at one with themselves.

When a human becomes conscious of his pure self-sufficiency, he rejects everything sensuous and arrives at a feeling of his rational freedom only through this separation from matter. But because the sensuous is persistent and resists powerfully, considerable strength and great effort are required on his part, without which it would not be possible to keep desire at bay or to silence the impulse that insists on expressing itself. Such a frame of mind lets the nature dependent on it know that it, the mind, is in charge, both when nature acts in the service of the mind's will and when nature tries to anticipate that will. Under its strict discipline, the sensuous will thus appear to be suppressed and the inner opposition will be evident from outside in constraint. Such a state of mind cannot be conducive to beauty, which nature can only produce freely, and it will also not be grace that makes itself known through the struggle of moral freedom against matter.

[NA 281] On the other hand, when a human, prey to desire, lets natural impulse rule him unrestrainedly, his inner self-sufficiency disappears as well as every trace of it in his physique. Brutishness alone speaks from his blurry, fading eyes, from his lecherous, open mouth, from his choked, quaking voice, from his short, rapid breathing, from his trembling limbs, from the whole of his languishing frame. All moral strength's opposition has subsided and the natural within him is released into total freedom. But just this complete suspension of self-motivation, which habitually occurs in the moment of sensual longing and, even more, of indulgence, also immediately sets free the raw matter that was constrained by the balance between the active and passive powers. Nature's inert powers begin to get the upper hand over the living ones in the organism; form is overcome by mass, humanity by common nature. The eye, through which the soul shines, becomes dull, or protrudes *glassy* and *fixed* from its socket, the fine complexion of the cheeks thickens to a coarse and undifferentiated wash, the mouth becomes a mere aperture, since its shape is no longer a consequence of the active but of the subsiding powers; the voice and sigh are nothing more than breath through which the laden chest tries to gain relief and which is now evidence simply of an automatic need and not of the soul. In a word: in the freedom that the sensuous *grasps by itself*, there is no thought of beauty. Coarse matter, which always gains as much ground as is lost by the will, *overwhelms* the freedom of forms, which the ethical will had merely *restricted*.

A human being in this condition not only outrages the *moral* sense that uncompromisingly demands an expression of humanity, but also the *aesthetic* sense, which is not satisfied with mere matter and seeks free enjoyment of form, will turn away in disgust at such a sight, in which *desire* alone is accommodated.

The first of these relationships between the two natures in the human is reminiscent of a *monarchy* in which [**NA 282**] the ruler's strict surveillance bridles every free stirring; the second is like a wild *ochlocracy*, in which the citizen, by refusing obedience to the rightful supremacy, fails to gain freedom, just as the human constitution, by suppressing moral self-motivation, fails to become beautiful; instead, he becomes a victim of the more brutal despotism of the lowest classes, just as form falls victim to mass. Just as *freedom* lies in the centre between anarchy and the suppression of law, we now find *beauty* in the middle between *dignity*, that is to say, the expression of dominant mind, and *lust*, as the expression of dominant impulse.

When neither *reason dominating the sensuous*, nor *sensuousness dominating reason* is compatible with beauty of expression, then (as there is no fourth alternative) the state of mind *in which reason and sensuousness —* duty and inclination — *coincide* will be the condition under which the beauty of play occurs.

In order to become the object of inclination, obedience to reason must deliver a source of enjoyment, because the impulse is only set in motion by pleasure or pain. In common experience it is the other way around, and pleasure is the reason for acting rationally. We have to thank the immortal author of the Critique, to whom fame is due for having reestablished healthy reason out of philosophical reason, for the fact that morality itself has finally stopped using this language.

But in the way the principles of this wise philosopher are generally presented by him and by others, inclination is a very unreliable companion to ethical sense and pleasure a dubious ingredient for moral determination. Even if the impulse to happiness does not maintain blind dominion over humans, it does want to *have a voice* in the ethical elections and to harm the purity of the will, which always wants to pursue the *law*, never the *impulse*. In order to be completely certain that inclination did not exercise its influence *as well*, we prefer to visualize it in conflict rather than in agreement with the law of reason because it can too easily [*NA* 283] happen that its intercession alone gives that law power over the will. For, because ethical behavior is not about the *legality* of the deeds but only about the *dutiful nature* of the attitude, it is right not to set any store by the observation that in the first case it is usually advantageous if the inclination is aligned with duty. This much seems certain, that sensuousness, in bestowing approval, may not actually make the dutiful nature of the will suspicious, but it is at least not in a position to *vouch for it*. The sensuous expression of this approval in grace will never bear adequate and valid witness to the ethical nature of the action in which it appears, and one will never learn of the moral worth of an attitude or action from the beautiful way it is presented.

Up until now I believe I am completely of one mind with the most *rigorous moralists* but I hope I will not be considered a *latitudinarian* for trying to assert the demands of the sensuous in the realm of appearance and in the actual fulfillment of ethical obligations, which are *completely* rejected in the sphere of pure reason and moral legislation.

Firmly persuaded as I am — and just because I am persuaded — that the part played by inclination in a free action demonstrates nothing about the purely dutiful nature of this action, I believe I can conclude *from this* that the ethical perfection of the human being can only become clear precisely because of the part played by the inclination in moral actions. The human being is not destined to perform individual ethical actions but to be an ethical being. *Virtue* is prescribed for him, rather than *virtues,* and virtue is nothing other than "an inclination for duty." However much actions from inclination and actions out of duty stand opposed to one another in an objective sense, this is not the case in the subjective sense, and humans not only *may*, but *should* combine enjoyment with duty; they should obey their reason with joy. Not in order to discard it like a burden or shrug it off like a coarse covering [*NA* 284], no, their purely intellectual nature is accompanied by a sensuous one so that the sensuous can agree as closely as possible with the higher self. In that it made him a rational, sensitive being, that is, a human, nature gave the human being notice of his obligation not to separate what it had bound together and, even in the purest expressions of his divine part, not to neglect the sensuous, and not to base the triumph of the one on the subjugation of the other. Only when it gushes forth from *mankind as a whole* as the combined effect of both principles, *when it has become his nature,* is the ethical spirit secure, since, as long as the ethical spirit still employs *force,* the natural impulse has to respond to it with *strength.* The enemy who has merely been *laid low* can get up again, but the one who is *reconciled* has been truly overcome.

In Kant's moral philosophy, the idea of *duty* is presented with a severity that repels all graces and might tempt a weak intellect to seek moral perfection by taking the path of a somber and monkish asceticism. However much this great philosopher tried to defend himself against this misinterpretation, which, to his serene and free spirit has to be the most outrageous one, he himself, it seems to me, has provided strong grounds for it (although, for his purpose, this was unavoidable), in his strict and harsh opposition of the two principles that have an effect on the human will. Among thoughtful people who are *open to persuasion,* there can no longer be any argument about the matter itself, considering the proofs he provides, and I would hardly think that one would not rather give up one's whole humanity than accept a different result from reason about this situation. However, although he meticulously undertook an *examination* of the truth, and however much everything proceeds on purely objective grounds here, nevertheless, in the *representation* of the truth discovered, a subjective maxim appears to have guided him, which is, to my mind, not difficult to explain by the circumstances of the time.

The moral state of his time, as he found it in theory and in practice, must have incensed him with, on the one hand, [*NA* 285] the coarse materialism of its moral principles, which the philosophers, inappropriately accommodating, had placed as a pillow under the lax character of the time. On the other hand, a no less questionable *principle of perfection,* which was not in doubt about the choice of means to bring about an abstract idea of universal world perfection, would also have had to arouse his attention. He directed his greatest powers of reasoning where the danger was greatest and the need for reform most urgent, and adopted the rule of relentlessly pursuing sensuousness, both where it impudently scorns ethical sensibility and under the impressive cover of morally praiseworthy aims, in which a certain enthusiastic spirit of a certain Order knows particularly well how to hide it. He did not have to instruct *ignorance,* but to set straight what was *wrong.* A shock was demanded as a cure, not flattery or persuasion, and the greater the discrepancy between the basis of truth and the prevailing maxims, the more he hoped to be able to promote reflection about this. He was the *Draco*[8] of his time, because he did not regard his time as worthy of a *Solon* or yet able to receive one. He brought the unfamiliar and yet, at the same time, so well-known moral law forth from the sanctuary of pure reason and displayed it in all its holiness to the unworthy century and barely inquired whether there were eyes that could not withstand its brightness.

How were the *children of the house* at fault, if he was only concerned about the *servants?* Must an unselfish emotion in the noblest of breasts come under suspicion just because impure inclinations often usurp the name of virtue?[9] Just because the moral weakling would like to introduce a certain *laxity* into the law of reason, to make it a toy for his own convenience, does this mean that a *rigidity* has to set in, transforming the most powerful expression of moral freedom into merely an honorable kind of servitude? Does the truly ethical human have a freer choice between self-regard and self-reproach than the slave of the senses between pleasure and pain? Is there perhaps less pressure on a pure will than on a depraved one? [*NA 286*] Does mankind have to be accused and humiliated simply by the *imperative* form of the moral law, and does the most sublime document of its greatness also have to be a certification of its frailty? Could one indeed, in this imperative form, have avoided a situation where a prescription given by humans to themselves as rational beings and therefore binding only on them and compatible only with their feeling of freedom took on the appearance of an unfamiliar and positive law — an appearance that could be reduced only with difficulty, because of their *radical* tendency (of which they stand accused) to work against it?*

---

[8] Draco was a seventh-century Athenian politician who codified the laws of Athens. His code is legendary for its severity.

[9] Some commentators point to biblical passages as Schiller's reference here (John 8:34, Romans 8:14, Cor. 7:22). However, Schiller may still have Roman law in mind. In any case, the suggestion that cultivation lends an appearance of virtue to unconscious acts emerges clearly enough.

* Cf. Kant's creed on human nature in his latest work: *Religion in the Bounds of Reason,* part 1.

It is certainly not advantageous for moral truths if there are sentiments *against* them which humans can admit to without blushing. But how should sentiments of beauty and freedom be accommodated to the austere spirit of a law that guides them more by *fear* than *confidence,* that constantly tries to *divide* them, although nature *made them one,* and can only secure its control over someone by arousing in him a mistrust towards one part of his being. Human nature is a more coherent whole in reality than a philosopher, who can only achieve results through separation, is permitted to reveal. It is inconceivable that reason can reject as beneath it emotions to which the heart assents with gladness, and if humans, however morally abject, are not incapable of rising at least in their own estimation. If sensuous nature were always the suppressed part and never belonged to the *effective* part of ethics, how could it wholeheartedly impart its fiery emotions to celebrate a triumph over itself? How could it be such a lively participant in the self-consciousness of pure mind if it could not, in the end, bind itself so securely to the mind that even analytical reason could not separate them without violence.

The will has a more direct connection with the powers of emotion, in any case, than with those of understanding, [**NA 287**] and in several situations it would be undesirable for it to have to orientate itself first in relation to pure reason. A person does not make a good impression on me if he can trust the voice of impulse so little as to feel obliged to test its tone against that of moral principles; one respects him more highly if he confidently trusts it and is not in danger of being misled by it. This is because it shows that in him both principles are already in that harmony that seals perfected humanity and that is understood as the *beautiful soul.*

One refers to a beautiful soul when the ethical sense has at last so taken control of all a person's feelings that it can leave affect to guide the will without hesitation and is never in danger of standing in contradiction of its decisions. For this reason the actions of a beautiful soul are not themselves ethical, but the character as a whole is so. One cannot give the beautiful soul credit for any action, since satisfying an impulse is never considered creditable. The beautiful soul has no other merit besides being. It carries out humankind's most exacting duties with such ease that they might simply be the actions of its inner instinct, and the most heroic sacrifice that it exacts from natural impulse appears to the eye as a free operation of this impulse. This is why the beautiful soul itself never knows about the beauty of its actions and it does not even occur to it that one could act and feel differently. A pupil well-schooled in the rules of ethics, as required by his master's instructions, on the other hand, will always be ready to give a precise account of the relation between his actions and the law. His life will resemble a drawing in which one can see the rules behind the precise lines and from which at most an apprentice could perhaps learn the principles of art. In a beautiful life, however, all the sharp dividing lines disappear, as in a painting by *Titian*,[10] and yet the whole impression comes across more faithfully, more harmoniously, and truer to life.

[*NA* 288] It is in a beautiful soul that sensuousness and reason, duty and inclination are in harmony, and grace is their expression as appearance. Only in the service of a beautiful soul can nature possess freedom and at the same time preserve its form, since freedom vanishes under the control of a strict disposition and form under the anarchy of sensuousness. A beautiful soul spreads an irresistible grace over a physique lacking in architectonic beauty and often one even sees it triumph over natural shortcomings. All movements that emanate from it become light and gentle, and yet lively. The eye shines bright and clear, and sentiment gleams in it. From the gentle heart, the mouth receives a grace that cannot be produced by dissimulation. No tension is perceptible in the features or constraint in the intentional movements, because the soul knows of none. The voice will be music and move the heart with the stream of its modulations. Architectonic beauty can give rise to pleasure, admiration, or amazement, but only grace will enrapture. Beauty has *worshippers;* only grace has *lovers,* because we pay homage to the Creator and love the people.

As a general rule, one finds more grace among *women* (more beauty, perhaps, among men), and the origin of this is not hard to find. The physical form has to contribute to grace, as well as the character; the physical through its flexible ability to receive impressions and to be set in motion, the character through the moral harmony of feelings. In both, nature was more favorable towards woman than towards man.

The more delicate feminine physique receives each impression more quickly and makes it disappear more quickly. Strong constitutions are only

---

[10] Titian (Tiziano Vecellio) 1488?–1576 is famous for his use of vigorous colors into which, in the later paintings, the form is all but entirely submerged.

set in motion by an assault, and when strong muscles are flexed, they cannot display the lightness demanded for grace. What in a woman's face is beautiful sensitivity, would, in a man, express suffering. The delicate fiber of a woman bends like a thin reed at the slightest breath of emotion. [*NA* 289] The soul glides in light, delightful waves over the expressive face, which then becomes as calm as a mirror again.

The contribution that the soul must make to grace can also be more easily fulfilled in a woman than a man. A woman's character seldom reaches the highest idea of ethical purity and seldom goes beyond acts of *affection*. It often resists sensuousness with heroic fortitude, but only *by means of* sensuousness. Now because the ethical disposition of woman is normally on the side of inclination, in the appearance it will seem as though the inclination were on the side of the ethical disposition. Grace will thus become the expression of womanly virtue, and very often might be missing from manly virtue.

Dignity

As grace is the expression of a beautiful soul, *dignity* is the expression of a superior mentality.

Human beings do have the task of establishing an intimate agreement between their two natures, of always being a harmonious whole, and of acting with their full human capacity. But this beauty of character, the ripest fruit of humanity, is only an idea that they can vigilantly strive to live up to, yet, despite all efforts, can never fully attain.

The reason they cannot reach it is the unchanging outlines of their nature; the physical conditions of their existence hinder them.

In order to safeguard their existence in the world of the senses, which depends upon natural conditions, humans, because they are beings that can change at will, had, for their self-preservation, to be enabled to perform actions through which the physical conditions of their existence can be fulfilled, or, when lacking, restored. However, although nature had to hand over to the human being this concern, which it alone takes care of in its plant life, [*NA* 290] the satisfaction of such an urgent need, a need that relates to his existence and that of his whole species, ought not to be trusted to his uncertain judgment. Thus, nature took this matter into its domain, where it belongs in terms of *content*, in terms of *form* as well, by introducing necessity into the conditions of free will. In this way, natural instinct arose, which is nothing other than natural necessity through the medium of sensation.

Natural instinct assails the faculty of sensation through the double forces of pain and pleasure: through pain, when it demands satisfaction, through pleasure, when it finds it.

Since nothing in natural necessity can be modified, humans, despite their freedom, feel what nature wants them to feel and, according to whether the feeling is pain or enjoyment, loathing or desire inevitably results. In this regard, humans are exactly the same as animals, and the most strong-willed Stoic feels hunger just as acutely and loathes it just as strongly as the worm at his feet.

But now this is where the main difference lies: in animals, action results from desire and loathing just as necessarily as desire results from sensation and sensation resulted from the outward impression. It is a constantly extending chain, in which each ring is necessarily linked to the next. In humans, there is an additional factor, namely, the *will*, which, as a suprasensual faculty, is not so subject either to the law of nature or to that of reason that it does not have complete freedom to choose whether to follow the one or the other. Animals *must* strive to free themselves from pain; humans can decide to hold on to it.

The human will is a noble concept, even when one does not consider its moral application. The will *alone* already elevates the human above animal nature; the *moral* will elevates him to divinity. He must have left animal nature behind before he can approach the divine state. For this reason it is no small step to the moral freedom of the will, which is achieved by breaking the natural necessity in oneself of exercising *pure* will, even in matters of indifference. [*NA 291*]

Nature's legislation extends to the will, where its legislation ends and the legislation of reason begins. The will stands between these two jurisdictions, and it alone decides which law to accept, but it does not stand in the same relation to them both. As a force of nature it is free in relation to the one as much as to the other; this means that it does not *have to* give an account to the one or to the other. It is not free as a moral force, however; in other words, it *should* be accountable to the force of reason. It is *bound* to neither but *indebted* to the law of reason. Thus, it truly exercises its freedom even when it acts in contradiction to reason, but it exercises it *unworthily*, because, despite its freedom, it remains *within nature* and does not add reality to the operation of pure instinct, since *to will* from *desire* is simply a more complicated way of saying to desire.*[11]

Nature's legislation through instinct can come into conflict with the legislation of reason through principle, if instinct demands, for its satisfaction, an action that goes against the moral principle. In such a case, it is the absolute duty of the will to place the demands of nature after the tenets of reason, since natural laws only bind conditionally but reason's laws bind absolutely and unconditionally.

Nature, however, emphatically claims its rights, and since it never makes arbitrary claims, it never withdraws unsatisfied claims. Because from the first cause that sets it in motion, up to the will, where its legislation ceases, everything is strictly necessary, it cannot retreat *backwards*, but must push *forwards* against the will, in which the satisfaction of its needs resides. Occasionally it does seem as though it had cut short its path, and, without first bringing its petition before the will, had immediate cause for the action through which its needs are relieved. In such a case, where the human [*NA* 292] did not *grant* free rein to instinct, but where instinct *took* it anyway, the human would *only* be an animal. However, it is very doubtful whether this could ever be his lot, and if it really were, whether this blind power of instinct is not a crime of the will.

The faculty of desire insists on satisfaction, and demands that the will provide it. But the will should receive its regulations from reason and only form a resolution in accordance with what reason allows or prescribes. If the will really does proceed directly to reason, before approving the demand of instinct, it acts ethically; if it decides immediately, it acts sensuously.**

---

* On this matter, the Theory of the Will in the second part of Reinhold's Letters is worthy of much attention.

[11] Karl Leonhard (1758–1823), a follower of Kant's, sought, in his philosophical works, to establish the common ground of the senses and understanding. Schiller refers here to his *Briefe über die Kantsche Philosophie*. A selection of Reinhold's works can be read in Sabine Roehr's *A Primer on German Enlightenment: With a Translation of Karl Leonhard Reinhold's The Fundamental Concepts and Principles of Ethics* (Columbia/London: U Missouri P, 1995).

** One should not confuse *this* inquiry made of reason by the will with the one about the *means* of satisfying desire. Here the question is not how to *attain* satisfaction

Whenever nature makes a demand, then, and wants to surprise the will by the blind power of feeling, the will is obliged to hold nature back until reason has spoken. What it cannot yet know is whether reason's statement will be *in the interests of* sensuousness or *against* it; that is why it has to regard this procedure without differentiating between feelings, and whenever nature is the *initiator,* the will must deny nature immediate causality. Only by crushing the power of desire, which rushes too eagerly towards satisfaction, and would prefer to skirt around the will's authority altogether, do human beings display their independence and prove themselves to be moral beings, which never simply desire or simply loathe, but have *to will* their loathing and desire in each instance.

The simple inquiry of reason is an encroachment on nature, which is an accomplished judge in its own matters, and does not wish to see its statements subjected to outside authority. [**NA 293**] An act of will that places the concerns of the faculty of desire before the ethical tribunal is, in truth, *unnatural,* because it makes what is necessary into something arbitrary and leaves the decision up to the laws of reason in a matter where only nature's laws can speak and have, in fact, spoken. This is because, however little attention pure reason pays, in her moral legislation, to the way the senses would receive her decisions, nature, in her own legislation, pays just as little attention to the means of making it acceptable to reason. In each of these, another necessity is valid and it would not be so if each were allowed to make arbitrary changes to the other. For this reason, the most courageous spirit, despite being completely opposed to sensuousness, can neither suppress feeling itself, nor desire itself, but can only reject their influence on the directions of his will; he can *disarm* instinct by moral means, but only through natural ones can he *appease* it. Although by his independent power he can prevent the laws of nature from being binding on his will, he cannot change anything at all about these laws.

In emotions, then, "where nature (instinct) acts *first* and tries either to *circumvent* the will completely or to bring it on side *with force,* the ethical nature of the character can do nothing else but reveal itself through *opposition,* and, can only prevent instinct from restricting the freedom of the will,

---

but whether satisfaction is to be *permitted.* Only the latter belongs in the moral sphere; the former belongs to prudence.

by restricting instinct." In the emotions, agreement with the law of reason is only possible by contravening the demands of nature. And since nature, for ethical reasons, never withdraws her demands, and therefore everything on her side remains the same, no matter how the will behaves in relation to her, so here there is no agreement possible between inclination and duty, between reason and sensuousness; so humans cannot here act with their whole nature in harmony, but only with their reason. In such cases, then, they also do not act with *moral beauty*, because inclination necessarily has to participate in the beauty of action as well, [*NA* 294] but here it stands in conflict. But they do act with *moral greatness* because all those things and only those are great that give evidence of superiority of the higher faculties over the sensuous.

The *beautiful* soul, then, must, in emotion, change into a *sublime* soul, and this is the foolproof test to distinguish it from *a good heart* or from *virtue born of temperament*. If a person's inclination is only on the side of justice because justice is, luckily, situated on the side of inclination, then natural instinct in the emotions will exercise a completely compulsive power over the will, and, when a sacrifice is necessary, it will be made by the ethical and not the sensuous. If, on the other hand, reason itself, as is the case in a beautiful character, has *taken over* the inclinations and *only entrusted* sensuousness with the helm, it will take it back the moment that instinct tries to abuse its power. Virtue of temperament, in the emotions, then, is reduced to a simple product of nature; the beautiful soul becomes heroic and elevates itself to pure intelligence.

Control of impulses through moral strength is *spiritual freedom,* and its expression in appearance is called *dignity.*

Strictly speaking, moral strength in humans is not capable of being represented, because the suprasensuous can never be made sensuous. But it can be presented to the understanding in an indirect way through sensuous signs, as indeed happens with dignity in the human constitution.

The stimulated natural instinct, like the heart in its moral movements, is accompanied by movements of the body, of which some run ahead of the will and some, as merely sympathetic, are not subject to its control. Because neither sentiment nor desire and loathing lie within the human being's arbitration, he cannot master those movements that are directly connected to them either. The instinct, however, does not rest at desire; it strives rashly and urgently to realize its objective and, [*NA* 295] as long as it is not strongly resisted by the independent spirit, will even *anticipate* those actions about which the will alone should speak. The instinct for preservation struggles unremittingly for the power of legislation in the area of the will, and it attempts to control humans just as unreservedly as animals.

Thus one finds movements of two kinds and origins in every emotion ignited by the human instinct for preservation; first, those that proceed directly from sentiment and are therefore completely determined; second, those which are of the type that should and could be arbitrary, but which blind natural instinct has won away from freedom. The former relate to emotion itself and are therefore necessarily connected with it; the latter correspond more to the origin and object of emotion, which is why they are accidental and changeable and cannot count as its reliable indicators. But because both are equally necessary to natural instinct as soon as the object is determined, both belong to the making of a complete and coherent whole out of an expression of emotion.*[12]

Now when the will possesses sufficient independence to set limits on the over-eager natural impulse and to impose its just power on the impetuous power of the other, all those appearances remain in power that the stimulated natural impulse brought about in its own sphere, but all those that it tried, illegitimately, to snatch for itself in a foreign jurisdiction are missing. Thus the appearances do not correspond, but the expression of moral strength lies precisely in their contradiction.

Let us imagine we were looking at the signs in a person of the most agonizing emotion from that first class of completely instinctive [*NA 296*] movements. But while his veins swell, his muscles become cramped and taut, his voice cracks, his chest is thrust out, and his lower body pressed in, his intentional movements are gentle, the facial features relaxed, and the eyes and brow serene. If a human were simply a creature of the senses, all

---

* If one encounters the second type of movement without the first, this indicates that the person wants the emotion and nature denies it. If one encounters movements of the first kind without the second, this proves that nature really is placed in the emotion, but that the person prevents it. One sees the first case every day in affected people and bad comedians, the second less often and only in the strong-willed.

[12] Schiller's two examples refer to movements that portray a sentiment but have no genuine basis in emotion.

his features would correspond with each other, since they would have a common source, and thus, in this case, they would all, equally, have to express suffering. But as there are peaceful signs among the pained signs, and since one cause cannot have opposite effects, this contradiction of signs demonstrates the existence and influence of a power independent of suffering and above the impressions to which we see the sensuous succumb. And in this way, *peace in suffering,* in which dignity actually consists, becomes the representation of intelligence in humans and the expression of their moral freedom, although only indirectly, through a conclusion on the part of reason.*[13]

Not only in suffering in the narrower sense, however, where this word simply means painful emotions, but in general, with every strong engagement of the faculty of desire, the mind must show its freedom, and dignity must be its expression. Pleasant emotions demand this as much as painful ones, because nature would like to play the master in both cases and should be checked by the will. Dignity applies to the *form* and not to the *content* of an emotion, so that it can often happen that emotions whose content is praiseworthy, descend, when a person gives himself blindly up to them, to become common or base, because of a lack of dignity; on the other hand, that despicable emotions not infrequently approach the sublime, as long as they show control of the mind over sensations, even if only in their form.

In dignity, then, the mind conducts itself in the body as *ruler,* because there it has to assert its independence against domineering instinct, which proceeds without it, [*NA 297*] and would like to escape from its yoke. In grace, on the other hand, the mind governs with *liberality,* because it is the mind that sets nature in action here, and it finds no opposition to quell. Leniency is due only to the obedient, however, and only *opposition* justifies severity.

Grace, then, lies in the *freedom of intentional movements,* dignity in the *mastery of instinctive ones.* Grace leaves nature with the appearance of free will where she carries out the commands of the mind; dignity, by

---

* This is more thoroughly discussed in the 3rd part of *Thalia* in an essay on Pathetic Representation.
[13] Schiller means the essay "Über das Pathetische."

contrast, subjugates her where she wants to be in command, to the mind. Whenever instinct begins to act and takes the liberty of encroaching on the offices of the will, the will may not allow *indulgence,* but must demonstrate its independence (autonomy) through the most insistent opposition. If, on the other hand, the will *begins,* and the sensuous *follows* it, then it should not show severity; it must show indulgence. This, in brief, is the law for the relationship between the two natures in humans, as represented in appearance.

Dignity is therefore demanded and demonstrated more in *suffering* (pathos), grace more in *conduct* (ethos), since a free disposition can only be revealed in suffering and a free body only in action.

Because dignity is an expression of opposition to natural instinct made by the independent mind, natural instinct must be seen as a power that makes opposition necessary; thus dignity, where there is no such power to fight against, is ridiculous, and where there *ought* no longer to be a force to fight against, is contemptible. We laugh at a comedian (whatever his class and dignity may be) who affects a certain dignity while carrying out perfectly normal tasks. We despise the small mind that accords itself dignity by performing a common task, which often amounts to no more than omitting to carry out a mean act.

As a rule, it is not actually dignity but grace that is required of virtue. Dignity is necessary to virtuous behavior, which, because of its content, presupposes a person's command over his impulses. [**NA 298**] In the exercise of ethical duties, it will be so much more likely for the sensuous to find itself pressured and suppressed, especially when a painful sacrifice is made. Since the ideal of perfected humanity does not demand an opposition but a consonance of the ethical and the sensuous, it is not compatible with a dignity that, as an expression of that opposition between the two, makes visible either the particular limits of the subject or those of mankind in general.

If the first is the case, even if it is simply on account of the inability of the subject that inclination and duty do not coincide in an action, this action will always forfeit ethical esteem to the extent that a struggle is involved in its exercise, that dignity is involved in its performance. Our moral judgment sets the standard of the species for each individual and no other limits will be placed upon a human than those of humanity.

If the second is the case, and if an action out of duty cannot be brought into harmony with the demands of nature without suspending the concept of human nature, then inclination's opposition is necessary and only when we see the struggle are we convinced that victory is possible. Thus we expect an expression of conflict in the appearance and will never be persuaded to believe there is virtue where humanity is not even present. When ethical duty demands an action that causes the sensuous to suffer, it is serious, and not a game; we would be irritated rather than gratified by ease in its performance; only dignity can be its expression, not grace. In general, the law is valid here that humans should do everything with grace that can be carried out within humanity, and everything with dignity that requires going beyond humanity.

Just as we demand grace from virtue, so we demand dignity from inclination. Grace is as necessary to inclination as dignity is to virtue, because in its content it is sensuous, favorable towards natural freedom and hostile to exertion. [*NA* 299] Even a coarse person does not lack a certain degree of grace, if love or a similar emotion inspires him, and where does one find more grace than in children, completely guided as they are by the sensuous? There is much more danger that inclination may in the end place the condition of suffering in power, suppress the mind's own activity and bring about a general lassitude. In order to gain esteem from a noble feeling, which can only happen when the origin is *ethical*, inclination must combine with dignity at all times. For this reason, the lover demands dignity in the object of his passion. Dignity alone guarantees that it was *not out of need* that he was chosen, but *freely* — that he is not *desired as a thing*, but *esteemed as a person*.

One demands grace from a person who places obligations, and dignity from someone who is placed under an obligation. The former, in order to avoid having a displeasing advantage over the other, should reduce the act of his impartial decision to a *benevolent* act, by allowing inclination to enter into it, and thus make himself appear to be the one who gains. To avoid, in his person, disrespecting humanity (whose holy Palladium is freedom) through the dependency into which he is entering, the latter should elevate the mere *drive* of an impulse to an act of his will, and, in this way, by receiving a favor, grant one.

One should criticize a mistake with grace, and confess one with dignity. If this is reversed, it will look as though one part is too aware of its advantage, and the other too little aware of its disadvantage.

If the strong wishes to be loved, he must temper his superiority with grace. If the weak wants respect, he must supplement his impotence with dignity. One is generally of the opinion that dignity belongs on the throne, and, as one knows, those who sit on the throne love to see grace in their advisors, confessors, and parliaments. But what is good and praiseworthy in a political realm is not always so in the realm of taste. [*NA* 300] Into this realm the King steps — as soon as he descends from his throne (since thrones have their privileges) and the creeping courtier also enters this holy freedom, as soon as he stands up straight as a person. But the one should be advised to make good his lack from the other's abundance, and to give the other as much dignity as he himself needs grace.

Since grace and dignity express themselves in different areas, they are not mutually exclusive in the same person and not even in the same condition of a person. Rather, it is only from grace that dignity acquires recognition and only from dignity that grace acquires value.

Dignity alone displays a certain restriction of desires and inclinations wherever we encounter it. Only the grace associated with it can establish beyond doubt whether what we take to be control is not actually a dullness (hardening) of sensibility and whether it is really one's own moral activity and not rather the preponderance of another emotion, deliberate exertion, that holds the outbreak of the present one in check. Grace gives evidence of a peaceful, harmonious disposition and a sensitive heart.

In this way as well, grace alone displays receptivity towards the faculty of feeling, and an agreement between sensations. Again, only the dignity associated with it can vouch for the fact that it is not mental slackness that allows the senses so much freedom and opens the heart to every impression, and that it is the ethical that brings sensations into this agreement. In dignity, the subject legitimizes itself as an independent power; and the will, by *harnessing* the *license* of instinctive movements, lets it be known that it simply *approves* the *freedom* of the intentional movements.

If grace, supported by architectonic beauty, and dignity, supported by strength, are *united* in the same person, then the expression of humanity is complete in that person, and he stands there, justified in the world of spirit and affirmed in appearance. The two legislations are [*NA* 301] in such close contact here that their boundaries flow together. The *freedom of reason* arises with a milder glow in the smiling mouth, in the gently animated glance, in the cheerful brow, and *natural necessity* retreats, with a sublime farewell, from the noble majesty of the countenance. Ancient works of art were formed according to this ideal of human beauty, and one recognizes it in the divine form of Niobe, in Apollo

Belvedere, in the winged Genius of Borghesi and in the Muse of the Barberini Palace.*[14]

[*NA* 302] Where grace and dignity combine, we are attracted and repelled in turn; attracted as intellects, repelled as sensuous natures.

---

* With the fine and grand sense characteristic of him, Winckelmann understood and described this extreme beauty, which emerges from the combination of grace and dignity (Geschichte der Kunst., Erster Theil, 480ff., Vienna edition). But he took what he found combined and portrayed it only as a unit, and contented himself with what sense alone taught him, without looking into whether it could be divided. He confuses the concept of grace by including in it characteristics that obviously only apply to dignity. But grace and dignity are essentially different and it is unjust to make what is actually a *restriction* on grace into one of its *characteristics*. What Winckelmann calls extreme, heavenly grace is nothing other than beauty and grace with a preponderance of dignity. "Heavenly grace," he says, "seems to be self-sufficient, and does not offer itself, but wants to be sought; it is too sublime to make itself very sensuous. It embraces movements of the soul and approaches the blessed serenity of the divine nature." "If through it," he says in another place, "the artist of Niobe dared to enter the realm of incorporeal ideas, and arrived at the secret of *how to combine the fear of death with the most extreme beauty,*" (it would be difficult to find meaning here if it were not obvious that only dignity is intended), "he became a creator of pure spirits that arouse no desires of the senses, since they seem not to be made for passion, only to have taken it on." Elsewhere he writes, "the soul only expressed itself under the calm surface of the water, and never stepped impetuously forth. In the idea of suffering, extreme pain remains hidden, and joy hovers like a gentle breeze, hardly touching the leaves, on the face of a Leukothea."

All these characteristics apply to dignity and not to grace, because grace does not close itself off, but comes forward, grace makes itself sensuous, and is not sublime, but beautiful. But it is dignity that holds nature's expressions back and, even in the fear of death and, in the most bitter suffering of a Laokoon, imparts serenity to a person's features.

Home makes the same mistake, but it is less surprising in his case. He too takes up characteristics of dignity into grace, although he expressly distinguishes grace from dignity. His observations are usually correct, and the rules he *initially* forms from them, true; but one should not follow him further than this (Grundsätze der Kritik, part 2, Anmuth und Würde).

[14] For a recent English edition of Winckelmann's best known work, see Johann Joachim, *Reflections on the Imitation of Greek Works in Painting and Sculpture,* trans. Elfriede Heyer, and Roger C. Norton (La Salle: Open Court, 1987).

In dignity we are presented with an example of the subjugation of the sensuous to the ethical, and although the rule demands that we imitate this, at the same time it exceeds our physical capacities. The opposition between the needs of nature and the demands of the law, whose validity we do admit, puts strain on the senses, and gives rise to the feeling that is called *respect* and that is inseparable from dignity.

In grace on the other hand, as in beauty generally, reason sees her demands fulfilled in sensuousness, and one of her ideas comes unexpectedly before her as an appearance. This unforeseen coincidence of the accidental in nature and the necessity of reason arouses a feeling of joyful appreciation (*approval*) that is relaxing for the senses, but stimulating and absorbing for the intellect, and attraction for the sensuous object must follow. We call this attraction favor — *love;* a feeling that is inseparable from grace and beauty.

With *charm* (not the charm of love, but that of voluptuousness, stimulus), the senses are presented with a sensuous substance that promises the fulfillment of a need; that is, lust. The senses are thus anxious to join with sensuousness, and *desire* is aroused, a feeling that tautens the consciousness, but slackens the spirit.

One can say of respect, that it *bows before* its object; of love, that it *inclines* towards its object; [**NA 303**] of desire, that it *falls upon* its object. For respect, the object is reason and the subject, sensuous nature.*[15] For

---

* One should not confuse *respect* with *admiration*. Respect (in its purest sense) only applies to the relation of sensuous nature to the demands of pure practical reason, without regard for their actual fulfillment. "The feeling of inadequacy as regards the attainment of an ideal that we accept as law is called respect" (Kant's Critique of Judgment). For this reason, respect is not a pleasant but a dispiriting feeling. It is a feeling of the distance of the empirical will from the pure will. — Therefore it also cannot be disconcerting to make sensuous nature the subject of respect, although this only applies to *pure reason;* because inadequacy in relation to the fulfillment of the law can only lie in sensuousness.

Admiration, on the other hand, does apply to the actual fulfillment of the law, and is not felt for the law, but for the person who adheres to it. Thus, there is something delightful about it, because the fulfillment of the law has to please rational beings. Respect is forced, admiration is a freer feeling. This, however, comes from love, the object is sensuous and the subject is moral nature. For desire, the object and the subject are sensuous.

Love alone is thus a free emotion, because its pure source flows forth from the seat of freedom, from our divine nature. It is not the small and the low that are being measured against the great and high here, not the senses looking dizzily upwards to the law of reason; it is *absolute greatness* itself, that finds itself imitated in grace and beauty and affirmed in the ethical. It is the legislator himself, the *God* in us, who plays with his own image in the world of senses. Thus the disposition is relaxed in love, as it is strained in respect; because there is nothing here to place restraints on it, since there is nothing above absolute greatness, and sensuousness, from which alone a restriction could come, coincides in grace and beauty with the ideas of intellect. Love is descent, as respect is an upwards climb. [*NA* 304] Therefore, a bad man cannot love anything, although he has to respect many things; therefore the good man can respect little that he does not at the same time embrace with love. Pure intellect can only love, not respect; the senses can only respect, but not love.

When a conscience-stricken person hovers in constant fear of encountering the legislator in himself in the world of senses, and sees his enemy in everything that is great and beautiful and exquisite, the beautiful soul knows no sweeter happiness than to see the sacred in itself imitated or realized and to embrace its immortal friend in the world of senses. Love is at the same time the most magnanimous and the most selfish thing in nature; the first, because it receives nothing from its object but gives it everything, since pure intellect can only give, not receive; the second, because it is always only its own self that it seeks and appreciates in its object.

But just because the lover only receives from the beloved what he himself gave, it often happens that he gives the beloved object what he did not receive from it. External sense believes it sees what only the inner sense looks at, the burning wish becomes belief, and the lover's own

---

love, which constitutes an ingredient of admiration. Even the least worthy person must respect the good, but in order to admire the person who performed it, he would have to cease to be unworthy.

[15] See the discussion of this passage in Jane V. Curran's essay in this volume.

excess conceals the poverty of the beloved. This is why love is so susceptible to deception, which seldom happens to respect or desire. The blissful
enchantment of platonic love endures for as long as the inner sense exalts
the external sense, and only needs permanence in order to become the
ecstasy of the immortals. However, as soon as the inner senses no longer
pass off their own views as those of the outer senses, the outer senses
assert their rights and demand their due: *matter.* The fire that heavenly
Venus ignited is used by the earthly Venus, and natural instinct not infrequently seeks to avenge its long neglect by means of a domination that is
all the more uninhibited. Because the senses are never deceived, they tri-
umphantly take this advantage over their nobler competitor and are bold
enough to claim that they have come up with what inspiration failed to
deliver.

Dignity prevents love from becoming desire. Grace protects respect
from becoming fear.

[*NA* 305] True beauty, true grace should never arouse desire. When
desire interferes, there must either be a lack of dignity in the object or of
morality in the feelings of the beholder.

True greatness should never arouse fear. When fear enters, one can be
certain that the object lacks taste or grace or that the beholder's conscience
lacks a favorable testimony.

Charm, grace, and gracefulness are normally used synonymously; but
they are not, or should not be, because the concept that they express can
be determined in several ways that warrant different designations.

There is a *stimulating* and a *calming* grace. The first borders on sensual attraction, and pleasure taken in it, when not restrained by dignity,
can easily decline into longing. It can be called *charm.* An exhausted person cannot set himself in motion through inner strength; he must receive
matter from without and seek to reestablish his lost energy through
gentle exercises of the imagination and swift transitions from sensation to
action. In the company of a *charming* person, who sets in motion the
stagnating sea of his imagination with conversation and glances, he suc-
ceeds in this.

Calming grace comes closer to dignity, since it expresses itself
through the moderation of agitated movements. The tense person turns
to it, and the wild storm of his emotion is unleashed on her peacefully
breathing breast. This can be called *grace.* Laughing wit and the sting of
scorn like to combine with charm; sympathy and love with grace. The

enervated Soliman[16] languishes at last in the chains of a Roxelane when the stormy spirit of Othello is rocked to rest on the gentle breast of a Desdemona.

Dignity has its various grades as well, and, where it comes close to grace and beauty, becomes *noble*, and, where it borders on the fearful, becomes *grandeur*.

The highest grade of grace is the *enchanting*; the [*NA* 306] highest grade of dignity is *majesty*. It is as if we lose ourselves in the enchanting, and flow over into the object. The highest enjoyment of freedom borders on the complete loss of it, and the intoxication of the intellect borders on the rapture of the senses. Majesty, on the other hand, presents us with a law that requires us to look into ourselves. We look down at the ground before the presence of God and forget everything outside ourselves, and feel nothing but the heavy burden of our own existence.

Only the sacred has majesty. If a person can represent this for us, he has majesty; even if our knees do not follow, at least our minds will bow before him. But the mind stands up again as soon as the slightest trace of *human guilt* is visible in the object of its devotion: nothing that is only *comparatively* great is permitted to cast down our spirits.

Simple power, however fearful and limitless, can never grant majesty. Power only impresses the creature of sense; majesty must grasp freedom from the intellect. A person who can condemn me to death does not yet possess majesty on that account in my eyes as soon as I am myself what I should be. His advantage over me is over as soon as I want it to be. But if someone represents pure will in his person, I will, if it is possible, even bow before him in worlds to come.

Grace and dignity are too highly valued for vanity and folly not to be tempted to imitate them. But there is only *one* path, imitation of the attitudes whose expression they are. Anything else is *mimicry* and will soon become evident as such, through exaggeration.

---

[16] The figures of Soliman and Roxelane come from a French comedy by Charles Simon Favart, *Soliman Second* (1762). Favart's plays and comic operas were popular with Schiller's contemporaries, particularly Lessing and Lenz. Soliman was regarded as the epitome of the enervated potentate, ruined by over-indulgence in the pleasures of the flesh.

Just as *bombast* arises from the affectation of the sublime, *preciosity* arises from the affectation of the noble, and from affected grace comes *fussiness* and from affected dignity, *ceremony* and *gravity*.

True grace *simply yields* and accommodates; false grace, on the other hand, *flows away*. True grace simply *protects* the tools of intentional movement and does not wish to offend natural freedom unnecessarily; [**NA 307**] false grace does not have the wits to use the tools of the will properly, and in order not to end in hardness or awkwardness, prefers to *sacrifice* something of the purpose of the movement, or seeks to gain it *by circumvention*. If the *clumsy* dancer uses as much strength in a minuet as it would take to pull a mill wheel, and forms sharp angles with the hands and feet, as though geometrical exactitude were here the task, the *affected* dancer will enter weakly, as though in fear of the floor, and will describe nothing but serpentine lines with the hands and feet, without even moving from the spot. The other sex, which characteristically possesses true grace, is most often guilty of false grace; but nowhere is this more offensive than when it serves as bait for desire. The smile of true grace becomes the ugliest grimace, the beautiful play of the eyes, so enchanting when true feelings speak from them, becomes perverted, the melting, modulated voice, so irresistible from a true mouth, becomes a studied, tremulous noise, and the entire music of feminine charms become a deceitful art of toiletry.

If, at theatres and balls, one has the opportunity to observe affected grace, one can often study false dignity in the cabinets of ministers and in the studies of scholars (particularly in higher schools). Whereas true dignity is satisfied with hindering affectation's dominance, and only setting limits to natural instinct when it wants to play the master, in unintentional movements, false dignity, with an iron scepter, rules the intentional movements as well, suppresses moral movements that are sacred to true dignity, as well as the sensuous ones, and obliterates the whole mimic play of the soul in the facial features. It is not simply severe towards the opposing nature, but also strict with groveling nature and seeks its ridiculous greatness by subjugating, and where this will not work, by concealing it. As though it had conceived an irredeemable hatred for everything that is called nature, it places the body in long, pleated robes [**NA 308**] that cover up the whole structure of the human limbs, restricts the use of the limbs with a cumbersome apparatus of useless ornament, and even cuts off the hair, in order to replace the gift of nature with a product of art. If true dignity, which is never ashamed of nature, but only of raw nature, is still always free and open, even when it holds itself back, and if feeling shines in the eyes and the cheerful, calm spirit rests on the eloquent brow, *gravity* places furrows on its brow, becomes withdrawn and mysterious, and, like a comedian, pays close attention to its features. All the facial muscles are tense, all true, natural expression disappears and the whole person is like a sealed letter. But false dignity is not always wrong to hold the mimic play of the features strictly in check, because it could perhaps express more than one wants said aloud; a caution that is clearly not necessary for true dignity. True dignity will only rule nature, never conceal it; on the other hand, nature only rules false dignity the more powerfully from *within* if it is forced from *without*.*

---

* Nevertheless, there is also a *ceremony*, in the good sense, that art can use. This does not come from the presumption of making oneself important, but has the intention of *preparing* the emotions for something important. When a great and deep impression is sought, and the poet must not let anything be lost, he prepares the emotions in advance to receive it, removes all distractions and places the imagination in a state of tense anticipation. *Ceremony* that consists of piling up many arrangements to no obvious end, and intentionally delaying progress just where impatience demands haste, is very well suited for this. In music, ceremony is produced by a *slow*, even succession of strong tones; the strength arouses and tenses the emotion, the slowness delays satisfaction, and the evenness of the rhythm leaves no end in sight for impatience.

Ceremony supports the impression of the great and sublime to no small extent and is therefore used in religious customs and mysteries with great success. The effects of bells, choral music, and organ are well known; but there is also a *ceremony* for the eye, namely *splendor*, connected with the *fearful*, as in funeral ceremonies and in all public acts that observe a great solemnity and slow rhythm.

Ueber Anmuth und Würde

Friedrich Schiller

[*NA* 251]¹

DIE GRIECHISCHE FABEL legt der Göttinn der Schönheit einen Gürtel bey, der die Kraft besitzt, dem, der ihn trägt, *Anmuth* zu verleyhen, und Liebe zu erwerben. Eben diese Gottheit wird von den Huldgöttinnen oder den *Grazien* begleitet.

Die Griechen *unterschieden* also die Anmuth und die Grazien noch von der Schönheit, da sie solche durch Attribute ausdrückten, die von der Schönheitsgöttinn zu trennen waren. Alle Anmuth ist schön, denn der Gürtel des Liebreizes ist ein *Eigenthum* der Göttinn von Gnidus; aber nicht alles Schöne ist Anmuth, denn auch ohne diesen Gürtel bleibt Venus, was sie ist.

Nach eben dieser Allegorie ist es die Schönheitsgöttinn *allein,* die den Gürtel des Reizes trägt und verleyht. *Juno,* die herrliche Königinn des Himmels, muß jenen Gürtel erst von der Venus *entlehnen,* wenn sie den Jupiter auf dem Ida bezaubern will. Hoheit also, selbst wenn ein gewisser Grad von Schönheit sie schmückt, (den man der Gattinn Jupiters keineswegs abspricht) ist ohne Anmuth nicht sicher, zu gefallen; denn nicht von ihren eignen Reizen, sondern von dem Gürtel der Venus erwartet die hohe Götterköniginn den Sieg über Jupiters Herz.

Die Schönheitsgöttinn kann aber doch ihren Gürtel entäussern und seine Kraft auf das Minderschöne *übertragen.* Anmuth ist also kein *ausschließendes* Prärogativ des Schönen, sondern kann auch, obgleich immer

---

¹ The notations in the form of [*NA* 251] indicate pages of the essay as printed in volume 20 of the Schiller *Nationalausgabe*, which is the source of the present version.

nur aus der Hand des Schönen, auf das Minderschöne, ja selbst auf das Nichtschöne, übergehen.

Die nehmlichen Griechen empfahlen demjenigen, dem bey allen übrigen Geistesvorzügen die Anmuth, das Gefällige, fehlte, den Grazien zu opfern. Diese Göttinnen wurden also von ihnen zwar als Begleiterinnen des schönen Geschlechts vorgestellt, aber doch als solche, die auch dem Mann gewogen werden können, und die ihm, wenn er gefallen will, unentbehrlich sind.

Was ist aber nun die Anmuth, wenn sie sich mit dem Schönen zwar am liebsten, aber doch nicht ausschließend, verbindet? [*NA* 252] wenn sie zwar von dem Schönen herstammt, aber die Wirkungen desselben auch an dem Nichtschönen offenbart? wenn die Schönheit zwar *ohne sie* bestehen, aber *durch sie* allein Neigung einflößen kann?

Das zarte Gefühl der Griechen unterschied frühe schon, was die Vernunft noch nicht zu *verdeutlichen* fähig war, und, nach einem Ausdruck strebend, erborgte es von der Einbildungskraft Bilder, da ihm der Verstand noch keine Begriffe darbieten konnte. Jener Mythus ist daher der Achtung des Philosophen werth, der sich ohnehin damit begnügen muß, zu den Anschauungen, in welchen der reine Natursinn seine Entdeckungen niederlegt, die Begriffe aufzusuchen, oder mit andern Worten, die Bilderschrift der Empfindungen zu erklären.

Entkleidet man die Vorstellung der Griechen von ihrer allegorischen Hülle, so scheint sie keinen andern, als folgenden Sinn einzuschließen.

Anmuth ist eine *bewegliche* Schönheit; eine Schönheit nehmlich, die an ihrem Subjekte zufällig entstehen und eben so aufhören kann. Dadurch unterscheidet sie sich von der *fixen* Schönheit, die mit dem Subjekte selbst nothwendig gegeben ist. Ihren Gürtel kann Venus abnehmen und der Juno augenblicklich überlassen; ihre Schönheit würde sie nur mit ihrer Person weggeben können. Ohne ihren Gürtel ist sie nicht mehr die reizende Venus, ohne Schönheit ist sie nicht Venus mehr.

Dieser Gürtel, als das Symbol der beweglichen Schönheit, hat aber das ganz besondere, daß er der Person, die damit geschmückt wird, die objektive Eigenschaft der Anmuth verleyht; und unterscheidet sich dadurch von jedem andern Schmuck, der nicht die Person selbst, sondern bloß den Eindruck derselben, subjektiv, in der Vorstellung eines Andern, verändert. Es ist der ausdrückliche Sinn des griechischen Mythus, daß sich die Anmuth in eine Eigenschaft der Person verwandle, und daß die Trägerinn des Gürtels wirklich liebenswürdig *sey*, nicht bloß so *scheine*.

Ein Gürtel, der nicht mehr ist als ein zufälliger äußerlicher Schmuck, scheint allerdings kein ganz passendes Bild zu seyn, die *persönliche* Eigenschaft der Anmuth zu bezeichnen; aber eine persönliche Eigenschaft, die zugleich als zertrennbar von dem Subjekte gedacht wird, konnte nicht wohl anders, als durch [*NA* 253] eine zufällige Zierde versinnlicht werden, die sich unbeschadet der Person von ihr trennen läßt.

Der Gürtel des Reizes wirkt also nicht *natürlich,* weil er in diesem Fall an der Person selbst nichts verändern könnte, sondern er wirkt *magisch,* das ist, seine Kraft wird über alle Naturbedingungen erweitert. Durch diese Auskunft (die freylich nicht mehr ist als ein Behelf) sollte der Widerspruch gehoben werden, in den das Darstellungsvermögen sich jederzeit unvermeidlich verwickelt, wenn es für das, was außerhalb der Natur im Reiche der Freyheit liegt, in der Natur einen Ausdruck sucht.

Wenn nun der Gürtel des Reizes eine objektive Eigenschaft ausdrückt, die sich von ihrem Subjekte absondern läßt, ohne deswegen etwas an der Natur desselben zu verändern, so kann er nichts anders als Schönheit der Bewegung bezeichnen; denn Bewegung ist die einzige Veränderung, die mit einem Gegenstand vorgehen kann, ohne seine Identität aufzuheben.

Schönheit der Bewegung ist ein Begriff, der beyden Foderungen Genüge leistet, die in dem angeführten Mythus enthalten sind. Sie ist *erstlich* objectiv und kommt dem Gegenstande selbst zu, nicht bloß der Art, wie wir ihn aufnehmen. Sie ist *zweytens* etwas zufälliges an demselben, und der Gegenstand bleibt übrig, auch wenn wir diese Eigenschaft von ihm wegdenken.

Der Gürtel des Reizes verliert auch bey dem Minderschönen, und selbst bey dem Nichtschönen seine magische Kraft nicht; das heißt, auch das Minderschöne, auch das Nichtschöne kann sich *schön bewegen.*

Die Anmuth, sagt der Mythus, ist etwas *zufälliges* an ihrem Subjekt; daher können nur zufällige Bewegungen diese Eigenschaft haben. An einem Ideal der Schönheit *müssen* alle *nothwendigen* Bewegungen schön seyn, weil sie, als nothwendig, zu seiner Natur gehören; die Schönheit *dieser* Bewegungen ist also schon mit dem Begriff der Venus *gegeben,* die Schönheit der zufälligen ist hingegen eine *Erweiterung* dieses Begriffs. Es giebt eine Anmuth der Stimme, aber keine Anmuth des Athemholens.

Ist aber jede Schönheit der zufälligen Bewegungen Anmuth? [*NA* 254]

Daß der griechische Mythus Anmuth und Grazien nur auf die Menschheit einschränke, wird kaum einer Erinnerung bedürfen; er geht sogar noch weiter, und schließt selbst die Schönheit der Gestalt in die Grenzen der Menschengattung ein, unter welcher der Grieche bekanntlich auch seine Götter begreift. Ist aber die Anmuth nur ein Vorrecht der Menschenbildung, so kann keine derjenigen Bewegungen darauf Anspruch machen, die der Mensch auch mit dem, was bloß Natur ist, gemein hat. Könnten also die Locken an einem schönen Haupte sich mit Anmuth bewegen, so wäre kein Grund mehr vorhanden, warum nicht auch die Äste eines Baumes, die Wellen eines Stroms, die Saaten eines Kornfeldes, die Gliedmaaßen der Thiere, sich mit Anmuth bewegen sollten. Aber die Göttinn von Gnidus repräsentirt nur die menschliche Gattung, und da, wo der Mensch weiter nichts als ein Naturding und Sinnenwesen ist, da hört sie auf, für ihn Bedeutung zu haben.

Willkührlichen Bewegungen allein kann also Anmuth zukommen, aber auch unter diesen nur denjenigen, die ein Ausdruck *moralischer* Empfindungen sind. Bewegungen, welche keine andere Quelle als die Sinnlichkeit haben, gehören bey aller Willkührlichkeit doch nur der Natur an, die für sich allein sich nie bis zur Anmuth erhebet. Könnte sich die Begierde mit Anmuth, der Instinkt mit Grazie äußern, so würden Anmuth und Grazie nicht mehr fähig und würdig seyn, der Menschheit zu einem Ausdruck zu dienen.

Und doch ist es die *Menschheit* allein, in die der Grieche alle Schönheit und Vollkommenheit einschließt. Nie darf sich ihm die Sinnlichkeit ohne Seele zeigen, und seinem *humanen* Gefühle ist es gleich unmöglich, die rohe Thierheit und die Intelligenz zu *vereinzeln*. Wie er jeder Idee sogleich einen Leib anbildet und auch das Geistigste zu verkörpern strebt, so fodert er von jeder Handlung des Instinkts an dem Menschen zugleich einen Ausdruck seiner sittlichen Bestimmung. Dem Griechen ist die Natur nie *bloß* Natur, darum darf er auch nicht erröthen, sie zu ehren; ihm ist die Vernunft niemals *bloß* Vernunft, darum darf er auch nicht zittern, unter ihren Maaßstab zu treten. Natur und Sittlichkeit, Materie und Geist, Erde und Himmel fließen wunderbar schön in seinen Dichtungen zu[*NA 255*]sammen. Er führte die Freyheit, die nur im Olympus zu Hause ist, auch in die Geschäfte der Sinnlichkeit ein, und dafür wird man es ihm hingehen lassen, daß er die Sinnlichkeit in den Olympus versetzte.

Dieser zärtliche Sinn der Griechen nun, der das Materielle immer nur unter der Begleitung des Geistigen duldet, weiß von keiner willkührlichen Bewegung am Menschen, die nur der Sinnlichkeit allein angehörte, ohne zugleich ein Ausdruck des moralisch empfindenden Geistes zu seyn. Daher ist ihm auch die Anmuth nichts anders als ein solcher schöner Ausdruck der Seele in den willkührlichen Bewegungen. Wo also Anmuth statt findet, da ist die Seele das bewegende Princip, und in *ihr* ist der Grund von der Schönheit der Bewegung enthalten. Und so löst sich denn jene mythische Vorstellung in folgenden Gedanken auf: „Anmuth ist eine Schönheit, die nicht von der Natur gegeben, sondern von dem Subjekte selbst hervorgebracht wird."

Ich habe mich bis jetzt darauf eingeschränkt, den Begriff der Anmuth aus der griechischen Fabel zu entwickeln, und, wie ich hoffe, ohne ihr Gewalt anzuthun. Jetzt sey mir erlaubt zu versuchen, was sich auf dem Weg der philosophischen Untersuchung darüber ausmachen läßt, und ob es auch hier, wie in soviel andern Fällen wahr ist, daß sich die philosophirende Vernunft weniger Entdeckungen rühmen kann, die der Sinn nicht schon dunkel *geahndet,* und die Poesie nicht *geoffenbart* hätte.

Venus, ohne ihren Gürtel und ohne die Grazien, repräsentirt uns das Ideal der Schönheit, so wie letztere aus den Händen *der bloßen Natur* kommen kann, und, *ohne die Einwirkung eines empfindenden Geistes,* durch die plastischen Kräfte erzeugt wird. Mit Recht stellt die Fabel für diese Schönheit eine eigene Göttergestalt zur Repräsentantin auf, denn schon das natürliche Gefühl unterscheidet sie auf das strengste von derjenigen, die dem Einfluß eines empfindenden Geistes ihren Ursprung verdankt.

Es sey mir erlaubt diese von der bloßen Natur, nach dem Gesetz der Nothwendigkeit gebildete Schönheit, zum Unterschied von der, welche sich nach Freyheitsbedingungen richtet, die Schönheit des Baues (*architektonische Schönheit*) zu benennen. Mit diesem Nahmen will ich also denjenigen Theil der [NA 256] menschlichen Schönheit bezeichnet haben, der nicht bloß durch Naturkräfte *ausgeführt* worden (was von jeder Erscheinung gilt), sondern der auch *nur allein durch Naturkräfte bestimmt ist.*

Ein glückliches Verhältniß der Glieder, fließende Umrisse, ein lieblicher Teint, eine zarte Haut, ein feiner und freyer Wuchs, eine wohlklingende Stimme u. s. f. sind Vorzüge, die man bloß der Natur und dem Glück zu verdanken hat; der *Natur,* welche die Anlage dazu hergab, und selbst entwickelte; dem *Glück* — welches das Bildungsgeschäft der Natur von jeder Einwirkung feindlicher Kräfte beschützte.

Diese Venus steigt schon *ganz vollendet* aus dem Schaume des Meers empor: vollendet, denn sie ist ein beschlossenes, streng abgewogenes Werk der Nothwendigkeit, und als solches, keiner Varietät, keiner Erweiterung fähig. Da sie nehmlich nichts anders ist, als ein schöner Vortrag der Zwecke, welche die Natur mit dem Menschen beabsichtet, und daher jede ihrer

Eigenschaften durch den Begriff, der ihr zum Grund liegt, vollkommen entschieden ist, so kann sie — der Anlage nach — als ganz gegeben beurtheilt werden, obgleich diese erst unter Zeitbedingungen zur Entwicklung kommt.

Die architektonische Schönheit der menschlichen Bildung muß von der technischen Vollkommenheit derselben wohl unterschieden werden. Unter der leztern hat man *das System der Zwecke selbst* zu verstehen, so wie sie sich unter einander zu einem obersten Endzweck vereinigen; unter der erstern hingegen bloß *eine Eigenschaft der Darstellung* dieser Zwecke, so wie sie sich dem anschauenden Vermögen in der Erscheinung offenbaren. Wenn man also von der Schönheit spricht, so wird weder der materielle Werth dieser Zwecke noch die formale Kunstmäßigkeit ihrer Verbindung dabei in Betrachtung gezogen. Das anschauende Vermögen hält sich einzig nur an die Art des Erscheinens, ohne auf die logische Beschaffenheit seines Objekts die geringste Rücksicht zu nehmen. Ob also gleich die architektonische Schönheit des menschlichen Baues durch den Begriff, der demselben zum Grund liegt, und durch die Zwecke bedingt ist, welche die Natur mit ihm beabsichtet, so *isolirt* doch das ästhetische Urtheil sie völlig von diesen Zwecken, und [*NA 257*] nichts, als was der Erscheinung unmittelbar und eigenthümlich angehört, wird in die Vorstellung der Schönheit aufgenommen.

Man kann daher auch nicht sagen, daß die Würde der Menschheit die Schönheit des menschlichen Baues *erhöhe.* In unser Urtheil über die letztere kann die Vorstellung der erstern zwar einfließen, aber alsdann hört es zugleich auf, ein reinästhetisches Urtheil zu seyn. Die Technik der menschlichen Gestalt ist allerdings ein Ausdruck seiner Bestimmung, und als ein solcher darf und soll sie uns mit Achtung erfüllen. Aber diese Technik wird nicht dem *Sinn* sondern dem *Verstande* vorgestellt; sie kann nur *gedacht werden,* nicht *erscheinen.* Die architektonische Schönheit hingegen kann nie ein Ausdruck seiner Bestimmung seyn, da sie sich an ein ganz andres Vermögen wendet, als dasjenige ist, welches über jene Bestimmung zu entscheiden hat.

Wenn daher dem Menschen, vorzugsweise vor allen übrigen technischen Bildungen der Natur, Schönheit beygelegt wird, so ist dieß nur in sofern wahr, als er schon in der *bloßen Erscheinung* diesen Vorzug behauptet, ohne daß man sich dabei seiner Menschheit zu erinnern braucht. Denn da dieses letzte nicht anders als vermittelst eines Begriffs geschehen könnte, so würde nicht der Sinn, sondern der Verstand über die Schönheit Richter seyn, welches einen Widerspruch einschließt. Die Würde seiner sittlichen Bestimmung kann also der Mensch nicht in Anschlag bringen, seinen Vorzug als Intelligenz kann er nicht geltend machen, wenn er den Preis der Schönheit behaupten will; hier ist er nichts als ein Ding im Raume, nichts als Erscheinung unter Erscheinungen. Auf seinen Rang in der Ideenwelt wird in der Sinnenwelt nicht geachtet, und wenn er in dieser die erste Stelle behaupten soll, so kann er sie nur *dem*, was in ihm *Natur ist*, zu verdanken haben.

Aber eben diese seine Natur ist, wie wir wissen, durch die Idee seiner Menschheit bestimmt worden, und so ist es denn mittelbar auch seine architektonische Schönheit. Wenn er sich also vor allen Sinnenwesen um ihn her durch höhere Schönheit unterscheidet, so ist er dafür unstreitig seiner menschlichen Bestimmung verpflichtet, welche den Grund enthält, warum er sich von den übrigen Sinnenwesen überhaupt nur unterscheidet. Aber nicht darum ist die menschliche Bildung schön, weil sie ein Aus-[*NA* **258**]druck dieser höheren Bestimmung ist, denn wäre dieses, so würde die nehmliche Bildung aufhören schön zu seyn, sobald sie eine niedrigere Bestimmung ausdrückte, so würde auch das Gegentheil dieser Bildung schön seyn, sobald man nur annehmen könnte, daß es jene höhere Bestimmung ausdrückte. Gesetzt aber, man könnte bey einer schönen Menschengestalt ganz und gar vergessen, was sie ausdrückt, man könnte ihr, ohne sie in der Erscheinung zu verändern, den rohen Instinkt eines Tigers unterschieben, so würde das Urtheil der Augen vollkommen dasselbe bleiben, und der Sinn würde den Tiger für das schönste Werk des Schöpfers erklären.

Die Bestimmung des Menschen, als einer Intelligenz, hat also an der Schönheit seines Baues nur in sofern einen Antheil, als ihre Darstellung, d. i. ihr Ausdruck in der Erscheinung zugleich mit den Bedingungen *zusammentrifft*, unter welchen das Schöne sich in der Sinnenwelt erzeugt. Die Schönheit selbst nehmlich muß jederzeit ein freyer Natureffekt bleiben, und die Vernunftidee, welche die Technik des menschlichen Baues bestimmte, kann ihm nie Schönheit *ertheilen*, sondern *bloß gestatten*.

Man könnte mir zwar einwenden, daß überhaupt alles, was in der Erscheinung sich darstellt, durch Naturkräfte ausgeführt werde, und daß dieses also kein ausschließendes Merkmal des Schönen seyn könne. Es ist wahr, alle technische Bildungen sind hervorgebracht durch Natur, aber durch Natur sind sie nicht technisch; wenigstens werden sie nicht so beurtheilt. Technisch sind sie nur durch den Verstand, und ihre technische Vollkommenheit hat also schon Existenz im Verstande, ehe sie in die

Sinnenwelt hinübertritt, und zur Erscheinung wird. Schönheit hingegen hat das ganz eigenthümliche, daß sie in der Sinnenwelt nicht bloß dargestellt wird, sondern auch in derselben zuerst entspringt; daß die Natur sie nicht bloß ausdrückt, sondern auch erschafft. Sie ist durchaus nur eine Eigenschaft des Sinnlichen, und auch der Künstler, der sie beabsichtet, kann sie nur in so weit erreichen, als er den Schein unterhält, daß die Natur gebildet habe.

Die Technik des menschlichen Baues zu beurtheilen, muß man die Vorstellung der Zwecke, denen sie gemäß ist, zu Hülfe neh[*NA 259*]men; dieß hat man gar nicht nöthig, um die Schönheit dieses Baues zu beurtheilen. Der Sinn allein ist hier ein völlig kompetenter Richter, und dieß könnte er nicht seyn, wenn nicht die Sinnenwelt (die sein einziges Objekt ist) alle Bedingungen der Schönheit enthielte, und also zu Erzeugung derselben vollkommen hinreichend wäre. *Mittelbar* freylich ist die Schönheit des Menschen in dem Begriff seiner Menschheit gegründet, weil seine ganze sinnliche Natur in diesem Begriffe gegründet ist, aber der Sinn, weiß man, hält sich nur an das *Unmittelbare*, und für ihn ist es also gerade soviel, als wenn sie ein ganz unabhängiger Natureffekt wäre.

Nach dem bisherigen sollte es nun scheinen, als wenn die Schönheit für die Vernunft durchaus kein Interesse haben könnte, da sie bloß in der Sinnenwelt entspringt, und sich auch nur an das sinnliche Erkenntnißvermögen wendet. Denn nachdem wir von dem Begriff derselben als fremdartig, abgesondert haben, was die *Vorstellung der Vollkommenheit* in unser Urtheil über die Schönheit zu mischen kaum unterlassen kann, so scheint dieser nichts mehr übrig zu bleiben, wodurch sie der Gegenstand eines vernünftigen Wohlgefallens seyn könnte. Nichts desto weniger ist es eben so ausgemacht, daß das Schöne *der Vernunft gefällt,* als es entschieden ist, daß es auf keiner solchen Eigenschaft des Objektes beruht, die nur durch Vernunft zu entdecken wäre.

Um diesen anscheinenden Widerspruch aufzulösen, muß man sich erinnern, daß es zweyerley Arten giebt, wodurch Erscheinungen Objekte der Vernunft werden, und Ideen ausdrücken können. Es ist nicht immer nöthig, daß die Vernunft diese Ideen aus den Erscheinungen *herauszieht,* sie kann sie auch in dieselben *hineinlegen.* In beyden Fällen wird die Erscheinung einem Vernunftbegriff adäquat seyn, nur mit dem Unterschied: daß in dem ersten Fall die Vernunft ihn schon objektiv darinn findet, und ihn gleichsam von dem Gegenstand nur empfängt, weil der Begriff gesetzt werden muß, um die Beschaffenheit und oft selbst um die

Möglichkeit des Objekts zu erklären; daß sie hingegen in dem zweyten Fall das, was unabhängig von ihrem Begriff in der Erscheinung gegeben ist, selbstthätig zu einem Ausdruck desselben *macht,* und also etwas bloß sinnliches über[*NA 260*]sinnlich behandelt. Dort ist also die Idee mit dem Gegenstande objektiv nothwendig, hier hingegen höchstens subjektiv nothwendig verknüpft. Ich brauche nicht zu sagen, daß ich jenes von der Vollkommenheit, dieses von der Schönheit verstehe.

Da es also in dem zweyten Fall, in Ansehung des sinnlichen Objektes ganz und gar zufällig ist, ob es eine Vernunft giebt, die mit der Vorstellung desselben eine ihrer Ideen verbindet, folglich die objektive Beschaffenheit des Gegenstandes von dieser Idee als völlig unabhängig muß betrachtet werden, so thut man ganz Recht, das Schöne, *objektiv,* auf lauter Naturbedingungen einzuschränken, und es für einen bloßen Effekt der Sinnenwelt zu erklären. Weil aber doch — auf der andern Seite — die Vernunft von diesem Effekt der bloßen Sinnenwelt einen transcendenten Gebrauch macht, und ihm dadurch, daß sie ihm eine höhere Bedeutung leiht, gleichsam ihren Stempel aufdrückt, so hat man ebenfalls Recht, das Schöne *subjektiv* in die intelligible Welt zu versetzen. Die Schönheit ist daher als die Bürgerin zwoer Welten anzusehen, deren einer sie durch *Geburt,* der andern durch *Adoption* angehört; sie empfängt ihre Existenz in der sinnlichen Natur, und *erlangt* in der Vernunftwelt das Bürgerrecht. Hieraus erklärt sich auch, wie es zugeht, daß der Geschmack, als ein Beurtheilungsvermögen des Schönen, zwischen Geist und Sinnlichkeit in die Mitte tritt, und diese beyden, einander verschmähenden Naturen, zu einer glücklichen Eintracht verbindet — wie er dem *Materiellen* die Achtung der Vernunft, wie er dem *Rationalen* die Zuneigung der Sinne erwirbt — wie er Anschauungen zu Ideen adelt, und selbst die Sinnenwelt gewißermaaßen in ein Reich der Freyheit verwandelt.

Wiewohl es aber — in Ansehung des Gegenstandes selbst — zufällig ist, ob die Vernunft mit der Vorstellung desselben eine ihrer Ideen verbindet, so ist es doch — für das vorstellende Subjekt — nothwendig, mit einer solchen Vorstellung eine solche Idee zu verknüpfen. Diese Idee und das ihr korrespondirende sinnliche Merkmal an dem Objekte müssen mit einander in einem solchen Verhältniß stehen, daß die Vernunft durch ihre eignen unveränderlichen Gesetze zu dieser Handlung genöthigt wird. In der Vernunft selbst muß also der Grund liegen, warum sie aus-[*NA 261*] schließend nur mit einer *gewissen* Erscheinungsart der Dinge eine bestimmte Idee verknüpft, und in dem Objekte muß wieder der Grund liegen, warum es ausschließend nur *diese* Idee und keine andre hervorruft. Was für eine Idee das nun sey, die die Vernunft in das Schöne hineinträgt, und durch welche objektive Eigenschaft der schöne Gegenstand fähig sey, dieser Idee zum Symbol zu dienen — dieß ist eine viel zu wichtige Frage, um hier bloß im Vorübergehen beantwortet zu werden, und deren Erörterung ich also auf eine Analytik des Schönen verspare.

Die architektonische Schönheit des Menschen ist also, auf die Art, wie ich eben erwähnte, *der sinnliche Ausdruck eines Vernunftbegriffs;* aber sie ist es in keinem andern Sinne und mit keinem größern Rechte, als überhaupt jede schöne Bildung der Natur. *Dem Grade nach* übertrifft sie zwar alle andere Schönheiten, aber *der Art nach* steht sie in der nehmlichen Reihe mit denselben, da auch sie von ihrem Subjekte nichts, als was sinnlich ist, offenbart, und erst in der Vorstellung eine übersinnliche Bedeutung empfängt.* Daß die Darstellung der Zwecke am Menschen schöner ausgefallen ist, als bey andern organischen Bildungen, ist als eine *Gunst* anzusehen, welche die Vernunft, als Gesetzgeberinn des menschlichen Baues, der Natur als Ausrichterinn ihrer Gesetze erzeigte. Die Vernunft verfolgt zwar bey der Technik des Menschen ihre Zwecke mit strenger Nothwendigkeit, aber glücklicherweise treffen ihre Foderungen mit der Noth[*NA 262*]wendigkeit der Natur *zusammen,* so daß die letztere den Auftrag der erstern vollzieht, indem sie bloß nach ihrer eigenen Neigung handelt.

Dieses kann aber nur von der *architektonischen* Schönheit des Menschen gelten, wo die Naturnothwendigkeit durch die Nothwendigkeit

---

* Denn — um es noch einmal zu wiederholen — in der *bloßen Anschauung* wird alles, was an der Schönheit *objektiv* ist, gegeben. Da aber das, was dem Menschen den Vorzug vor allen übrigen Sinnenwesen giebt, in der bloßen Anschauung *nicht* vorkommt, so kann eine Eigenschaft, die sich schon in der bloßen Anschauung offenbart, diesen Vorzug nicht sichtbar machen. Seine höhere Bestimmung, die allein diesen Vorzug begründet, wird also durch seine Schönheit nicht ausgedrückt, und die Vorstellung von jener kann daher nie ein Ingredienz von dieser abgeben, nie in das ästhetische Urtheil mit aufgenommen werden. Nicht der Gedanke selbst, dessen Ausdruck die menschliche Bildung ist, bloß die Wirkungen desselben in der Erscheinung offenbaren sich dem Sinn. Zu dem übersinnlichen Grund dieser Wirkungen erhebt der bloße Sinn sich eben so wenig, als (wenn man mir dieß Beyspiel verstatten will) als der bloß sinnliche Mensch zu der Idee der obersten Welturssache hinaufsteigt, wenn er seine Triebe befriedigt.

des sie bestimmenden teleologischen Grundes unterstützt wird. Hier allein konnte die Schönheit gegen die Technik des Baues *berechnet* werden, welches aber nicht mehr statt findet, sobald die Nothwendigkeit nur einseitig ist und die übersinnliche Ursache, welche die Erscheinung bestimmt, sich zufällig verändert. Für die architektonische Schönheit des Menschen sorgt also die Natur *allein,* weil ihr hier, gleich in der ersten Anlage, die Vollziehung alles dessen, was der Mensch zu Erfüllung seiner Zwecke *bedarf,* einmal für immer von dem schaffenden Verstand *übergeben* wurde, und sie also in diesem ihrem *organischen* Geschäfte keine Neuerung zu befürchten hat.

Der Mensch aber ist zugleich eine *Person,* ein Wesen also, welches *selbst* Ursache, und zwar absolut letzte Ursache seiner Zustände seyn, welches sich nach Gründen, die es aus sich selbst nimmt, verändern kann. Die Art seines Erscheinens ist abhängig von der Art seines Empfindens und Wollens, also von Zuständen, die er selbst in seiner Freyheit, und nicht die Natur nach ihrer Nothwendigkeit bestimmt.

Wäre der Mensch bloß ein Sinnenwesen, so würde die Natur zugleich die *Gesetze* geben und die *Fälle* der Anwendung bestimmen; jetzt theilt sie das Regiment mit der Freyheit, und obgleich ihre Gesetze Bestand haben, so ist es nunmehr doch der Geist, der über die Fälle entscheidet.

Das Gebiet des Geistes erstreckt sich *so weit, als die Natur lebendig* ist, und endigt nicht eher, als wo das organische Leben sich in die formlose Masse verliert, und die animalischen Kräfte aufhören. Es ist bekannt, daß alle bewegenden Kräfte im Menschen unter einander zusammenhängen, und so läßt sich einsehen, wie der Geist — auch nur als Princip der willkührlichen Bewegung betrachtet — seine Wirkungen durch das ganze System derselben fortpflanzen kann. Nicht bloß die Werkzeuge des Willens, auch diejenigen, über welche der Wille nicht un[*NA 263*]mittelbar zu gebieten hat, erfahren wenigstens mittelbar seinen Einfluß. Der Geist bestimmt sie nicht bloß absichtlich, wenn er handelt, sondern auch unabsichtlich, wenn er empfindet.

Die Natur für sich allein kann, wie aus dem obigen klar ist, nur für die Schönheit derjenigen Erscheinungen sorgen, die sie selbst, uneingeschränkt, nach dem Gesetz der Nothwendigkeit zu bestimmen hat. Aber mit der *Willkühr* tritt der *Zufall* in ihre Schöpfung ein, und obgleich die Veränderungen, welche sie unter dem Regiment der Freyheit erleidet, *nach* keinen andern als ihren eignen Gesetzen erfolgen, so erfolgen sie doch nicht mehr *aus* diesen Gesetzen. Da es jetzt auf den Geist ankommt, welchen Gebrauch er von seinen Werkzeugen machen will, so kann die Natur über denjenigen Theil der Schönheit, welcher von diesem Gebrauche abhängt, nichts mehr zu gebieten, und also auch nichts mehr zu verantworten haben.

Und so würde denn der Mensch in Gefahr schweben, gerade da, wo er sich durch den Gebrauch seiner Freyheit zu den reinen Intelligenzen erhebt, als Erscheinung zu *sinken,* und in dem Urtheile des Geschmacks zu verlieren, was er vor dem Richterstuhl der Vernunft gewinnt. Die durch sein Handeln *erfüllte* Bestimmung würde ihm einen Vorzug kosten, den die in seinem Bau bloß *angekündigte* Bestimmung begünstigte; und wenn gleich dieser Vorzug nur sinnlich ist, so haben wir doch gefunden, daß ihm die Vernunft eine höhere Bedeutung ertheilt. Eines so groben Widerspruchs macht sich die Übereinstimmung liebende Natur nicht schuldig, und was in dem Reiche der Vernunft harmonisch ist, wird sich durch keinen Mißklang in der Sinnenwelt offenbaren.

Indem also die Person oder das freye Principium im Menschen es auf sich nimmt, das Spiel der Erscheinungen zu bestimmen, und durch seine Dazwischenkunft der Natur die Macht entzieht, die Schönheit ihres Werks zu beschützen, so tritt es selbst an die Stelle der Natur, und übernimmt, (wenn mir dieser Ausdruck erlaubt ist) mit den Rechten derselben einen Theil ihrer Verpflichtungen. Indem der Geist die ihm untergeordnete Sinnlichkeit in sein Schicksal verwickelt, und von seinen Zuständen abhängen läßt, macht er sich gewißermaaßen selbst zur Erscheinung, und bekennt sich als einen Unterthan des Gesetzes, welches [**NA 264**] an alle Erscheinungen ergehet. Um seiner selbst willen macht er sich verbindlich, die von ihm abhängende Natur auch noch in seinem Dienste Natur bleiben zu lassen, und sie ihrer früheren Pflicht nie *entgegen* zu behandeln. Ich nenne die Schönheit eine *Pflicht* der Erscheinungen, weil das ihr entsprechende Bedürfniß im Subjekte in der Vernunft selbst gegründet, und daher allgemein und nothwendig ist. Ich nenne sie eine *frühere* Pflicht, weil der Sinn schon geurtheilt hat, ehe der Verstand sein Geschäft beginnt.

Die Freyheit regiert also jetzt die Schönheit. Die Natur gab die Schönheit des Baues, die Seele giebt die Schönheit des Spiels. Und nun wissen wir auch, was wir unter Anmuth und Grazie zu verstehen haben. Anmuth ist die Schönheit der Gestalt unter dem Einfluß der Freyheit; die Schönheit derjenigen Erscheinungen, die die Person bestimmt. Die architektonische Schönheit macht dem Urheber der Natur, Anmuth und Grazie machen ihrem Besitzer Ehre. Jene ist ein *Talent,* diese ein *persönliches Verdienst.*

Anmuth kann nur der *Bewegung* zukommen, denn eine Veränderung im Gemüth kann sich nur als Bewegung in der Sinnenwelt offenbaren. Dieß hindert aber nicht, daß nicht auch feste und ruhende Züge Anmuth zeigen könnten. Diese festen Züge waren ursprünglich nichts als Bewegungen, die endlich bey oftmaliger Erneuerung habituell wurden, und bleibende Spuren eindrückten.*[*NA* 265]

Aber nicht alle Bewegungen am Menschen sind der Grazie fähig. Grazie ist immer nur die Schönheit der *durch Freyheit bewegten Gestalt,* und Bewegungen, *die bloß der Natur angehören,* können nie diesen Nahmen verdienen. Es ist zwar an dem, daß ein lebhafter Geist sich zuletzt beinahe aller Bewegungen seines Körpers bemächtigt, aber wenn die Kette sehr lang wird, wodurch sich ein schöner Zug an moralische Empfindungen anschließt, so wird er eine Eigenschaft des Baues, und läßt sich kaum mehr zur Grazie zählen. Endlich *bildet* sich der Geist sogar seinen Körper, und der *Bau* selbst muß dem *Spiele* folgen, so daß sich die Anmuth zuletzt nicht selten in architektonische Schönheit verwandelt.

---

* Daher nimmt Home den Begriff der Anmuth viel zu *eng* an, wenn er (Grundsätze d. Kritik II. 39. Neueste Ausgabe) sagt: „daß, wenn die anmuthigste Person in *Ruhe* sey, und sich weder bewege noch spreche, wir die Eigenschaft der Anmuth, wie die Farbe im Finstern, aus den Augen verlieren." Nein, wir verlieren sie nicht aus den Augen, so lange wir an der schlafenden Person die Züge wahrnehmen, die ein wohlwollender sanfter Geist gebildet hat; und gerade der schätzbarste Theil der Grazie bleibt übrig, derjenige nehmlich, der sich aus *Gebärden zu Zügen* verfestete, und also die *Fertigkeit* des Gemüths in schönen Empfindungen an den Tag legt. Wenn aber der Herr *Berichtiger* des *Homischen* Werks seinen Autor durch die Bemerkung zurecht zu weisen glaubte, (siehe in demselben Band S. 459.) „daß sich die Anmuth nicht bloß auf willkührliche Bewegungen einschränke, daß eine schlafende Person nicht aufhöre reizend zu seyn" — und warum? „weil während dieses Zustandes die unwillkührlichen, sanften und eben deswegen desto anmuthigern Bewegungen erst recht sichtbar werden," so hebt er den Begriff der Grazie ganz auf, den Home bloß zu sehr einschränkte. Unwillkührliche Bewegungen im Schlafe, wenn es nicht mechanische Wiederholungen von willkührlichen sind, können nie anmuthig seyn, weit entfernt, daß sie es vorzugsweise seyn könnten, und wenn eine schlafende Person reizend ist, so ist sie es keineswegs durch die Bewegungen, die sie macht, sondern durch ihre Züge, die von vorhergegangenen Bewegungen zeugen.

So, wie ein feindseliger, mit sich uneiniger Geist selbst die erhabenste
Schönheit des Baues zu Grund richtet, daß man unter den unwürdigen
Händen der Freyheit das herrliche Meisterstück der Natur zuletzt nicht
mehr erkennen kann, so sieht man auch zuweilen das heitre und in sich
harmonische Gemüth der durch Hindernisse gefesselten Technik zu
Hülfe kommen, die Natur in Freyheit setzen, und die noch eingewickelte,
gedrückte Gestalt mit göttlicher Glorie *auseinander breiten*. Die plastische
Natur des Menschen hat unendlich viele Hülfsmittel in sich selbst, ihr
Versäumniß herein zu bringen, und ihre Fehler zu verbessern, so bald nur
der sittliche Geist sie in ihrem Bildungswerk unterstützen, oder auch
manchmal nur nicht beunruhigen will.

Da auch die *verfesteten Bewegungen* (in Züge übergegangene Gebärden)
von der Anmuth nicht ausgeschlossen sind, so könnte es das Ansehen haben,
als ob überhaupt auch die Schönheit der *anscheinenden* oder *nachgeahmten*
Bewegungen (die flammigten oder geschlängelten Linien) gleichfalls mit
dazu gerechnet werden müßte, wie Mendelsohn auch wirklich [*NA 266*]
behauptet.* Aber dadurch würde der Begriff der Anmuth zu dem Begriff
der Schönheit überhaupt erweitert; denn *alle* Schönheit ist zuletzt bloß eine
Eigenschaft der wahren oder anscheinenden (objektiven oder subjektiven)
Bewegung, wie ich in einer Zergliederung des Schönen zu beweisen hoffe.
Anmuth aber können nur solche Bewegungen zeigen, die zugleich einer
Empfindung entsprechen.

Die Person — man weiß, was ich damit andeuten will — schreibt dem
Körper die Bewegungen entweder durch ihren Willen vor, wenn sie eine
vorgestellte Wirkung in der Sinnenwelt realisiren will, und in diesem Fall
heißen die Bewegungen *willkührlich* oder abgezweckt; oder solche erfolgen,
ohne den Willen der Person, nach einem Gesetz der Nothwendigkeit — aber
auf Veranlassung einer Empfindung; diese nenne ich *sympathetische* Bewegungen. Ob die letztern gleich unwillkührlich und in einer Empfindung gegründet sind, so darf man sie doch mit denjenigen nicht verwechseln, welche das
sinnliche Gefühlvermögen, und der Naturtrieb, bestimmt; denn der Naturtrieb ist kein freyes Princip, und was er verrichtet, das ist keine Handlung der
Person. Unter den sympathetischen Bewegungen, von denen hier die Rede
ist, will ich also nur diejenigen verstanden haben, welche der moralischen
Empfindung, oder der moralischen Gesinnung zur Begleitung dienen.

---

* [Mendelssohn,] Philos. Schriften. I. 90.

Die Frage entsteht nun, welche von diesen beyden Arten der in der Person gegründeten Bewegungen ist der Anmuth fähig?

Was man beym Philosophiren nothwendig von einander trennen muß, ist darum nicht immer auch in der Wirklichkeit getrennt. So findet man abgezweckte Bewegungen selten ohne sympathetische, weil der Wille als die Ursache von *jenen* sich nach moralischen Empfindungen bestimmt, aus welchen *diese* entspringen. Indem eine Person spricht, sehen wir zugleich ihre Blicke, ihre Gesichtszüge, ihre Hände, ja oft den ganzen Körper *mit-sprechen,* und der *mimische* Theil der Unterhaltung wird nicht selten für den beredtsten geachtet. Aber auch selbst eine abgezweckte Bewegung kann zugleich als eine sympathetische anzusehen seyn, und dieß geschieht alsdann, wenn sich etwas unwillkührliches in das willkührliche derselben mit einmischt. [*NA 267*]

Die Art und Weise nehmlich, wie eine willkührliche Bewegung voll-zogen wird, ist durch ihren Zweck nicht so genau bestimmt, daß es nicht mehrere Arten geben sollte, nach denen sie kann verrichtet wer-den. Dasjenige nun, was durch den Willen oder den Zweck dabey unbestimmt gelassen ist, kann durch den Empfindungszustand der Per-son, sympathetisch bestimmt werden, und also zu einem Ausdruck des-selben dienen. Indem ich meinen Arm ausstrecke, um einen Gegenstand in Empfang zu nehmen, so führe ich einen Zweck aus, und die Bewe-gung, die ich mache, wird durch die Absicht, die ich damit erreichen will, vorgeschrieben. Aber welchen Weg ich meinen Arm zu dem Gegenstand nehmen und wie weit ich meinen übrigen Körper will nach-folgen lassen — wie geschwind oder langsam; und mit wie viel oder wenig Kraftaufwand ich die Bewegung verrichten will, in diese genaue Berechnung lasse ich mich in dem Augenblick nicht ein, und der Natur in mir wird also hier etwas anheim gestellt. Auf irgend eine Art und Weise muß aber doch dieses durch den bloßen Zweck nicht bestimmte, entschieden werden, und hier also kann meine Art zu empfinden den Ausschlag geben, und durch den *Ton,* den sie angiebt, die Art und Weise der Bewegung bestimmen. Der Antheil nun, den der Empfind-ungszustand der Person an einer willkührlichen Bewegung hat, ist das Unwillkührliche an derselben, und er ist auch das, worinn man die Gra-zie zu suchen hat.

Eine *willkührliche* Bewegung, wenn sie sich nicht zugleich mit einer sympathetischen verbindet, oder was eben so viel sagt, nicht mit etwas *unwillkührlichem,* das in dem moralischen Empfindungszustand der Person seinen Grund hat, vermischet, kann *niemals Grazie* zeigen, wozu immer ein Zustand im Gemüth, als Ursache erfordert wird. Die willkührliche Bewegung *erfolgt* auf eine Handlung des Gemüths, welche also vergangen ist, wenn die Bewegung geschieht.

Die sympathetische Bewegung hingegen *begleitet* die Handlung des Gemüths, und den Empfindungszustand desselben, durch den es zu dieser Handlung vermocht wird, und muß daher mit beyden als *gleichlaufend* betrachtet werden.

Es erhellt schon daraus, daß die erste, die nicht von der Gesinnung der Person unmittelbar ausfließt, auch keine Darstellung [*NA* 268] derselben seyn kann. Denn zwischen die Gesinnung und die Bewegung selbst tritt der *Entschluß*, der für sich betrachtet etwas ganz gleichgültiges ist; die Bewegung ist Wirkung des *Entschlusses* und des Zweckes, nicht aber der Person und der Gesinnung.

Die willkührliche Bewegung ist mit der ihr vorangehenden Gesinnung zufällig, die begleitende hingegen nothwendig damit verbunden. Jene verhält sich zum Gemüth wie das conventionelle Sprachzeichen zu dem Gedanken, den es ausdrückt; die sympathetische oder begleitende hingegen wie der leidenschaftliche Laut zu der Leidenschaft. Jene ist daher nicht ihrer *Natur,* sondern bloß ihrem *Gebrauch* nach, Darstellung des Geistes. Also kann man auch nicht wohl sagen, daß der Geist in einer willkührlichen Bewegung sich offenbare, da sie nur die *Materie des Willens* (den Zweck) nicht aber die *Form des Willens* (die Gesinnung) ausdrückt. Von der Letztern kann uns nur die begleitende Bewegung belehren.*

Daher wird man aus den Reden eines Menschen zwar abnehmen können, für *was er will gehalten seyn,* aber das, *was er wirklich* ist, muß man

---

* Wenn sich eine Begebenheit vor einer zahlreichen Gesellschaft ereignet, so kann es sich treffen, daß jeder Anwesende von der Gesinnung der handelnden Personen seine eigene Meinung hat; so zufällig sind willkührliche Bewegungen mit ihrer moralischen Ursache verbunden. Wenn hingegen einem aus dieser Gesellschaft ein sehr geliebter Freund oder ein sehr verhaßter Feind unerwartet in die Augen fiele, so würde der unzweydeutige Ausdruck seines Gesichts die Empfindungen seines Herzens schnell und bestimmt an den Tag legen, und das Urtheil der ganzen Gesellschaft über den gegenwärtigen Empfindungszustand dieses Menschen würde wahrscheinlich völlig einstimmig seyn: denn der Ausdruck ist hier mit seiner Ursache im Gemüth durch Naturnothwendigkeit verbunden.

aus dem mimischen Vortrag seiner Worte und aus seinen Gebärden, also aus Bewegungen, *die er nicht will,* zu errathen suchen. Erfährt man aber, daß ein Mensch auch seine Gesichtszüge *wollen* kann, so traut man seinem Gesicht, von dem Augenblick dieser Entdeckung an, nicht mehr, und läßt jene auch nicht mehr für einen Ausdruck seiner Gesinnungen gelten.

[*NA* 269]

Nun mag zwar ein Mensch durch Kunst und Studium es zuletzt wirklich dahin bringen, daß er auch die begleitenden Bewegungen seinem Willen unterwirft, und gleich einem geschickten Taschenspieler, welche Gestalt er will, auf den mimischen Spiegel seiner Seele fallen lassen kann. Aber an einem solchen Menschen ist dann auch alles Lüge, und alle Natur wird von der Kunst verschlungen. Grazie hingegen muß jederzeit Natur, d. i. unwillkührlich seyn (wenigstens so scheinen), und das Subjekt selbst darf nie so aussehen, als wenn es *um seine Anmuth wüßte.*

Daraus ersieht man auch beiläufig, was man von der *nachgeahmten* oder *gelernten* Anmuth (die ich die theatralische und die Tanzmeistergrazie nennen möchte) zu halten habe. Sie ist ein würdiges Gegenstück zu derjenigen *Schönheit,* die am Putztisch aus Karmin und Bleyweiß, falschen Locken, Fausses Gorges, und Wallfischrippen hervorgeht, und verhält sich ohngefähr eben so zu der wahren Anmuth, wie die *Toiletten-Schönheit* sich zu der *architektonischen* verhält.* Auf [*NA* 270] einen ungeübten

---

* Ich bin eben so weit entfernt, bey dieser Zusammenstellung dem Tanzmeister sein Verdienst um die wahre Grazie, als dem Schauspieler seinen Anspruch darauf abzustreiten. Der Tanzmeister kommt der wahren Anmuth unstreitig zu Hülfe, indem er dem Willen die Herrschaft über seine Werkzeuge verschaft, und die Hindernisse hinwegräumt, welche die *Masse* und *Schwerkraft* dem Spiel der lebendigen Kräfte entgegensetzen. Er kann dieß nicht anders als nach *Regeln* verrichten, welche den Körper in einer heilsamen Zucht erhalten, und, so lange die Trägheit widerstrebt, *steif,* d. i. *zwingend* seyn und auch so aussehen dürfen. Entläßt er aber den Lehrling aus seiner Schule, so muß die Regel bey diesem ihren Dienst schon geleistet haben, daß sie ihn nicht in die Welt *zu begleiten braucht:* kurz das Werk der Regel muß in Natur übergehen.

Die Geringschätzung, mit der ich von der theatralischen Grazie rede, gilt nur der *nachgeahmten,* und diese, nehme ich keinen Anstand, auf der Schaubühne wie im Leben zu verwerfen. Ich bekenne, daß mir der Schauspieler nicht gefällt, der seine *Grazie,* gesetzt daß ihm die Nachahmung auch noch so sehr gelungen sey, an der Toilette studirt hat. Die Foderungen, die wir an den Schauspieler machen,

Sinn können beyde völlig denselben Effekt machen, wie das Original, das sie nachahmen, und ist die Kunst groß, so kann sie auch zuweilen den Kenner betrügen. Aber aus irgend einem Zuge blickt endlich doch der Zwang und die Absicht hervor, und dann ist Gleichgültigkeit, wo nicht gar Verachtung und Ekel, die unvermeidliche Folge. Sobald wir merken, daß die architektonische Schönheit *gemacht* ist, so sehen wir gerade so viel von der Menschheit (als Erscheinung) verschwunden, als aus einem fremden Naturgebiet zu derselben geschlagen worden ist — und wie sollten wir, die wir nicht einmal Wegwerfung eines zufälligen Vorzugs verzeihen, mit Vergnügen, ja auch nur mit Gleichgültigkeit einen Tausch betrachten, wobey ein Theil der Menschheit für gemeine Natur ist hingegeben worden? Wie sollten wir, wenn wir auch die Wirkung verzeihen könnten, den Betrug nicht verachten? — Sobald wir merken, daß die *Anmuth* erkünstelt ist, so schließt sich plötzlich unser Herz, und zurücke flieht die ihr entgegenwallende Seele. Aus Geist sehen wir plötzlich Materie geworden, und ein Wolkenbild aus einer himmlischen Juno.

Ob aber gleich die Anmuth etwas unwillkührliches seyn oder scheinen muß, so suchen wir sie doch nur bey Bewegungen, die, [*NA* 271] mehr

---

sind: 1) *Wahrheit* der Darstellung und 2) *Schönheit* der Darstellung. Nun behaupte ich, daß der Schauspieler, *was die Wahrheit der Darstellung betrift,* alles durch Kunst und nichts durch Natur hervorbringen müsse, weil er sonst gar nicht Künstler ist; und ich werde ihn bewundern, wenn ich höre oder sehe, daß er, der einen wüthenden Guelfo meisterhaft spielte, ein Mensch von sanftem Charakter ist; auf der andern Seite hingegen behaupte ich, daß er, *was die Anmuth der Darstellung betrift,* der Kunst gar nichts zu danken haben dürfe, und daß hier alles an ihm freiwilliges Werk der Natur seyn müsse. Wenn es mir bey der Wahrheit seines Spiels beyfällt, daß ihm dieser Charakter nicht natürlich ist, so werde ich ihn nur um so höher schätzen; wenn es mir bey der Schönheit seines Spiels beyfällt, daß ihm diese anmuthigen Bewegungen nicht natürlich sind, so werde ich mich nicht enthalten können, über den *Menschen* zu zürnen, der hier den *Künstler* zu Hülfe nehmen mußte. Die Ursache ist, weil das Wesen der Grazie mit ihrer Natürlichkeit verschwindet, und weil die Grazie doch eine Foderung ist, die wir uns an den bloßen Menschen zu machen berechtigt glauben. Was werde ich aber nun dem mimischen Künstler antworten, der gern wissen möchte, wie er, da er sie nicht *erlernen* darf, zu der Grazie kommen soll? Er soll, ist meine Meinung, zuerst dafür sorgen, daß die Menschheit in ihm selbst zur Zeitigung komme, und dann soll er hingehen und (wenn es sonst sein Beruf ist) sie auf der Schaubühne repräsentiren.

oder weniger, von dem Willen abhängen. Man legt zwar auch einer gewissen Gebärdensprache Grazie bey, und spricht von einem anmuthigen Lächeln und einem reizenden Erröthen, welches doch beydes sympathetische Bewegungen sind, worüber nicht der Wille, sondern die Empfindung entscheidet. Allein nicht zu rechnen, daß jenes doch in unserer Gewalt ist, und daß noch gezweifelt werden kann, ob dieses auch eigentlich zur Anmuth gehöre, so sind doch bey weitem die mehrern Fälle, in welchen sich die Grazie offenbart, aus dem Gebiet der willkührlichen Bewegungen. Man fodert Anmuth von der Rede und vom Gesang, von dem willkührlichen Spiele der Augen und des Mundes, von den Bewegungen der Hände und der Arme bey jedem freyen Gebrauch derselben, von dem Gange, von der Haltung des Körpers und der Stellung, von dem ganzen Bezeugen eines Menschen, in sofern es in seiner Gewalt ist. Von denjenigen Bewegungen am Menschen, die der Naturtrieb oder ein herrgewordener Affekt *auf seine eigene Hand* ausführet, und die also auch ihrem Ursprung nach sinnlich sind, verlangen wir etwas ganz anders als Anmuth, wie sich nachher entdecken wird. Dergleichen Bewegungen gehören der *Natur* und nicht der *Person* an, aus der doch allein alle Grazie quellen muß.

Wenn also die Anmuth eine Eigenschaft ist, die wir von willkührlichen Bewegungen fodern, und wenn auf der andern Seite von der Anmuth selbst doch alles willkührliche verbannt seyn muß, so werden wir sie in demjenigen, was bey absichtlichen Bewegungen unabsichtlich, zugleich aber einer moralischen Ursache im Gemüth entsprechend ist, aufzusuchen haben.

Dadurch wird übrigens bloß die Gattung von Bewegungen bezeichnet, unter welcher man die Grazie zu suchen hat; aber eine Bewegung kann alle diese Eigenschaften haben, ohne deswegen anmuthig zu seyn. Sie ist dadurch bloß *sprechend*, (mimisch).

Sprechend (im weitesten Sinne) nenne ich jede Erscheinung am Körper, die einen Gemüthszustand begleitet, und ausdrückt. In dieser Bedeutung sind also alle sympathetische Bewegungen sprechend, selbst diejenigen, welche bloßen Affektionen der Sinnlichkeit zur Begleitung dienen.

Auch thierische Bildungen sprechen, indem ihr äußres das innre offenbart. Hier aber spricht bloß die *Natur,* nie die *Frey*[NA 272]*heit*. In der permanenten Gestalt und in den festen architektonischen Zügen des Thieres kündigt die Natur ihren *Zweck,* in den mimischen Zügen das erwachte oder gestillte *Bedürfniß* an. Der Ring der Nothwendigkeit geht durch das Thier wie durch die Pflanze, ohne durch eine *Person* unterbrochen zu werden. Die Individualität seines Daseyns ist nur die besondre

Vorstellung eines allgemeinen Naturbegriffs; die Eigenthümlichkeit seines gegenwärtigen Zustandes bloß Beyspiel einer Ausführung des Naturzwecks unter bestimmten Naturbedingungen.

Sprechend im *engern* Sinn ist nur die menschliche Bildung und diese auch nur in denjenigen ihrer Erscheinungen, die seinen moralischen Empfindungszustand begleiten, und demselben zum Ausdruck dienen.

Nur in *diesen* Erscheinungen: denn in allen andern steht der Mensch in gleicher Reihe mit den übrigen Sinnenwesen. In seiner permanenten Gestalt und in seinen architektonischen Zügen legt bloß die *Natur,* wie beym Thier und allen organischen Wesen, ihre Absicht vor. Die Absicht der Natur mit ihm kann zwar viel weiter gehen, als bey diesen, und die Verbindung der Mittel zu Erreichung derselben kunstreicher und verwikelter seyn; dieß alles kommt bloß auf Rechnung der *Natur,* und kann ihm selbst zu keinem Vorzug gereichen.

Bey dem Thiere und der Pflanze giebt die Natur nicht bloß die Bestimmung an, sondern *führt sie auch allein aus.* Dem Menschen aber giebt sie bloß die Bestimmung, und überläßt *ihm selbst* die Erfüllung derselben. Dieß allein macht ihn zum Menschen.

Der Mensch allein hat als Person unter allen bekannten Wesen das Vorrecht, in den Ring der Nothwendigkeit, der für bloße Naturwesen unzerreißbar ist, durch seinen Willen zu greifen, und eine ganz frische Reihe von Erscheinungen in sich selbst anzufangen. Der Akt, durch den er dieses wirkt, heißt vorzugsweise eine *Handlung,* und diejenigen seiner Verrichtungen, die aus einer solchen Handlung herfließen, ausschließungsweise, seine *Thaten.* Er kann also, daß er eine Person ist, bloß durch seine Thaten beweisen.

Die Bildung des Thiers drückt nicht nur den Begriff seiner Bestimmung, sondern auch das Verhältniß seines gegenwärtigen [*NA* **273**] Zustandes zu dieser Bestimmung aus. Da nun bey dem Thiere die Natur die Bestimmung zugleich giebt, und erfüllt, so kann die Bildung des Thiers nie etwas anders als das Werk der Natur ausdrücken.

Da die Natur dem Menschen zwar die Bestimmung *giebt,* aber die Erfüllung derselben *in seinen Willen stellt,* so kann das gegenwärtige Verhältniß seines Zustandes zu seiner Bestimmung nicht Werk der Natur, sondern muß sein eigenes Werk seyn. Der Ausdruck dieses Verhältnisses in seiner Bildung gehört also nicht der Natur, sondern ihm selbst an, das ist, es ist ein persönlicher Ausdruck. Wenn wir also aus dem architektonischen Theil seiner Bildung erfahren, was die *Natur* mit ihm beabsichtet hat, so erfahren wir aus dem mimischen Theil derselben, was *er selbst* zu Erfüllung dieser Absicht *gethan hat.*

Bey der Gestalt des Menschen begnügen wir uns also nicht damit, daß sie uns bloß den allgemeinen Begriff der Menschheit, oder was etwa die *Natur* zu Erfüllung desselben an diesem Individuum wirkte, vor Augen stelle, denn das würde er mit jeder technischen Bildung gemein haben. Wir erwarten noch von seiner Gestalt, daß sie uns zugleich offenbare, in wie weit er in seiner Freyheit dem Naturzweck entgegen kam, d. i. daß sie Charakter zeige. In dem erstern Fall sieht man wohl, daß die Natur es mit ihm auf einen Menschen *anlegte,* aber nur aus dem zweyten ergiebt sich, ob er es *wirklich* geworden ist.

Die Bildung eines Menschen ist also nur in so weit seine Bildung, als sie mimisch ist; aber auch *so weit sie mimisch* ist, ist sie sein. Denn, wenn gleich der größere Theil dieser mimischen Züge, ja wenn gleich alle bloßer Ausdruck der Sinnlichkeit wären, und ihm also schon als bloßem Thiere zukommen könnten, so war er bestimmt und fähig, die Sinnlichkeit durch seine Freyheit einzuschränken. Die Gegenwart solcher Züge beweist also den Nichtgebrauch jener Fähigkeit, und die Nichterfüllung jener Bestimmung; ist also eben so gewiß moralisch sprechend, als die Unterlassung einer Handlung, welche die Pflicht gebietet, eine Handlung ist.

Von den sprechenden Zügen, die immer ein Ausdruck der Seele sind, muß man die stummen Züge unterscheiden, die bloß die plastische Natur, in sofern sie von jedem Einfluß der Seele [*NA 274*] unabhängig wirkt, in die menschliche Bildung zeichnet. Ich nenne diese Züge *stumm,* weil sie als unverständliche Chiffern der Natur von dem Charakter schweigen. Sie zeigen bloß die Eigenthümlichkeit der Natur im Vortrag der Gattung, und reichen oft für sich allein schon hin, das *Individuum* zu unterscheiden, aber von der *Person* können sie nie etwas offenbaren. Für den Physiognomen sind diese stummen Züge keines.wegs bedeutungleer, weil der Physiognome nicht bloß wissen will, was der Mensch selbst aus sich gemacht, sondern auch, was die Natur für und gegen ihn gethan hat.

Es ist nicht so leicht, die Grenzen anzugeben, wo die stummen Züge aufhören, und die sprechenden beginnen. Die gleichförmig wirkende Bildungskraft und der gesetzlose Affekt streiten unaufhörlich um ihr Gebiet; und was die *Natur* mit unermüdeter stiller Thätigkeit erbaute, wird oft wieder umgerissen von der *Freyheit,* die gleich einem anschwellenden Strome über ihre Ufer tritt. Ein reger Geist verschaft sich auf *alle* körperlichen Bewegungen Einfluß, und kommt zuletzt mittelbar dahin, auch selbst die festen

Formen der Natur, die dem Willen unerreichbar sind, durch die Macht des sympathetischen Spiels zu verändern. An einem solchen Menschen wird endlich alles Charakterzug, wie wir an manchen Köpfen finden, die ein langes Leben, außerordentliche Schicksale und ein thätiger Geist völlig *durchgearbeitet* haben. Der plastischen Natur gehört an solchen Formen nur das *Generische,* die ganze *Individualität* der Ausführung aber der Person an; daher sagt man sehr richtig, daß an einer solchen Gestalt alles Seele sey.

Dagegen zeigen uns jene zugestutzten Zöglinge der *Regel,* (die zwar die Sinnlichkeit zur Ruhe bringen, aber die Menschheit nicht wecken kann) in ihrer flachen und ausdruckslosen Bildung überall nichts, als den Finger der Natur. Die geschäftlose Seele ist ein bescheidener Gast in ihrem Körper und ein friedlicher stiller Nachbar der sich selbst überlassenen Bildungskraft. Kein anstrengender Gedanke, keine Leidenschaft greift in den ruhigen Takt des physischen Lebens; nie wird der *Bau* durch das *Spiel* in Gefahr gesetzt, nie die Vegetation durch die Freyheit beunruhigt. Da die tiefe Ruhe des Geistes keine beträchtliche Konsumtion der Kräfte verursacht, so wird die Ausgabe nie die Ein[*NA 275*]nahme übersteigen, vielmehr die thierische Ökonomie immer Überschuß haben. Für den schmalen Gehalt von Glückseligkeit, den sie ihm auswirft, macht der Geist den pünktlichen Hausverwalter der Natur, und sein ganzer Ruhm ist, ihr *Buch* in Ordnung zu halten. Geleistet wird also werden, was die Organisation immer leisten kann, und floriren wird das Geschäft der Ernährung und Zeugung. Ein so glückliches Einverständniß zwischen der Naturnothwendigkeit und der Freyheit kann der architektonischen Schönheit nicht anders als günstig seyn, und hier ist es auch, wo sie in ihrer ganzen Reinheit kann beobachtet werden. Aber die allgemeinen Naturkräfte führen, wie man weiß, einen ewigen Krieg mit den besondern, oder den organischen, und die kunstreichste Technik wird endlich von der *Kohäsion* und *Schwerkraft* bezwungen. Daher hat auch die Schönheit des Baues, *als bloßes Naturprodukt,* ihre bestimmten Perioden der Blüthe, der Reife und des Verfalles, die das Spiel zwar beschleunigen, aber niemals verzögern kann; und ihr gewöhnliches Ende ist, daß die *Masse* allmählig über die *Form* Meister wird, und der lebendige Bildungstrieb in dem *aufgespeicherten* Stoff sich sein eigenes Grab bereitet.* [*NA 276*]

---

* Daher man auch mehrentheils finden wird, daß solche Schönheiten des Baues sich schon im mittlern Alter durch Obesität sehr merklich vergröbern, daß, anstatt

Ob indessen gleich kein *einzelner* stummer Zug Ausdruck des Geistes ist, so ist eine solche stumme Bildung doch *im Ganzen* charakteristisch; und zwar aus eben dem Grunde, warum eine sinnlich sprechende es ist. Der

---

jener kaum angedeuteten zarten Lineamente der Haut, sich Gruben einsenken und wurstförmige Falten aufwerfen, daß das *Gewicht* unvermerkt auf die Form Einfluß bekömmt, und das reizende mannichfache Spiel schöner Linien auf der Oberfläche sich in einem gleichförmig schwellenden Polster von Fette verliert. Die Natur nimmt wieder, was sie gegeben hat.

Ich bemerke beiläufig, daß etwas ähnliches zuweilen mit dem *Genie* vorgeht, welches überhaupt in seinem Ursprunge, wie in seinen Wirkungen mit der architektonischen Schönheit vieles gemein hat. Wie diese, so ist auch jenes ein bloßes *Naturerzeugniß,* und nach der verkehrten Denkart der Menschen, die, was nach keiner Vorschrift nachzuahmen, und durch kein Verdienst zu erringen ist, gerade am höchsten schätzen, wird die Schönheit mehr als der Reiz, das Genie mehr als erworbene Kraft des Geistes bewundert. Beyde *Günstlinge der Natur* werden bey allen ihren Unarten (wodurch sie nicht selten ein Gegenstand verdienter Verachtung sind) als ein gewißer Geburtsadel, als eine höhere Kaste betrachtet, weil ihre Vorzüge von Naturbedingungen abhängig sind, und daher über alle Wahl hinaus liegen.

Aber wie es der architektonischen Schönheit ergeht, wenn sie nicht zeitig dafür Sorge trägt, sich an der *Grazie* eine Stütze und eine Stellvertreterinn heranzuziehen, eben so ergeht es auch dem Genie, wenn es sich durch Grundsätze, Geschmack und Wissenschaft zu stärken verabsäumt. War seine ganze Ausstattung eine lebhafte und blühende Einbildungskraft (und die Natur kann nicht wohl andre als sinnliche Vorzüge ertheilen) so mag es bey Zeiten darauf denken, sich dieses zweydeutigen Geschenks durch den einzigen Gebrauch zu versichern, wodurch Naturgaben Besitzungen des Geistes werden können; dadurch, meyne ich, daß es der Materie Form ertheilt; denn der Geist kann nichts, als was Form ist, sein eigen nennen. Durch keine verhältnißmäßige Kraft der Vernunft beherrscht, wird die wildaufgeschossene üppige *Naturkraft* über die Freyheit des Verstandes hinauswachsen, und sie eben so ersticken, wie bey der architektonischen Schönheit die Masse endlich die Form unterdrückt.

Die Erfahrung, denke ich, liefert hievon reichlich Belege, besonders an denjenigen Dichtergenien, die früher berühmt werden, als sie mündig sind, und wo, wie bey mancher Schönheit, das ganze Talent oft die *Jugend* ist. Ist aber der kurze Frühling vorbey, und fragt man nach den Früchten, die er hoffen ließ, so sind es schwammigte und oft verkrüppelte Geburten, die ein mißgeleiteter blinder

Geist nehmlich soll thätig seyn und soll moralisch empfinden; und also zeugt es von seiner Schuld, wenn seine Bildung davon keine Spuren aufweist. Wenn uns also gleich der reine und schöne Ausdruck seiner Bestimmung in der Architektur seiner Gestalt mit Wohlgefallen und mit Ehrfurcht gegen die höchste Vernunft, als ihre Ursache, erfüllt, so werden beyde Empfindungen nur so lange ungemischt bleiben, als er uns bloße Naturerzeugung ist. Denken wir ihn [*NA* 277] uns aber als moralische Person, so sind wir berechtigt, einen Ausdruck derselben in seiner Gestalt zu erwarten, und schlägt diese Erwartung fehl, so wird Verachtung unausbleiblich erfolgen. Bloß organische Wesen sind uns ehrwürdig als *Geschöpfe*, der Mensch aber kann es uns nur als *Schöpfer*, (d. i. als Selbsturheber seines Zustandes) seyn. Er soll nicht bloß, wie die übrigen Sinnenwesen, die Strahlen fremder Vernunft zurückwerfen, wenn es gleich die Göttliche wäre, sondern er soll, gleich einem Sonnenkörper, von seinem eigenen Lichte glänzen.

Eine sprechende Bildung wird also von dem Menschen gefodert, sobald man sich seiner sittlichen Bestimmung bewußt wird; aber es muß zugleich eine Bildung seyn, die zu seinem Vortheile spricht, d. i. die eine, seiner Bestimmung gemäße Empfindungsart, eine moralische Fertigkeit, ausdrückt. Diese Anfoderung macht die Vernunft an die Menschenbildung.

Der Mensch ist aber als Erscheinung zugleich Gegenstand des Sinnes. Wo das *moralische* Gefühl Befriedigung findet, da will das *ästhetische* nicht verkürzt seyn, und die Übereinstimmung mit einer Idee darf in der Erscheinung kein Opfer kosten. So streng also auch immer die Vernunft einen Ausdruck der Sittlichkeit fodert, so unnachläßlich fodert das Auge Schönheit. Da diese beyden Foderungen an dasselbe Objekt, obgleich von verschiedenen Instanzen der Beurtheilung, ergehen, so muß auch durch eine und dieselbe Ursache für beider Befriedigung gesorgt seyn. Diejenige Gemüthsverfassung des Menschen, wodurch er am fähigsten wird, seine

---

Bildungstrieb erzeugte. Gerade da, wo man erwarten kann, daß der Stoff sich zur Form veredelt und der bildende Geist in der Anschauung Ideen niedergelegt habe, sind sie, wie jedes andre Naturprodukt, der Materie anheim gefallen, und die vielversprechenden Meteore erscheinen als ganz gewöhnliche Lichter — wo nicht gar als noch etwas weniger. Denn die poetisirende Einbildungskraft sinkt zuweilen auch ganz zu dem Stoff zurück, aus dem sie sich losgewickelt hatte, und verschmäht es nicht, der Natur bey einem andern *solidern* Bildungswerk zu dienen, wenn es ihr mit der poetischen Zeugung nicht recht mehr gelingen will.

Bestimmung als moralische Person zu erfüllen, muß einen solchen Ausdruck gestatten, der ihm auch, als bloßer Erscheinung, am vortheilhaftesten ist. Mit andern Worten: seine sittliche Fertigkeit muß sich durch Grazie offenbaren.

Hier ist es nun, wo die große Schwierigkeit eintritt. Schon aus dem Begriff moralischsprechender Bewegungen ergiebt sich, daß sie eine moralische Ursache haben müssen, die über die Sinnenwelt hinaus liegt; eben so ergiebt sich aus dem Begriffe der Schönheit, daß sie keine andre als sinnliche Ursache habe, und ein völlig freyer Natureffekt seyn oder doch so erscheinen müsse. Wenn aber der letzte Grund moralischsprechender Bewegungen nothwendig *außerhalb,* der letzte Grund der Schön[*NA 278*]heit eben so nothwendig *innerhalb* der Sinnenwelt liegt, so scheint die *Grazie,* welche beydes verbinden soll, einen offenbaren Widerspruch zu enthalten.

Um ihn zu heben, wird man also annehmen müssen, „daß die moralische Ursache im Gemüthe, die der Grazie zum Grunde liegt, in der von ihr abhängenden Sinnlichkeit gerade denjenigen Zustand nothwendig hervorbringe, der die *Naturbedingungen* des Schönen in sich enthält." Das Schöne setzt nehmlich, wie sich von allem Sinnlichen versteht, gewisse Bedingungen, und, in sofern es das Schöne ist, auch bloß sinnliche Bedingungen voraus. Daß nun der Geist, (nach einem Gesetz, das wir nicht ergründen können) durch den Zustand, worinn er sich selbst befindet, der ihn begleitenden Natur den ihrigen vorschreibt, und daß der Zustand moralischer Fertigkeit in ihm gerade derjenige ist, durch den die sinnlichen Bedingungen des Schönen in Erfüllung gebracht werden, dadurch macht er das Schöne *möglich,* und das allein ist *seine* Handlung. Daß aber *wirklich* Schönheit daraus wird, das ist Folge jener sinnlichen Bedingungen, also freye *Naturwirkung.* Weil aber die Natur bey *willkührlichen* Bewegungen, wo sie als Mittel behandelt wird, um einen Zweck auszuführen, nicht wirklich frey heißen kann, und weil sie bey den *unwillkührlichen* Bewegungen, die das Moralische ausdrücken, wiederum nicht frey heißen kann, so ist die Freyheit, mit der sie sich in ihrer Abhängigkeit von dem Willen demungeachtet äußert, eine *Zulassung* von Seiten des Geistes. Man kann also sagen, daß die Grazie eine *Gunst* sey, die das Sittliche dem Sinnlichen erzeigt, so wie die architektonische Schönheit als die *Einwilligung* der Natur zu ihrer technischen Form kann betrachtet werden.

Man erlaube mir dieß durch eine bildliche Vorstellung zu erläutern. Wenn ein monarchischer Staat auf eine solche Art verwaltet wird, daß, obgleich alles nach eines Einzigen Willen geht, der einzelne Bürger sich doch überreden kann, daß er nach seinem eigenen Sinne lebe, und bloß seiner Neigung gehorche, so nennt man dieß eine liberale Regierung. Man würde aber großes Bedenken tragen, ihr diesen Nahmen zu geben, wenn *entweder* der Regent seinen Willen gegen die Neigung des Bürgers, oder der Bürger seine Neigung gegen den Willen des [NA 279] Regenten behauptete; denn in dem ersten Fall wäre die Regierung nicht *liberal*, in dem zweyten wäre sie gar nicht *Regierung*.

Es ist nicht schwer, die Anwendung davon auf die menschliche Bildung unter dem Regiment des Geistes zu machen. Wenn sich der Geist in der von ihm abhängenden sinnlichen Natur auf eine solche Art äußert, daß sie seinen Willen aufs treuste ausrichtet und seine Empfindungen auf das sprechendste ausdrückt, ohne doch gegen die Anfoderungen zu verstoßen, welche der Sinn an sie, als an Erscheinungen, macht, so wird dasjenige entstehen, was man Anmuth nennt. Man würde aber gleich weit entfernt seyn, es Anmuth zu nennen, wenn entweder der Geist sich in der Sinnlichkeit durch Zwang offenbare, oder wenn dem freyen Effekt der Sinnlichkeit der Ausdruck des Geistes fehlte. Denn in dem ersten Fall wäre keine Schönheit vorhanden, in dem zweyten wäre es keine Schönheit des Spiels.

Es ist also immer nur der übersinnliche Grund im Gemüthe, der die Grazie sprechend, und immer nur ein bloß sinnlicher Grund in der Natur, der sie schön macht. Es läßt sich eben so wenig sagen, daß der Geist die Schönheit *erzeuge,* als man, im angeführten Fall, von dem Herrscher sagen kann, daß er Freyheit *hervorbringe;* denn Freyheit kann man einem zwar *lassen,* aber nicht *geben.*

So wie aber doch der Grund, warum ein Volk unter dem Zwang eines fremden Willens sich frey fühlt, größtentheils in der Gesinnung des Herrschers liegt, und eine entgegengesetzte Denkart des Letztern jener Freyheit nicht sehr günstig seyn würde, eben so müssen wir auch die Schönheit der freyen Bewegungen in der sittlichen Beschaffenheit des sie diktirenden Geistes aufsuchen. Und nun entsteht die Frage, was dieß wohl für eine *persönliche Beschaffenheit* seyn mag, die den sinnlichen Werkzeugen des Willens die größere Freyheit verstattet, und was für moralische Empfindungen sich am besten mit der Schönheit im Ausdruck vertragen?

Soviel leuchtet ein, daß sich weder der Wille, bey der absichtlichen, noch der Affekt bey der sympathetischen Bewegung, gegen die von ihm abhängende Natur als eine *Gewalt* verhalten dürfe, wenn sie ihm mit Schönheit gehorchen soll. Schon [NA 280] das allgemeine Gefühl der

Menschen macht die *Leichtigkeit* zum Hauptcharakter der Grazie, und was angestrengt wird, kann niemals Leichtigkeit zeigen. Eben so leuchtet ein, daß auf der andern Seite, die Natur sich gegen den Geist nicht als Gewalt verhalten dürfe, wenn ein schöner moralischer Ausdruck statt haben soll; denn wo die bloße Natur *herrscht,* da muß die Menschheit verschwinden.

Es lassen sich in allem dreyerley Verhältnisse denken, in welchen der Mensch zu sich selbst d. i. sein sinnlicher Theil zu seinem vernünftigen, stehen kann. Unter diesen haben wir dasjenige aufzusuchen, welches ihn in der Erscheinung am besten kleidet, und dessen Darstellung Schönheit ist.

Der Mensch unterdrückt entweder die Foderungen seiner sinnlichen Natur, um sich den höhern Foderungen seiner vernünftigen gemäß zu verhalten; oder er kehrt es um, und ordnet den vernünftigen Theil seines Wesens dem sinnlichen unter, und folgt also bloß dem Stoße, womit ihn die Naturnothwendigkeit, gleich den andern Erscheinungen forttreibt; oder die Triebe des letztern setzen sich mit den Gesetzen des erstern in Harmonie, und der Mensch ist einig mit sich selbst.

Wenn sich der Mensch seiner reinen Selbstständigkeit bewußt wird, so stößt er alles von sich, was sinnlich ist, und nur durch diese Absonderung von dem Stoffe gelangt er zum Gefühl seiner rationalen Freyheit. Dazu aber wird, weil die Sinnlichkeit hartnäckig und kraftvoll widersteht, von seiner Seite eine merkliche Gewalt und große Anstrengung erfodert, ohne welche es ihm unmöglich wäre, die Begierde von sich zu halten, und den nachdrücklich sprechenden Instinkt zum Schweigen zu bringen. Der so gestimmte Geist läßt die von ihm abhängende Natur, sowohl da, wo sie im Dienst seines Willens handelt, als da, wo sie seinem Willen vorgreifen will, erfahren, daß er ihr Herr ist. Unter seiner strengen Zucht wird also die Sinnlichkeit unterdrückt erscheinen, und der innere Widerstand wird sich von außen durch Zwang verrathen. Eine solche Verfassung des Gemüths kann also der Schönheit nicht günstig seyn, welche die Natur nicht anders als in ihrer Freyheit hervorbringt, und es wird daher auch nicht Grazie seyn können, wodurch die mit dem Stoffe kämpfende moralische Freyheit sich kenntlich macht. [*NA* 281]

Wenn hingegen der Mensch, unterjocht vom Bedürfniß, den Naturtrieb ungebunden über sich herrschen läßt, so verschwindet mit seiner innern Selbstständigkeit auch jede Spur derselben in seiner Gestalt. Nur die Thierheit redet aus dem schwimmenden ersterbenden Auge, aus dem lüstern geöfneten Munde, aus der erstickten bebenden Stimme, aus dem kurzen geschwinden Athem, aus dem Zittern der Glieder, aus dem ganzen erschlaffenden Bau. Nachgelassen hat aller Widerstand der moralischen Kraft, und die Natur in ihm ist in volle Freyheit gesetzt. Aber eben dieser gänzliche Nachlaß der Selbstthätigkeit, der im Moment des sinnlichen Verlangens und noch mehr im Genuß zu erfolgen pflegt, setzt augenblicklich auch die rohe Materie in Freyheit, die durch das Gleichgewicht der thätigen und leidenden Kräfte bisher gebunden war. Die todten Naturkräfte fangen an, über die lebendigen der Organisation die Oberhand zu bekommen, die Form von der Masse, die Menschheit von gemeiner Natur unterdrückt zu werden. Das seelestrahlende Auge wird matt, oder quillt auch *gläsern* und *stier* aus seiner Höhlung hervor, der feine Inkarnat der Wangen verdickt sich zu einer groben und gleichförmigen Tüncherfarbe, der Mund wird zur bloßen Oefnung, denn seine Form ist nicht mehr Folge der wirkenden sondern der nachlassenden Kräfte, die Stimme und der seufzende Athem sind nichts als Hauche, wodurch die beschwerte Brust sich erleichtern will, und die nun bloß ein mechanisches Bedürfniß, keine Seele verrathen. Mit einem Worte: bey der Freyheit, welche die Sinnlichkeit *sich selbst nimmt,* ist an keine Schönheit zu denken. Die Freyheit der Formen, die der sittliche Wille bloß *eingeschränkt* hatte, *überwältigt* der grobe Stoff, welcher stets soviel Feld gewinnt, als dem Willen entrissen wird.

Ein Mensch in diesem Zustand empört nicht bloß den *moralischen* Sinn, der den Ausdruck der Menschheit unnachläßlich fodert; auch der *ästhetische* Sinn, der sich nicht mit dem bloßen Stoffe befriedigt, sondern in der Form ein freyes Vergnügen sucht, wird sich mit Ekel von einem solchen Anblick abwenden, bey welchem nur die *Begierde* ihre Rechnung finden kann.

Das erste dieser Verhältnisse zwischen beyden Naturen im Menschen erinnert an eine *Monarchie,* wo die strenge Aufsicht [*NA* **282**] des Herrschers jede freye Regung im Zaum hält; das zweite an eine wilde *Ochlokratie,* wo der Bürger durch Aufkündigung des Gehorsams gegen den rechtmäßigen Oberherrn, so wenig frey, als die menschliche Bildung, durch Unterdrückung der moralischen Selbstthätigkeit, schön wird; vielmehr nur dem brutaleren Despotismus der untersten Klassen, wie hier die Form der Masse, anheimfällt. So wie die *Freyheit* zwischen dem gesetzlichen Druck und der Anarchie mitten inne liegt, so werden wir jetzt auch die *Schönheit* zwischen der *Würde,* als dem Ausdruck des herrschenden Geistes, und der *Wollust,* als dem Ausdruck des herrschenden Triebes, in der Mitte finden.

Wenn nehmlich weder *die über die Sinnlichkeit herrschende Vernunft,* noch *die über die Vernunft herrschende Sinnlichkeit* sich mit Schönheit des Ausdrucks vertragen, so wird (denn es giebt keinen vierten Fall) so wird derjenige Zustand des Gemüths, wo *Vernunft und Sinnlichkeit* — Pflicht und Neigung — *zusammenstimmen,* die Bedingung seyn, unter der die Schönheit des Spiels erfolgt.

Um ein Objekt der Neigung werden zu können, muß der Gehorsam gegen die Vernunft einen Grund des Vergnügens abgeben, denn nur durch Lust und Schmerz wird der Trieb in Bewegung gesetzt. In der gewöhnlichen Erfahrung ist es zwar umgekehrt, und das Vergnügen ist der Grund, warum man vernünftig handelt. Daß die Moral selbst endlich aufgehört hat, diese Sprache zu reden, hat man dem unsterblichen Verfasser der Kritik zu verdanken, dem der Ruhm gebührt, die gesunde Vernunft aus der philosophirenden wieder hergestellt zu haben.

Aber so wie die Grundsätze dieses Weltweisen von ihm selbst, und auch von andern, pflegen vorgestellt zu werden, so ist die Neigung eine sehr zweideutige Gefährtin des Sittengefühls, und das Vergnügen eine bedenkliche Zugabe zu moralischen Bestimmungen. Wenn der Glückseligkeitstrieb auch keine blinde Herrschaft über den Menschen behauptet, so wird er doch bey dem sittlichen Wahlgeschäfte gerne *mitsprechen* wollen, und so der Reinheit des Willens schaden, der immer nur dem *Gesetze* und nie dem *Triebe* folgen soll. Um also völlig sicher zu seyn, daß die Neigung nicht *mit* bestimmte, sieht man sie lieber im Krieg, als im Einverständniß mit dem Vernunftgesetze, weil es gar zu [*NA 283*] leicht seyn kann, daß ihre Fürsprache allein ihm seine Macht über den Willen verschaffte. Denn da es beym Sittlichhandeln nicht auf die *Gesetzmäßigkeit* der Thaten, sondern einzig nur auf die *Pflichtmäßigkeit* der Gesinnungen ankommt, so legt man mit Recht keinen Werth auf die Betrachtung, daß es für die erste gewöhnlich vortheilhafter sey, wenn sich die Neigung auf Seiten der Pflicht befindet. Soviel scheint also wohl gewiß zu seyn, daß der Beyfall der Sinnlichkeit, wenn er die Pflichtmäßigkeit des Willens auch nicht verdächtig macht, doch wenigstens nicht im Stand ist, sie zu *verbürgen.* Der sinnliche Ausdruck dieses Beyfalls in der Grazie, wird also für die Sittlichkeit der Handlung, bey der er angetroffen wird, nie ein hinreichendes und gültiges Zeugniß ablegen, und aus dem schönen Vortrag einer Gesinnung oder Handlung wird man nie ihren moralischen Werth erfahren.

Bis hieher glaube ich, mit den *Rigoristen* der Moral vollkommen einstimmig zu seyn, aber ich hoffe dadurch noch nicht zum *Latitudinarier* zu werden, daß ich die Ansprüche der Sinnlichkeit, die im Felde der reinen Vernunft, und bey der moralischen Gesetzgebung, *völlig* zurückgewiesen sind, im Feld der Erscheinung, und bey der wirklichen Ausübung der Sittenpflicht, noch zu behaupten versuche.

So gewiß ich nehmlich überzeugt bin — und eben darum, weil ich es bin — daß der Antheil der Neigung an einer freyen Handlung für die reine Pflichtmäßigkeit dieser Handlung nichts beweist, so glaube ich *eben daraus* folgern zu können, daß die sittliche Vollkommenheit des Menschen gerade nur aus diesem Antheil seiner Neigung an seinem moralischen Handeln erhellen kann. Der Mensch nehmlich ist nicht dazu bestimmt, einzelne sittliche Handlungen zu verrichten, sondern ein sittliches Wesen zu seyn. Nicht *Tugenden* sondern die *Tugend* ist seine Vorschrift, und Tugend ist nichts anders „als eine Neigung zu der Pflicht." Wie sehr also auch Handlungen aus Neigung und Handlungen aus Pflicht in objektivem Sinne einander entgegenstehen; so ist dieß doch in subjektivem Sinn nicht also, und der Mensch *darf* nicht nur, sondern *soll* Lust und Pflicht in Verbindung bringen; er soll seiner Vernunft mit Freuden gehorchen. Nicht um sie wie eine Last wegzuwerfen, oder wie eine grobe Hülle [*NA* 284] von sich abzustreifen, nein, um sie aufs innigste mit seinem höhern Selbst zu vereinbaren, ist seiner reinen Geisternatur eine sinnliche beygesellt. Dadurch schon, daß sie ihn zum vernünftig sinnlichen Wesen, d. i. zum Menschen machte, kündigte ihm die Natur die Verpflichtung an, nicht zu trennen, was sie verbunden hat, auch in den reinsten Äusserungen seines göttlichen Theiles den sinnlichen nicht hinter sich zu lassen, und den Triumph des einen nicht auf Unterdrückung des andern zu gründen. Erst alsdann, wenn sie *aus seiner gesammten Menschheit* als die vereinigte Wirkung beyder Principien, hervorquillt, *wenn sie ihm zur Natur geworden ist,* ist seine sittliche Denkart geborgen, denn so lange der sittliche Geist noch *Gewalt* anwendet, so muß der Naturtrieb ihm noch *Macht* entgegenzusetzen haben. Der bloß *niedergeworfene* Feind kann wiederaufstehen, aber der *versöhnte* ist wahrhaft überwunden.

In der Kantischen Moralphilosophie ist die Idee der *Pflicht* mit einer Härte vorgetragen, die alle Grazien davon zurückschreckt, und einen schwachen Verstand leicht versuchen könnte, auf dem Wege einer finstern und mönchischen Ascetik die moralische Vollkommenheit zu suchen. Wie sehr sich auch der große Weltweise gegen diese Mißdeutung zu verwahren suchte, die seinem heitern und freyen Geist unter allen gerade die empörendste seyn muß, so hat er, deucht mir, doch selbst durch die strenge und grelle Entgegensetzung beyder auf den Willen des Menschen wirkenden Principien, einen starken (obgleich bey seiner Absicht vielleicht kaum zu vermeidenden) Anlaß dazu gegeben. Über die Sache selbst kann, nach den von ihm geführten Beweisen, unter denkenden Köpfen, *die überzeugt seyn wollen,* kein Streit mehr seyn, und ich wüßte kaum, wie man nicht lieber sein ganzes Menschseyn aufgeben, als über diese Angelegenheit ein anderes Resultat von der Vernunft erhalten wollte. Aber so rein er bey *Untersuchung* der Wahrheit zu Werke gieng, und so sehr sich hier alles aus bloß objektiven Gründen erklärt, so scheint ihn doch in *Darstellung* der gefundenen Wahrheit eine mehr subjektive Maxime geleitet zu haben, die, wie ich glaube, aus den Zeitumständen nicht schwer zu erklären ist.

So wie er nehmlich die Moral seiner Zeit, im Systeme und in der Ausübung, vor sich fand, so mußte ihn auf der einen Seite [*NA 285*] ein grober Materialismus in den moralischen Principien empören, den die unwürdige Gefälligkeit der Philosophen dem schlaffen Zeitcharakter zum Kopfkißen untergelegt hatte. Auf der andern Seite mußte ein nicht weniger bedenklicher *Perfektionsgrundsatz,* der, um eine abstrakte Idee von allgemeiner Weltvollkommenheit zu realisiren, über die Wahl der Mittel nicht sehr verlegen war, seine Aufmerksamkeit erregen. Er richtete also dahin, wo die Gefahr am meisten erklärt, und die Reform am dringendsten war, die stärkste Kraft seiner Gründe, und machte es sich zum Gesetze, die Sinnlichkeit sowohl da, wo sie mit frecher Stirne dem Sittengefühl Hohn spricht, als in der imposanten Hülle moralischlöblicher Zwecke, worein besonders ein gewisser enthusiastischer Ordensgeist sie zu verstecken weiß, ohne Nachsicht zu verfolgen. Er hatte nicht die *Unwissenheit* zu belehren, sondern die *Verkehrtheit* zurecht zu weisen. Erschütterung foderte die Kur, nicht Einschmeichelung und Überredung; und je härter der Abstich war, den der Grundsatz der Wahrheit mit den herrschenden Maximen machte, desto mehr konnte er hoffen, Nachdenken darüber zu erregen. Er ward der *Drako* seiner Zeit, weil sie ihm eines *Solons* noch nicht werth und empfänglich schien. Aus dem Sanktuarium der reinen Vernunft brachte er das fremde und doch wieder so bekannte Moralgesetz, stellte es in seiner ganzen Heiligkeit aus vor dem entwürdigten Jahrhundert, und fragte wenig darnach, ob es Augen giebt, die seinen Glanz nicht vertragen.

Womit aber hatten es die *Kinder des Hauses* verschuldet, daß er nur für die *Knechte* sorgte? Weil oft sehr unreine Neigungen den Namen der Tugend usurpiren, mußte darum auch der uneigennützige Affekt in der edelsten Brust verdächtig gemacht werden? Weil der moralische Weichling

dem Gesetz der Vernunft gern eine *Laxität* geben möchte, die es zum
Spielwerk seiner Konvenienz macht, mußte ihm darum eine *Rigidität*
beygelegt werden, die die kraftvolleste Äußerung moralischer Freyheit nur
in eine rühmlichere Art von Knechtschaft verwandelt? Denn hat wohl der
wahrhaft sittliche Mensch eine freiere Wahl zwischen Selbstachtung und
Selbstverwerfung, als der Sinnensklave zwischen Vergnügen und Schmerz?
Ist dort etwa weniger Zwang für den reinen Willen, als hier für den
ver[*NA 286*]dorbenen? Mußte schon durch die *imperatife* Form des
Moralgesetzes die Menschheit angeklagt und erniedriget werden, und das
erhabenste Dokument ihrer Größe zugleich die Urkunde ihrer Gebrech-
lichkeit seyn? War es wohl bey dieser imperatifen Form zu vermeiden, daß
eine Vorschrift, die sich der Mensch als Vernunftwesen selbst giebt, die
deswegen allein für ihn bindend, und dadurch allein mit seinem Freyheits-
gefühle verträglich ist, nicht den Schein eines fremden und positiven
Gesetzes annahm — einen Schein, der durch seinen *radikalen* Hang,
demselben entgegen zu handeln (wie man ihm schuld giebt) schwerlich
vermindert werden dürfte!*

Es ist für moralische Wahrheiten gewiß nicht vortheilhaft, Empfindungen *gegen* sich zu haben, die der Mensch ohne Erröthen sich gestehen
darf. Wie sollen sich aber die Empfindungen der Schönheit und Freyheit
mit dem austeren Geist eines Gesetzes vertragen, das ihn mehr durch
Furcht als durch *Zuversicht* leitet, das ihn, den die Natur doch *vereinigte,*
stets zu *vereinzeln* strebt, und nur dadurch, daß es ihm Mistrauen gegen
den einen Theil seines Wesens erweckt, sich der Herrschaft über den
andern versichert. Die menschliche Natur ist ein verbundeneres Ganze in
der Wirklichkeit, als es dem Philosophen, der nur durch Trennen was vermag, erlaubt ist, sie erscheinen zu lassen. Nimmermehr kann die Vernunft
Affekte als ihrer unwerth verwerfen, die das Herz mit Freudigkeit bekennt,
und der Mensch da, wo er moralisch gesunken wäre, nicht wohl in seiner
eigenen Achtung steigen. Wäre die sinnliche Natur im Sittlichen immer
nur die unterdrückte und nie die *mitwirkende* Parthey, wie könnte sie das
ganze Feuer ihrer Gefühle zu einem Triumph hergeben, der über sie selbst

---

* Siehe das Glaubensbekenntniß des V. d. K. von der menschlichen Natur in
seiner neuesten Schrift: *Die Offenbarung in den Grenzen der Vernunft.* Erster
Abschnitt.

gefeyert wird? Wie könnte sie eine so lebhafte Theilnehmerin an dem Selbstbewußtseyn des reinen Geistes seyn, wenn sie sich nicht endlich so innig an ihn anschließen könnte, daß selbst der analytische Verstand sie nicht ohne Gewaltthätigkeit mehr von ihm trennen kann.

Der Wille hat ohnehin einen unmittelbarern Zusammenhang mit dem Vermögen der Empfindungen als dem der Erkenntniß, [*NA* 287] und es wäre in manchen Fällen schlimm, wenn er sich bey der reinen Vernunft erst orientiren müßte. Es erweckt mir kein gutes Vorurtheil für einen Menschen, wenn er der Stimme des Triebes so wenig trauen darf, daß er gezwungen ist, ihn jedesmal erst vor dem Grundsatze der Moral abzuhören; vielmehr achtet man ihn hoch, wenn er sich demselben, ohne Gefahr, durch ihn mißgeleitet zu werden, mit einer gewissen Sicherheit vertraut. Denn das beweist, daß beyde Principien in ihm sich schon in derjenigen Übereinstimmung befinden, welche das Siegel der vollendeten Menschheit, und dasjenige ist, was man unter einer *schönen Seele* verstehet.

Eine schöne Seele nennt man es, wenn sich das sittliche Gefühl aller Empfindungen des Menschen endlich bis zu dem Grad versichert hat, daß es dem Affekt die Leitung des Willens ohne Scheu überlassen darf, und nie Gefahr läuft, mit den Entscheidungen desselben im Widerspruch zu stehen. Daher sind bey einer schönen Seele die einzelnen Handlungen eigentlich nicht sittlich, sondern der ganze Charakter ist es. Man kann ihr auch keine einzige darunter zum Verdienst anrechnen, weil eine Befriedigung des Triebes nie verdienstlich heißen kann. Die schöne Seele hat kein andres Verdienst, als daß sie ist. Mit einer Leichtigkeit, als wenn bloß der Instinkt aus ihr handelte, übt sie der Menschheit peinlichste Pflichten aus, und das heldenmüthigste Opfer, das sie dem Naturtriebe abgewinnt, fällt, wie eine freiwillige Wirkung eben dieses Triebes, in die Augen. Daher weiß sie selbst auch niemals um die Schönheit ihres Handelns, und es fällt ihr nicht mehr ein, daß man anders handeln und empfinden könnte; dagegen ein schulgerechter Zögling der Sittenregel, so wie das Wort des Meisters ihn fodert, jeden Augenblick bereit seyn wird, vom Verhältniß seiner Handlungen zum Gesetz die strengste Rechnung abzulegen. Das Leben des Letztern wird einer Zeichnung gleichen, worin man die Regel durch harte Striche angedeutet sieht, und an der allenfalls ein Lehrling die Principien der Kunst lernen könnte. Aber in einem schönen Leben sind, wie in einem Titianischen Gemählde, alle jene schneidenden Grenzlinien verschwunden, und doch tritt die ganze Gestalt nur desto wahrer, lebendiger, harmonischer hervor.

[*NA* 288]

In einer schönen Seele ist es also, wo Sinnlichkeit und Vernunft, Pflicht und Neigung harmoniren, und Grazie ist ihr Ausdruck in der Erscheinung. Nur im Dienst einer schönen Seele kann die Natur zugleich Freyheit besitzen, und ihre Form bewahren, da sie erstere unter der Herrschaft eines strengen Gemüths, letztere unter der Anarchie der Sinnlichkeit einbüßt. Eine schöne Seele gießt auch über eine Bildung, der es an architektonischer Schönheit mangelt, eine unwiderstehliche Grazie aus, und oft sieht man sie selbst über Gebrechen der Natur triumphiren. Alle Bewegungen, die von ihr ausgehen, werden leicht, sanft und dennoch belebt seyn. Heiter und frey wird das Auge strahlen, und Empfindung wird in demselben glänzen. Von der Sanftmuth des Herzens wird der Mund eine Grazie erhalten, die keine Verstellung erkünsteln kann. Keine Spannung wird in den Minen, kein Zwang in den willkührlichen Bewegungen zu bemerken seyn, denn die Seele weiß von keinem. Musik wird die Stimme seyn, und mit dem reinen Strom ihrer Modulationen das Herz bewegen. Die architektonische Schönheit kann Wohlgefallen, kann Bewunderung, kann Erstaunen erregen, aber nur die Anmuth wird hinreißen. Die Schönheit hat *Anbeter, Liebhaber* hat nur die Grazie; denn wir huldigen dem Schöpfer, und lieben den Menschen.

Man wird, im Ganzen genommen, die Anmuth mehr bey dem *weiblichen* Geschlecht (die Schönheit vielleicht mehr bey dem männlichen) finden, wovon die Ursache nicht weit zu suchen ist. Zur Anmuth muß sowohl der körperliche Bau, als der Charakter beitragen; jener durch seine Biegsamkeit, Eindrücke anzunehmen und ins Spiel gesetzt zu werden, dieser durch die sittliche Harmonie der Gefühle. In beydem war die Natur dem Weibe günstiger als dem Manne.

Der zärtere weibliche Bau empfängt jeden Eindruck schneller und läßt ihn schneller wieder verschwinden. Feste Constitutionen kommen nur durch einen Sturm in Bewegung, und wenn starke Muskeln angezogen werden, so können sie die Leichtigkeit nicht zeigen, die zur Grazie erfodert wird. Was in einem weiblichen Gesicht noch schöne Empfindsamkeit ist, würde in einem männlichen schon Leiden ausdrücken. Die zarte Fiber des Weibes neigt sich wie dünnes Schilfrohr unter dem leisesten Hauch des [*NA* 289] Affekts. In leichten und lieblichen Wellen gleitet die Seele über das sprechende Angesicht, das sich bald wieder zu einem ruhigen Spiegel ebnet.

Auch der Beytrag, den die Seele zu der Grazie geben muß, kann bey dem Weibe leichter als bey dem Manne erfüllt werden. Selten wird sich der weibliche Charakter zu der höchsten Idee sittlicher Reinheit erheben, und es selten weiter als zu *affektionirten* Handlungen bringen. Er wird der Sinnlichkeit oft mit heroischer Stärke, aber nur *durch* die Sinnlichkeit widerstehen. Weil nun die Sittlichkeit des Weibes gewöhnlich auf Seiten der Neigung ist, so wird es sich in der Erscheinung eben so ausnehmen, als wenn die Neigung auf Seiten der Sittlichkeit wäre. Anmuth wird also der Ausdruck der weiblichen Tugend seyn, der sehr oft der männlichen fehlen dürfte.

Würde

So wie die Anmuth der Ausdruck einer schönen Seele ist, so ist *Würde* der Ausdruck einer erhabenen Gesinnung.

Es ist dem Menschen zwar aufgegeben, eine innige Übereinstimmung zwischen seinen beyden Naturen zu stiften, immer ein harmonirendes Ganze zu seyn, und mit seiner vollstimmigen ganzen Menschheit zu handeln. Aber diese Charakterschönheit, die reifste Frucht seiner Humanität, ist bloß eine Idee, welcher gemäß zu werden, er mit anhaltender Wachsamkeit streben, aber die er bey aller Anstrengung nie ganz erreichen kann.

Der Grund, warum er es nicht kann, ist die unveränderliche Einrichtung seiner Natur; es sind die physischen Bedingungen seines Daseyns selbst, die ihn daran verhindern.

Um nehmlich seine Existenz in der Sinnenwelt, die von Naturbedingungen abhängt, sicher zu stellen, mußte der Mensch, da er, als ein Wesen, das sich nach Willkühr verändern kann, für seine Erhaltung selbst zu sorgen hat, zu Handlungen vermocht werden, wodurch jene physischen Bedingungen seines Daseyns erfüllt, und wenn sie aufgehoben sind, wieder hergestellt werden können. Obgleich aber die Natur diese Sorge, die sie in ihren vegetabilischen Erzeugungen ganz allein über sich nimmt, ihm [**NA 290**] selbst übergeben mußte, so durfte doch die Befriedigung eines so dringenden Bedürfnisses, wo es sein und seines Geschlechts ganzes Daseyn gilt, seiner ungewissen Einsicht nicht anvertraut werden. Sie zog also diese Angelegenheit, die *dem Inhalte nach* in ihr Gebiet gehört, auch *der Form nach* in dasselbe, indem sie in die Bestimmungen der Willkühr Nothwendigkeit legte. So entstand der Naturtrieb, der nichts anders ist, als eine Naturnothwendigkeit durch das Medium der Empfindung.

Der Naturtrieb bestürmt das Empfindungsvermögen durch die gedoppelte Macht von Schmerz und Vergnügen; durch Schmerz, wo er Befriedigung fodert, durch Vergnügen, wo er sie findet.

Da einer Naturnothwendigkeit nichts abzudingen ist, so muß auch der Mensch, seiner Freyheit ungeachtet, empfinden, was die Natur ihn empfinden lassen will, und je nachdem die Empfindung Schmerz oder Lust ist, so muß bey ihm eben so unabänderlich Verabscheuung oder Begierde erfolgen. In diesem Punkte steht er dem Thiere vollkommen gleich, und der starkmüthigste Stoiker fühlt den Hunger eben so empfindlich und verabscheut ihn eben so lebhaft, als der Wurm zu seinen Füßen.

Jetzt aber fängt der große Unterschied an. Auf die Begierde und Verabscheuung erfolgt bey dem Thiere eben so nothwendig Handlung, als Begierde auf Empfindung, und Empfindung auf den äußern Eindruck erfolgte. Es ist hier eine stetig fortlaufende Kette, wo jeder Ring nothwendig in den andern greift. Bey dem Menschen ist noch eine Instanz mehr, nehmlich der *Wille,* der als ein übersinnliches Vermögen weder dem Gesetz der Natur, noch dem der Vernunft, so unterworfen ist, daß ihm nicht vollkommen freye Wahl bliebe, sich entweder nach diesem oder nach jenem zu richten. Das Thier *muß* streben den Schmerz los zu seyn, der Mensch kann sich entschließen, ihn zu behalten.

Der Wille des Menschen ist ein erhabener Begriff, auch dann, wenn man auf seinen moralischen Gebrauch nicht achtet. Schon der *bloße* Wille erhebt den Menschen über die Thierheit; der *moralische* erhebt ihn zur Gottheit. Er muß aber jene zuvor verlassen haben, eh' er sich dieser nähern kann; daher ist es kein geringer Schritt zur moralischen Freyheit des Willens, durch Brechung der Naturnothwendigkeit in sich, auch in gleichgültigen Dingen, den *bloßen* Willen zu üben. [*NA* 291]

Die Gesetzgebung der Natur hat Bestand bis zum Willen, wo sie sich endigt, und die vernünftige anfängt. Der Wille steht hier zwischen beyden Gerichtsbarkeiten, und es kommt ganz auf ihn selbst an, von welcher er das Gesetz empfangen will; aber er steht nicht in gleichem Verhältniß gegen beyde. Als Naturkraft ist er gegen die eine, wie gegen die andere, frey; das heißt, er *muß* sich weder zu dieser noch zu jener schlagen. Er ist aber nicht frey, als moralische Kraft, das heißt, er *soll* sich zu der vernünftigen schlagen. *Gebunden* ist er an keine, aber *verbunden* ist er dem Gesetz der Vernunft. Er gebraucht also seine Freyheit wirklich, wenn er gleich der Vernunft widersprechend handelt, aber er gebraucht sie *unwürdig,* weil er ungeachtet seiner Freyheit doch nur *innerhalb der Natur* stehen bleibt, und zu der Operation des bloßen Triebes gar keine Realität hinzuthut; denn aus *Begierde wollen* heißt nur umständlicher begehren.*

Die Gesetzgebung der Natur durch den Trieb kann mit der Gesetzgebung der Vernunft aus Principien in Streit gerathen, wenn der Trieb zu seiner Befriedigung eine Handlung fodert, die dem moralischen Grundsatz zuwider läuft. In diesem Fall ist es unwandelbare Pflicht für den Willen, die Foderung der Natur dem Ausspruch der Vernunft nachzusetzen, da Naturgesetze nur bedingungsweise, Vernunftgesetze aber schlechterdings und unbedingt verbinden.

Aber die Natur behauptet mit Nachdruck ihre Rechte, und da sie niemals willkührlich fodert, so nimmt sie, unbefriedigt, auch keine Foderung zurück. Weil von der ersten Ursache an, wodurch sie in Bewegung gebracht wird, bis zu dem Willen, wo ihre Gesetzgebung aufhört, alles in ihr streng nothwendig ist, so kann sie *rückwärts* nicht nachgeben, sondern muß *vorwärts* gegen den Willen drängen, bey dem die Befriedigung ihres Bedürfnisses steht. Zuweilen scheint es zwar, als ob sie sich ihren Weg verkürzte, und, ohne zuvor ihr Gesuch vor den Willen zu bringen, unmittelbare Kausalität für die Handlung hätte, durch die ihrem Bedürfniße abgeholfen wird. In einem solchen Falle, wo der [NA 292] Mensch dem Triebe nicht bloß freyen Lauf *ließe*, sondern wo der Trieb diesen Lauf selbst *nähme*, würde der Mensch auch *nur* Thier seyn; aber es ist sehr zu zweifeln, ob dieses jemals sein Fall seyn kann, und wenn er es wirklich wäre, ob diese blinde Macht seines Triebes nicht ein Verbrechen seines Willens ist.

Das Begehrungsvermögen dringt also auf Befriedigung, und der Wille wird aufgefodert, ihm diese zu verschaffen. Aber der Wille soll seine Bestimmungsgründe von der Vernunft empfangen, und nur nach demjenigen, was diese erlaubt oder vorschreibt, seine Entschließung fassen. Wendet sich nun der Wille wirklich an die Vernunft, ehe er das Verlangen des Triebes genehmigt, so handelt er sittlich; entscheidet er aber unmittelbar, so handelt er sinnlich.**

---

* Man lese über diese Materie die aller Aufmerksamkeit würdige Theorie des Willens im zweyten Theil der *Reinholdischen Briefe.*

** Man darf aber *diese* Anfrage des Willens bey der Vernunft nicht mit derjenigen verwechseln, wo sie über die *Mittel* zu Befriedigung einer Begierde erkennen soll. Hier ist nicht davon die Rede, wie die Befriedigung zu *erlangen*, sondern ob sie zu

So oft also die Natur eine Foderung macht, und den Willen durch die blinde Gewalt des Affekts überraschen will, kommt es diesem zu, ihr so lange Stillstand zu gebieten, bis die Vernunft gesprochen hat. Ob der Ausspruch der Vernunft *für* oder *gegen* das Interesse der Sinnlichkeit ausfallen werde, das ist, was er jetzt noch nicht wissen kann; eben deswegen aber muß er dieses Verfahren in jedem Affekt ohne Unterschied beobachten, und der Natur, in jedem Falle, wo sie der *anfangende* Theil ist, die unmittelbare Kausalität versagen. Dadurch allein, daß er die Gewalt der Begierde bricht, die mit Vorschnelligkeit ihrer Befriedigung zueilt, und die Instanz des Willens lieber ganz vorbeygehen möchte, zeigt der Mensch seine Selbstständigkeit, und beweist sich als ein moralisches Wesen, welches nie bloß begehren oder bloß verabscheuen, sondern seine Verabscheuung und Begierde jederzeit *wollen* muß.

Aber schon die bloße Anfrage bey der Vernunft ist eine Beeinträchtigung der Natur, die in ihrer eigenen Sache kompetente Richterin ist, und ihre Aussprüche keiner neuen und auswärtigen [*NA 293*] Instanz unterworfen sehen will. Jener Willensakt, der die Angelegenheit des Begehrungsvermögens vor das sittliche Forum bringt, ist also im eigentlichen Sinn *naturwidrig,* weil er das Nothwendige wieder zufällig macht, und Gesetzen der Vernunft die Entscheidung in einer Sache anheimstellt, wo nur Gesetze der Natur sprechen können, und auch wirklich gesprochen haben. Denn so wenig die reine Vernunft in ihrer moralischen Gesetzgebung darauf Rücksicht nimmt, wie der Sinn wohl ihre Entscheidungen aufnehmen möchte, eben so wenig richtet sich die Natur in ihrer Gesetzgebung darnach, wie sie es einer reinen Vernunft recht machen möchte. In jeder von beyden gilt eine andre Nothwendigkeit, die aber keine seyn würde, wenn es der einen erlaubt wäre, willkührliche Veränderungen in der andern zu treffen. Daher kann auch der tapferste Geist bey allem Widerstande, den er gegen die Sinnlichkeit ausübt, nicht die Empfindung selbst, nicht die Begierde selbst unterdrücken, sondern ihr bloß den Einfluß auf seine Willensbestimmungen verweigern; *entwaffnen* kann er den Trieb durch moralische Mittel, aber nur durch natürliche ihn *besänftigen.* Er kann durch seine selbstständige Kraft zwar verhindern, daß Naturgesetze für seinen Willen nicht zwingend werden, aber an diesen Gesetzen selbst kann er schlechterdings nichts verändern.

---

gestatten ist. Nur das letzte gehört ins Gebiet der Moralität; das erste gehört zur Klugheit.

In Affekten also „wo die Natur (der Trieb) *zuerst* handelt und den Willen entweder ganz zu *umgehen* oder ihn *gewaltsam* auf ihre Seite zu ziehen strebt, kann sich die Sittlichkeit des Charakters nicht anders, als durch *Widerstand* offenbaren, und daß der Trieb die Freyheit des Willens nicht einschränke, nur durch Einschränkung des Triebes verhindern." Übereinstimmung mit dem Vernunftgesetz ist also im Affekte nicht anders möglich, als durch einen Widerspruch mit den Foderungen der Natur. Und da die Natur ihre Foderungen, aus sittlichen Gründen, nie zurücknimmt, folglich auf ihrer Seite alles sich gleich bleibt, wie auch der Wille sich in Ansehung ihrer verhalten mag, so ist hier keine Zusammenstimmung zwischen Neigung und Pflicht, zwischen Vernunft und Sinnlichkeit möglich, so kann der Mensch hier nicht mit seiner ganzen harmonirenden Natur, sondern ausschließungsweise nur mit seiner vernünftigen handeln. Er handelt also in diesen Fällen auch nicht *moralisch schön,* [*NA 294*] weil an der Schönheit der Handlung auch die Neigung nothwendig Theil nehmen muß, die hier vielmehr widerstreitet. Er handelt aber *moralisch groß,* weil alles das, und das allein groß ist, was von einer Überlegenheit des höhern Vermögens über das sinnliche Zeugniß gibt.

Die *schöne* Seele muß sich also im Affekt in eine *erhabene* verwandeln, und das ist der untrügliche Probierstein, wodurch man sie von dem *guten Herzen* oder der *Temperamentstugend* unterscheiden kann. Ist bey einem Menschen die Neigung nur darum auf Seiten der Gerechtigkeit, weil die Gerechtigkeit sich glücklicherweise auf Seiten der Neigung befindet, so wird der Naturtrieb im Affekt eine vollkommene Zwangsgewalt über den Willen ausüben, und, wo ein Opfer nöthig ist, so wird es die Sittlichkeit und nicht die Sinnlichkeit bringen. War es hingegen die Vernunft selbst, die, wie bey einem schönen Charakter der Fall ist, die Neigungen *in Pflicht nahm,* und der Sinnlichkeit das Steuer *nur anvertraute,* so wird sie es in demselben Moment zurücknehmen, als der Trieb seine Vollmacht mißbrauchen will. Die Temperamentstugend sinkt also im Affekt zum bloßen Naturprodukt herab; die schöne Seele geht ins heroische über, und erhebt sich zur reinen Intelligenz.

Beherrschung der Triebe durch die moralische Kraft ist *Geistesfreiheit,* und *Würde* heißt ihr Ausdruck in der Erscheinung.

Streng genommen ist die moralische Kraft im Menschen keiner Darstellung fähig, da das Übersinnliche nie versinnlicht werden kann. Aber mittelbar kann sie durch sinnliche Zeichen dem Verstande vorgestellt werden, wie bey der Würde der menschlichen Bildung wirklich der Fall ist.

Der aufgeregte Naturtrieb wird eben so, wie das Herz in seinen morali-schen Rührungen, von Bewegungen im Körper begleitet, die theils dem Willen zuvoreilen, theils, als bloß sympathetische, seiner Herrschaft gar nicht unterworfen sind. Denn da weder Empfindung, noch Begierde und Verabscheuung, in der Willkühr des Menschen liegen, so kann er denjenigen Bewegungen, welche damit unmittelbar zusammenhängen, nicht zu gebie-ten haben. Aber der Trieb bleibt nicht bey der bloßen Begierde stehen; vorschnell und dringend strebt er sein Objekt zu verwirklichen, [*NA 295*] und wird, wenn ihm von dem selbstständigen Geiste nicht nachdrücklich widerstanden wird, selbst solche Handlungen *anticipiren,* worüber der Wille allein zu sagen haben soll. Denn der Erhaltungstrieb ringt ohne Unterlaß nach der gesetzgebenden Gewalt im Gebiete des Willens, und sein Bestreben ist, eben so ungebunden über den Menschen, wie über das Thier, zu schalten.

Man findet also Bewegungen von zweyerley Art und Ursprung in jedem Affekte, den der Erhaltungstrieb in dem Menschen entzündet; erstlich solche, welche unmittelbar von der Empfindung ausgehen, und daher ganz unwillkührlich sind; zweitens solche, welche der Art nach willkührlich seyn sollten und könnten, die aber der blinde Naturtrieb der Freyheit abgewinnt. Die ersten beziehen sich auf den Affekt selbst, und sind daher nothwendig mit demselben verbunden; die zweyten entsprechen mehr der Ursache und dem Gegenstande des Affekts, daher sie auch zufällig und veränderlich sind, und nicht für untrügliche Zeichen desselben gelten können. Weil aber beyde, sobald das Objekt bestimmt ist, dem Naturtriebe gleich nothwendig sind, so gehören auch beyde dazu, um den Ausdruck des Affekts zu einem vollständigen und übereinstimmenden Ganzen zu machen.*

Wenn nun der Wille Selbstständigkeit genug besitzt, dem vorgreifenden Naturtriebe Schranken zu setzen, und gegen die ungestüme Macht desselben seine Gerechtsame zu behaupten, so bleiben zwar alle jene Erscheinungen in

---

* Findet man nur die Bewegungen der zweyten Art, ohne die der erstern, so zeigt dieses an, daß die Person den Affekt will, und die Natur ihn verweigert. Findet man die Bewegungen der erstern Art, ohne die der zweyten, so beweist dieß, daß die Natur in den Affekt wirklich versetzt ist, aber die Person ihn verbietet. Den ersten Fall sieht man alle Tage bey affektirten Personen und schlechten Komö-dianten; den zweyten Fall desto seltener und nur bey starken Gemüthern.

Kraft, die der aufgeregte Naturtrieb in seinem eigenen Gebiet bewirkte, aber alle diejenigen werden fehlen, die er in einer fremden Gerichtsbarkeit eigenmächtig hatte an sich reißen wollen. Die Erscheinungen stimmen also nicht mehr überein, aber eben in ihrem Widerspruch liegt der Ausdruck der moralischen Kraft.

Gesetzt, wir erblicken an einem Menschen Zeichen des quaalvollesten Affekts aus der Klasse jener ersten ganz unwillkühr[*NA 296*]lichen Bewegungen. Aber indem seine Adern auflaufen, seine Muskel krampfhaft angespannt werden, seine Stimme erstickt, seine Brust emporgetrieben, sein Unterleib einwärts gepreßt ist, sind seine willkührlichen Bewegungen sanft, seine Gesichtszüge frey, und es ist heiter um Aug und Stirne. Wäre der Mensch bloß ein Sinnenwesen, so würden alle seine Züge, da sie dieselbe gemeinschaftliche Quelle hätten, mit einander übereinstimmend seyn, und also in dem gegenwärtigen Fall alle ohne Unterschied Leiden ausdrücken müssen. Da aber Züge der Ruhe unter die Züge des Schmerzens gemischt sind, einerley Ursache aber nicht entgegengesetzte Wirkungen haben kann, so beweist dieser Widerspruch der Züge das Daseyn und den Einfluß einer Kraft, die von dem Leiden unabhängig, und den Eindrücken überlegen ist, unter denen wir das Sinnliche erliegen sehen. Und auf diese Art nun wird die *Ruhe im Leiden,* als worinn die Würde eigentlich besteht, obgleich nur mittelbar durch einen Vernunftschluß, Darstellung der Intelligenz im Menschen und Ausdruck seiner moralischen Freyheit.*

Aber nicht bloß beym Leiden im engern Sinn, wo dieses Wort nur schmerzhafte Rührungen bedeutet, sondern überhaupt bey jedem starken Interesse des Begehrungsvermögens muß der Geist seine Freyheit beweisen, also Würde der Ausdruck seyn. Der angenehme Affekt erfodert sie nicht weniger als der peinliche, weil die Natur in beyden Fällen gern den Meister spielen möchte, und von dem Willen gezügelt werden soll. Die Würde bezieht sich auf die *Form* und nicht auf den *Inhalt* des Affekts, daher es geschehen kann, daß oft, dem Inhalt nach, lobenswürdige Affekte, wenn der Mensch sich ihnen blindlings überläßt, aus Mangel der Würde, ins Gemeine und Niedrige fallen; daß hingegen nicht selten verwerfliche Affekte sich sogar dem Erhabenen nähern, sobald sie nur in ihrer Form Herrschaft des Geistes über seine Empfindungen zeigen.

---

* In einer Untersuchung über Pathetische Darstellungen ist im 3ten Stück der Thalia umständlicher davon gehandelt worden.

Bey der Würde also führt sich der Geist in dem Körper als *Herrscher* auf, denn hier hat er seine Selbstständigkeit gegen den gebieterischen Trieb zu behaupten, der ohne ihn zu Hand[*NA* 297]lungen schreitet, und sich seinem Joch gern entziehen möchte. Bey der Anmuth hingegen regiert er mit *Liberalität,* weil er es hier ist, der die Natur in Handlung setzt, und keinen Widerstand zu besiegen findet. Nachsicht verdient aber nur der Gehorsam, und Strenge kann nur die *Widersetzung* rechtfertigen.

Anmuth liegt also in der *Freyheit der willkührlichen Bewegungen;* Würde in der *Beherrschung der unwillkührlichen.* Die Anmuth läßt der Natur da, wo sie die Befehle des Geistes ausrichtet, einen Schein von Freywilligkeit; die Würde hingegen unterwirft sie da, wo sie herrschen will, dem Geist. Ueberall, wo der Trieb anfängt zu handeln, und sich herausnimmt, in das Amt des Willen zu greifen, da darf der Wille keine *Indulgenz,* sondern muß durch den nachdrücklichsten Widerstand seine Selbstständigkeit (Avtonomie) beweisen. Wo hingegen der Wille *anfängt,* und die Sinnlichkeit ihm *folgt,* da darf er keine Strenge, sondern muß Indulgenz beweisen. Dieß ist mit wenigen Worten das Gesetz für das Verhältniß beyder Naturen im Menschen, so wie es in der Erscheinung sich darstellet.

Würde wird daher mehr im *Leiden* ($\pi\alpha\theta o\zeta$); Anmuth mehr im *Betragen* ($\eta\theta o\zeta$) gefodert und gezeigt; denn nur im Leiden kann sich die Freyheit des Gemüths, und nur im Handeln die Freyheit des Körpers offenbaren.

Da die Würde ein Ausdruck des Widerstandes ist, den der selbstständige Geist dem Naturtriebe leistet, dieser also als eine Gewalt muß angesehen werden, welche Widerstand nöthig macht, so ist sie da, wo keine solche Gewalt zu bekämpfen ist, lächerlich, und wo keine mehr zu bekämpfen seyn *sollte,* verächtlich. Man lacht über den Komödianten, (weß Standes und Würden er auch sey,) der auch bey gleichgültigen Verrichtungen eine gewisse Dignität affektirt. Man verachtet die kleine Seele, die sich für die Ausübung einer gemeinen Pflicht, die oft nur Unterlassung einer Niederträchtigkeit ist, mit Würde bezahlt macht.

Überhaupt ist es nicht eigentlich Würde, sondern Anmuth, was man von der Tugend fodert. Die Würde giebt sich bey der Tugend von selbst, die schon ihrem Inhalt nach Herrschaft des Menschen über seine Triebe voraussetzt. Weit eher wird sich [*NA* 298] bey Ausübung sittlicher Pflichten die Sinnlichkeit in einem Zustand des Zwangs und der Unterdrückung befinden, da besonders, wo sie ein schmerzhaftes Opfer bringt.

Da aber das Ideal vollkommener Menschheit keinen Widerstreit, sondern Zusammenstimmung zwischen dem Sittlichen und Sinnlichen fodert, so verträgt es sich nicht wohl mit der Würde, die, als ein Ausdruck jenes Widerstreits zwischen beyden, entweder die besondern Schranken des Subjekts oder die allgemeinen der Menschheit sichtbar macht.

Ist das erste, und liegt es bloß an dem Unvermögen des Subjekts, daß bey einer Handlung Neigung und Pflicht nicht zusammenstimmen, so wird diese Handlung jederzeit soviel an sittlicher Schätzung verlieren, als sich Kampf in ihre Ausübung, also Würde in ihren Vortrag mischt. Denn unser moralisches Urtheil bringt jedes Individuum unter den Maaßstab der Gattung, und dem Menschen werden keine andre als die Schranken der Menschheit vergeben.

Ist aber das zweyte, und kann eine Handlung der Pflicht mit den Foderungen der Natur nicht in Harmonie gebracht werden, ohne den Begriff der menschlichen Natur aufzuheben, so ist der Widerstand der Neigung nothwendig, und es ist bloß der Anblick des Kampfes, der uns von der Möglichkeit des Sieges überführen kann. Wir erwarten hier also einen Ausdruck des Widerstreits in der Erscheinung, und werden uns nie überreden lassen, da an eine Tugend zu glauben, wo wir nicht einmal Menschheit sehen. Wo also die sittliche Pflicht eine Handlung gebietet, die das sinnliche nothwendig leiden macht, da ist Ernst und kein Spiel, da würde uns die Leichtigkeit in der Ausübung vielmehr empören als befriedigen; da kann also nicht Anmuth, sondern Würde der Ausdruck seyn. Überhaupt gilt hier das Gesetz, daß der Mensch alles mit Anmuth thun müsse, was er innerhalb seiner Menschheit verrichten kann, und alles mit Würde, welches zu verrichten er über seine Menschheit hinaus gehen muß.

So wie wir Anmuth von der Tugend fodern, so fodern wir Würde von der Neigung. Der Neigung ist die Anmuth so natürlich, als der Tugend die Würde, da sie schon ihrem Inhalt nach sinnlich, der Naturfreyheit günstig, und aller Anspannung feind [*NA* 299] ist. Auch dem rohen Menschen fehlt es nicht an einem gewissen Grade von Anmuth, wenn ihn die Liebe oder ein ähnlicher Affekt beseelt, und wo findet man mehr Anmuth als bey Kindern, die doch ganz unter sinnlicher Leitung stehen? Weit mehr Gefahr ist da, daß die Neigung den Zustand des Leidens endlich zum herrschenden mache, die Selbstthätigkeit des Geistes ersticke, und eine allgemeine Erschlaffung herbeyführe. Um sich also bey einem edeln Gefühl in Achtung zu setzen, die ihr nur allein ein *sittlicher* Ursprung verschaffen kann, muß die Neigung sich jederzeit mit Würde verbinden. Daher fodert der

Liebende Würde von dem Gegenstand seiner Leidenschaft. Würde allein ist ihm Bürge, daß nicht *das Bedürfniß zu ihm nöthigte,* sondern daß *die Freyheit ihn wählte* — daß man ihn nicht *als Sache begehrt,* sondern *als Person hochschätzt.*

Man fodert Anmuth von dem, der verpflichtet, und Würde von dem, der verpflichtet wird. Der erste soll, um sich eines kränkenden Vortheils über den andern zu begeben, die Handlung seines uninteressirten Entschlusses durch den Antheil, den er die Neigung daran nehmen läßt, zu einer *affektionirten* Handlung heruntersetzen, und sich dadurch den Schein des gewinnenden Theiles geben. Der andre soll, um durch die Abhängigkeit, in die er tritt, die Menschheit (deren heiliges Palladium Freyheit ist) nicht in seiner Person zu entehren, das bloße *Zufahren* des Triebes zu einer Handlung seines Willens erheben, und auf diese Art, indem er eine Gunst empfängt, eine erzeigen.

Man muß einen Fehler mit Anmuth rügen, und mit Würde bekennen. Kehrt man es um, so wird es das Ansehen haben, als ob der eine Theil seinen Vortheil zu sehr, der andre seinen Nachtheil zu wenig empfände.

Will der Starke geliebt seyn, so mag er seine Überlegenheit durch Grazie mildern. Will der Schwache geachtet seyn, so mag er seiner Ohnmacht durch Würde aufhelfen. Man ist sonst der Meinung, daß auf den Thron Würde gehöre, und bekanntlich lieben die, welche darauf sitzen, in ihren Räthen, Beichtvätern und Parlamenten — die Anmuth. Aber was in einem politischen Reiche gut und löblich seyn mag, ist es nicht immer in einem [*NA* 300] Reiche des Geschmacks. In dieses Reich tritt auch der König — sobald er von seinem Throne herabsteigt, (denn Throne haben ihre Privilegien,) und auch der kriechende Höfling begiebt sich unter seine heilige Freyheit, sobald er sich zum Menschen aufrichtet. Alsdann aber möchte Ersterm zu rathen seyn, mit dem Überfluß des Andern seinen Mangel zu ersetzen, und ihm soviel an Würde abzugeben, als er selbst an Grazie nöthig hat.

Da Würde und Anmuth ihre verschiedenen Gebiete haben, worinn sie sich äußern, so schließen sie einander in derselben Person, ja in demselben Zustand einer Person nicht aus; vielmehr ist es nur die Anmuth, von der die Würde ihre Beglaubigung, und nur die Würde, von der die Anmuth ihren Werth empfängt.

Würde allein beweist zwar überall, wo wir sie antreffen, eine gewisse Einschränkung der Begierden und Neigungen. Ob es aber nicht vielmehr Stumpfheit des Empfindungsvermögens (Härte) sey, was wir für

Beherrschung halten, und ob es wirklich moralische Selbstthätigkeit und nicht vielmehr Übergewicht eines andern Affektes, also absichtliche Anspannung sey, was den Ausbruch des gegenwärtigen im Zaume hält, das kann nur die damit verbundene Anmuth außer Zweifel setzen. Die Anmuth nehmlich zeugt von einem ruhigen, in sich harmonischen Gemüth, und von einem empfindenden Herzen.

Eben so beweist auch die Anmuth schon für sich allein eine Empfänglichkeit des Gefühlvermögens, und eine Übereinstimmung der Empfindungen. Daß es aber nicht Schlaffheit des Geistes sey, was dem Sinn so viel Freyheit läßt, und das Herz jedem Eindruck öffnet, und daß es das Sittliche sey, was die Empfindungen in diese Übereinstimmung brachte, das kann uns wiederum nur die damit verbundne Würde verbürgen. In der Würde nehmlich legitimirt sich das Subjekt als eine selbstständige Kraft; und indem der Wille die *Licenz* der unwillkührlichen Bewegungen *bändigt,* giebt er zu erkennen, daß er die *Freyheit* der willkührlichen bloß *zuläßt.*

Sind Anmuth und Würde, jene noch durch architektonische Schönheit, diese durch Kraft unterstützt, in derselben Person *vereinigt,* so ist der Ausdruck der Menschheit in ihr vollendet, und sie steht da, gerechtfertigt in der Geisterwelt, und freygesprochen in der Erscheinung. Beyde Gesetzgebungen berühren [**NA 301**] einander hier so nahe, daß ihre Grenzen zusammenfließen. Mit gemildertem Glanze steigt in dem Lächeln des Mundes, in dem sanftbelebten Blick, in der heitern Stirne die *Vernunftfreyheit* auf, und mit erhabenem Abschied geht die *Naturnothwendigkeit* in der edeln Majestät des Angesichts unter. Nach diesem Ideal menschlicher Schönheit sind die Antiken gebildet, und man erkennt es in der göttlichen Gestalt einer Niobe, im belvederischen Apoll, in dem borghesischen geflügelten Genius, und in der Muse des Barberinischen Pallastes.*

---

* Mit dem feinen und großen Sinn, der ihm eigen ist, hat Winkelmann (Geschichte der Kunst. Erster Theil. S. 480 folg. Wiener Ausgabe) diese hohe Schönheit, welche aus der Verbindung der Grazie mit der Würde hervorgeht, aufgefaßt und beschrieben. Aber was er vereinigt fand, nahm und gab er auch nur für Eines, und er blieb bey dem stehen, was der bloße Sinn ihn lehrte, ohne zu untersuchen, ob es nicht vielleicht noch zu scheiden sey. Er verwirrt den Begriff der Grazie, da er Züge, die offenbar nur der Würde zukommen, in diesen Begriff mit aufnimmt. Grazie und Würde sind aber wesentlich verschieden, und man thut unrecht, das zu einer

[NA 302]

Wo sich Grazie und Würde vereinigen, da werden wir abwechselnd angezogen und zurückgestoßen; angezogen als Geister, zurückgestoßen als sinnliche Naturen.

In der Würde nehmlich wird uns ein Beyspiel der Unterordnung des Sinnlichen unter das Sittliche vorgehalten, welchem nachzuahmen für uns Gesetz, zugleich aber für unser physisches Vermögen übersteigend ist. Der Widerstreit zwischen dem Bedürfniß der Natur und der Foderung des Gesetzes, deren Gültigkeit wir doch eingestehen, spannt die Sinnlichkeit an, und erweckt das Gefühl, welches *Achtung* genannt wird, und von der Würde unzertrennlich ist.

Eigenschaft der Grazie zu machen, was vielmehr eine *Einschränkung* derselben ist. Was Winkelmann die hohe, himmlische Grazie nennt, ist nichts anders, als Schönheit und Grazie mit überwiegender Würde. „Die himmlische Grazie," sagt er, „scheint sich allgenügsam, und bietet sich nicht an, sondern will gesucht werden; sie ist zu erhaben, um sich sehr sinnlich zu machen. Sie verschließt in sich die Bewegungen der Seele, und nähert sich der seligen Stille der göttlichen Natur. — Durch sie," sagt er an einem andern Ort, „wagte sich der Künstler der Niobe in das Reich unkörperlicher Ideen, und erreichte das Geheimniß, die *Todesangst mit der höchsten Schönheit zu verbinden,*" (es würde schwer seyn, hierinn einen Sinn zu finden, wenn es nicht augenscheinlich wäre, daß hier nur die Würde gemeynt ist) „er wurde ein Schöpfer reiner Geister, die keine Begierden der Sinne erwecken, denn sie scheinen nicht zur Leidenschaft gebildet zu seyn, sondern dieselbe nur angenommen zu haben." — Anderswo heißt es „die Seele äußerte sich nur unter einer stillen Fläche des Wassers, und trat niemals mit Ungestüm hervor. In Vorstellung des Leidens bleibt die größte Pein verschlossen, und die Freude schwebet wie eine sanfte Luft, die kaum die Blätter rühret, auf dem Gesicht einer Leukothea."

Alle diese Züge kommen der Würde und nicht der Grazie zu, denn die Grazie verschließt sich nicht, sondern kommt entgegen, die Grazie macht sich sinnlich, und ist auch nicht erhaben sondern schön. Aber die Würde ist es, was die Natur in ihren Aeußerungen zurückhält, und den Zügen, auch in der Todesangst und in dem bittersten Leiden eines Laokoon, Ruhe gebietet.

Home verfällt in denselben Fehler, was aber bey diesem Schriftsteller weniger zu verwundern ist. Auch er nimmt Züge der Würde in die Grazie mit auf, ob er gleich Anmuth und Würde ausdrücklich von einander unterscheidet. Seine Beobachtungen sind gewöhnlich richtig, und die *nächsten* Regeln, die er sich daraus bildet, wahr; aber weiter darf man ihm auch nicht folgen. Grundsätze d. Krit. II. Theil. Anmuth und Würde.

In der Anmuth hingegen, wie in der Schönheit überhaupt, sieht die Vernunft ihre Foderung in der Sinnlichkeit erfüllt, und überraschend tritt ihr eine ihrer Ideen in der Erscheinung entgegen. Diese unerwartete Zusammenstimmung des Zufälligen der Natur mit dem Nothwendigen der Vernunft, erweckt ein Gefühl frohen Beyfalls, (*Wohlgefallen*) welches auflösend für den Sinn, für den Geist aber belebend und beschäftigend ist, und eine Anziehung des sinnlichen Objekts muß erfolgen. Diese Anziehung nennen wir Wohlwollen — *Liebe;* ein Gefühl, das von Anmuth und Schönheit unzertrennlich ist.

Bey dem *Reiz* (nicht dem Liebreiz, sondern dem Wollustreiz, stimulus,) wird dem Sinn ein sinnlicher Stoff vorgehalten, der ihm Entledigung von einem Bedürfniß, d. i. Lust verspricht. Der Sinn ist also bestrebt, sich mit dem Sinnlichen zu vereinbaren, und *Begierde* entsteht; ein Gefühl, das anspannend für den Sinn, für den Geist hingegen erschlaffend ist.

Von der Achtung, kann man sagen, sie *beugt sich vor* ihrem Gegenstande; von der Liebe, sie *neigt sich zu* dem [NA 303] ihrigen; von der Begierde, sie *stürzt auf* den ihrigen. Bey der Achtung ist das Objekt die Vernunft und das Subjekt die sinnliche Natur.* Bey der Liebe ist das Objekt sinnlich, und das Subjekt die moralische Natur. Bey der Begierde sind Objekt und Subjekt sinnlich.

---

* Man darf die *Achtung* nicht mit der *Hochachtung* verwechseln. Achtung (nach ihrem reinen Begriff) geht nur auf das Verhältniß der sinnlichen Natur zu den Foderungen reiner praktischer Vernunft überhaupt, ohne Rücksicht auf eine wirkliche Erfüllung. „Das Gefühl der Unangemessenheit zu Erreichung einer Idee, die für uns Gesetz ist, heißt Achtung" (Kants Kr. d. Urtheilskraft). Daher ist Achtung keine angenehme, eher drückende Empfindung. Sie ist ein Gefühl des Abstandes des empirischen Willens von dem reinen. — Es kann daher auch nicht befremdlich seyn, daß ich die sinnliche Natur zum Subjekt der Achtung mache, obgleich diese nur auf *reine Vernunft* geht; denn die Unangemessenheit zu Erreichung des Gesetzes kann nur in der Sinnlichkeit liegen.

Hochachtung hingegen geht schon auf die wirkliche Erfüllung des Gesetzes, und wird nicht für das Gesetz, sondern für die Person, die demselben gemäß handelt, empfunden. Daher hat sie etwas ergötzendes, weil die Erfüllung des Gesetzes Vernunftwesen erfreuen muß. Achtung ist Zwang, Hochachtung schon ein freyeres Gefühl. Aber das rührt von der Liebe her, die ein Ingredienz der Hochachtung ausmacht. Achten muß auch der Nichtswürdige das Gute, aber um denjenigen hochzuachten, der es gethan hat, müßte er aufhören, ein Nichtswürdiger zu seyn.

Die Liebe allein ist also eine freye Empfindung, denn ihre reine Quelle strömt hervor aus dem Sitz der Freyheit, aus unsrer göttlichen Natur. Es ist hier nicht das Kleine und Niedrige, was sich mit dem Großen und Hohen mißt, nicht der Sinn, der an dem Vernunftgesetz schwindelnd hinaufsieht; es ist das *absolut Große* selbst, was in der Anmuth und Schönheit sich nachgeahmt und in der Sittlichkeit sich befriedigt findet, es ist der Gesetzgeber selbst, der *Gott* in uns, der mit seinem eigenen Bilde in der Sinnenwelt spielt. Daher ist das Gemüth aufgelöst in der Liebe, da es angespannt ist in der Achtung; denn hier ist nichts, das ihm Schranken setzte, da das absolut große nichts über sich hat, und die Sinnlichkeit, von der hier allein die Einschränkung kommen könnte, in der Anmuth und Schönheit mit den Ideen des Geistes zusammenstimmt. Liebe ist ein Herabsteigen, da die Achtung ein Hinaufklimmen ist. [*NA* 304] Daher kann der Schlimme nichts lieben, ob er gleich vieles achten muß; daher kann der Gute wenig achten, was er nicht zugleich mit Liebe umfienge. Der reine Geist kann nur lieben, nicht achten; der Sinn kann nur achten, aber nicht lieben.

Wenn der schuldbewußte Mensch in ewiger Furcht schwebt, dem Gesetzgeber in ihm selbst, in der Sinnenwelt zu begegnen, und in allem, was groß und schön und treflich ist, seinen Feind erblickt, so kennt die schöne Seele kein süßeres Glück, als das Heilige in sich außer sich nachgeahmt oder verwirklicht zu sehen, und in der Sinnenwelt ihren unsterblichen Freund zu umarmen. Liebe ist zugleich das Großmüthigste und das Selbstsüchtigste in der Natur; das erste: denn sie empfängt von ihrem Gegenstande nichts, sondern giebt ihm alles, da der reine Geist nur geben, nicht empfangen kann; das zweyte: denn es ist immer nur ihr eigenes Selbst, was sie in ihrem Gegenstande sucht und schätzet.

Aber eben darum, weil der Liebende von dem Geliebten nur empfängt, was er ihm selber gab, so begegnet es ihm öfters, daß er ihm giebt, was er nicht von ihm empfieng. Der äußre Sinn glaubt zu sehen, was nur der innere anschaut, der feurige Wunsch wird zum Glauben und der eigne Überfluß des Liebenden verbirgt die Armuth des Geliebten. Daher ist die Liebe so leicht der Täuschung ausgesetzt, was der Achtung und Begierde selten begegnet. So lange der innre Sinn den äußern exaltirt, so lange dauert auch die selige Bezauberung der platonischen Liebe, der zur Wonne der Unsterblichen, nur die Dauer fehlt. Sobald aber der innere Sinn dem äußern *seine* Anschauungen nicht mehr unterschiebt, so tritt der äußere wieder in seine Rechte und fodert, was ihm zukommt, *Stoff.* Das Feuer, welches die himmlische Venus entzündete, wird von der irrdischen benutzt, und der Naturtrieb rächt seine lange Vernachlässigung nicht selten durch eine desto unumschränktere Herrschaft. Da der Sinn nie getäuscht wird, so macht er diesen Vortheil mit grobem Übermuth gegen seinen edleren Nebenbuhler geltend, und ist kühn genug zu behaupten, daß er gehalten habe, was die Begeisterung schuldig blieb.

Die Würde hindert, daß die Liebe nicht zur Begierde wird. Die Anmuth verhütet, daß die Achtung nicht Furcht wird. [*NA* 305]

Wahre Schönheit, wahre Anmuth soll niemals Begierde erregen. Wo diese sich einmischt, da muß es entweder dem Gegenstand an Würde, oder dem Betrachter an Sittlichkeit der Empfindungen mangeln.

Wahre Größe soll niemals Furcht erregen. Wo diese eintritt, da kann man gewiß seyn, daß es entweder dem Gegenstand an Geschmack und an Grazie, oder dem Betrachter an einem günstigen Zeugniß seines Gewissens fehlt.

Reiz, Anmuth und Grazie werden zwar gewöhnlich als gleichbedeutend gebraucht; sie sind es aber nicht, oder sollten es doch nicht seyn, da der Begriff den sie ausdrücken, mehrerer Bestimmungen fähig ist, die eine verschiedene Bezeichnung verdienen.

Es giebt eine *belebende* und eine *beruhigende* Grazie. Die erste grenzt an den Sinnenreiz, und das Wohlgefallen an derselben kann, wenn es nicht durch Würde zurückgehalten wird, leicht in Verlangen ausarten. Diese kann *Reiz* genannt werden. Ein abgespannter Mensch kann sich nicht durch innre Kraft in Bewegung setzen, sondern muß Stoff von aussen empfangen, und durch leichte Übungen der Phantasie, und schnelle Übergänge vom Empfinden zum Handeln seine verlorene Schnellkraft wieder herzustellen suchen. Dieses erlangt er im Umgang mit einer *reizenden* Person, die das stagnirende Meer seiner Einbildungskraft durch Gespräch und Anblick in Schwung bringt.

Die beruhigende Grazie gränzt näher an die Würde, da sie sich durch Mäßigung unruhiger Bewegungen äußert. Zu ihr wendet sich der angespannte Mensch, und der wilde Sturm des Gemüths löst sich auf an ihrem friedeathmenden Busen. Diese kann *Anmuth* genannt werden. Mit dem Reize verbindet sich gern der lachende Scherz und der Stachel des Spotts; mit der Anmuth das Mitleid und die Liebe. Der entnervte Soliman schmachtet zulezt in den Ketten einer Roxelane, wenn sich der brausende

Geist eines Othello an der sanften Brust einer Desdemona zur Ruhe wiegt.

Auch die Würde hat ihre verschiedenen Abstuffungen, und wird da, wo sie sich der Anmuth und Schönheit nähert, zum *Edeln,* und wo sie an das Furchtbare gränzt, zur *Hoheit.*

Der höchste Grad der Anmuth ist das *Bezaubernde;* der [**NA 306**] höchste Grad der Würde die *Majestät.* Bey dem Bezaubernden verlieren wir uns gleichsam selbst, und fließen hinüber in den Gegenstand. Der höchste Genuß der Freyheit gränzt an den völligen Verlust derselben, und die Trunkenheit des Geistes an den Taumel der Sinnenlust. Die Majestät hingegen hält uns ein Gesetz vor, das uns nöthigt, in uns selbst zu schauen. Wir schlagen die Augen vor dem gegenwärtigen Gott zu Boden, vergessen alles außer uns, und empfinden nichts als die schwere Bürde unsers eigenen Daseyns.

Majestät hat nur das Heilige. Kann ein Mensch uns dieses repräsentiren, so hat er Majestät; und wenn auch unsre Kniee nicht nachfolgen, so wird doch unser Geist vor ihm niederfallen. Aber er richtet sich schnell wieder auf, sobald nur die kleinste Spur *menschlicher Schuld* an dem Gegenstand seiner Anbetung sichtbar wird; denn nichts, was nur *vergleichungsweise* groß ist, darf unsern Muth darniederschlagen.

Die bloße Macht, sey sie auch noch so furchtbar und grenzenlos, kann nie Majestät verleihen. Macht imponiert nur dem Sinnenwesen, die Majestät muß dem Geist seine Freyheit nehmen. Ein Mensch, der mir das Todesurtheil schreiben kann, hat darum noch keine Majestät für mich, sobald ich selbst nur bin, was ich seyn soll. Sein Vortheil über mich ist aus, sobald ich will. Wer mir aber in seiner Person den reinen Willen darstellt, vor dem werde ich mich, wenns möglich ist, auch noch in künftigen Welten beugen.

Anmuth und Würde stehen in einem zu hohen Werth, um die Eitelkeit und Thorheit nicht zur Nachahmung zu reizen. Aber es giebt dazu nur *Einen* Weg, nehmlich Nachahmung der Gesinnungen, deren Ausdruck sie sind. Alles andre ist *Nachäffung,* und wird sich als solche durch Übertreibung bald kenntlich machen.

So wie aus der Affektation des Erhabenen *Schwulst,* aus der Affektation des Edeln das *Kostbare* entsteht, so wird aus der affektirten Anmuth *Ziererey* und aus der affektirten Würde steife *Feyerlichkeit* und *Gravität.*

Die ächte Anmuth *giebt bloß nach* und kommt entgegen, die falsche hingegen *zerfließt.* Die wahre Anmuth *schont* bloß die Werkzeuge der

willkührlichen Bewegung, und will der Freyheit der Natur nicht unnöthiger-
weise zu nahe treten; die [NA 307] falsche Anmuth hat gar nicht das Herz,
die Werkzeuge des Willens gehörig zu gebrauchen, und um ja nicht ins Harte
und Schwerfällige zu fallen, *opfert* sie lieber etwas von dem Zweck der Bewegung auf, oder sucht ihn *durch Umschweife* zu erreichen. Wenn der *unbe-
hülfliche* Tänzer bey einer Menuet soviel Kraft aufwendet, als ob er ein
Mühlrad zu ziehen hätte, und mit Händen und Füßen so scharfe Ecken
schneidet, als wenn es hier um eine geometrische Genauigkeit zu thun
wäre, so wird der *affektirte* Tänzer so schwach auftreten, als ob er den Fuß-
boden fürchtete, und mit Händen und Füßen nichts als Schlangenlinien
beschreiben, wenn er auch darüber nicht von der Stelle kommen sollte. Das
andre Geschlecht, welches vorzugsweise im Besitze der wahren Anmuth ist,
macht sich auch der falschen am meisten schuldig; aber nirgends beleidigt
diese mehr, als wo sie der Begierde zum Angel dienet. Aus dem Lächeln
der wahren Grazie wird dann die widrigste Grimasse, das schöne Spiel der
Augen, so bezaubernd, wenn wahre Empfindung daraus spricht, wird zur
Verdrehung, die schmelzend modulirende Stimme, so unwiderstehlich in
einem wahren Munde, wird zu einem studirten tremulirenden Klang, und die
ganze Musik weiblicher Reizungen zu einer betrüglichen Toilettenkunst.

Wenn man auf Theatern und Ballsälen Gelegenheit hat, die affektirte
Anmuth zu beobachten, so kann man oft in den Kabineten der Minister,
und in den Studierzimmern der Gelehrten (auf hohen Schulen besonders)
die falsche Würde studiren. Wenn die wahre Würde zufrieden ist, den
Affekt an seiner Herrschaft zu hindern, und dem Naturtriebe bloß da, wo
er den Meister spielen will, in den unwillkührlichen Bewegungen,
Schranken setzt, so regiert die falsche Würde auch die willkührlichen mit
einem eisernen Zepter, unterdrückt die moralischen Bewegungen, die der
wahren Würde heilig sind, so gut als die sinnlichen, und löscht das ganze
mimische Spiel der Seele in den Gesichtszügen aus. Sie ist nicht bloß
streng gegen die widerstrebende, sondern hart gegen die unterwürfige
Natur, und sucht ihre lächerliche Größe in Unterjochung, und wo dieß
nicht angehen will, in Verbergung derselben. Nicht anders, als wenn sie
allem, was Natur heißt, einen unversöhnlichen Haß gelobt hätte, steckt sie
den Leib in lange faltigte Gewänder, die [NA 308] den ganzen Glieder-
bau des Menschen verbergen, beschränkt den Gebrauch der Glieder durch
einen lästigen Apparat unnützer Zierrath und schneidet sogar die Haare
ab, um das Geschenk der Natur durch ein Machwerk der Kunst zu ersetzen. Wenn die wahre Würde, die sich nie der Natur, nur der rohen Natur

schämt, auch da, wo sie an sich hält, noch stets frey und offen bleibt, wenn in den Augen Empfindung strahlt, und der heitre stille Geist auf der beredten Stirne ruht, so legt die *Gravität* die ihrige in Falten, wird verschlossen und mysteriös, und bewacht sorgfältig wie ein Komödiant ihre Züge. Alle ihre Gesichtsmuskeln sind angespannt, aller wahre natürliche Ausdruck verschwindet, und der ganze Mensch ist wie ein versiegelter Brief. Aber die falsche Würde hat nicht immer Unrecht, das mimische Spiel ihrer Züge in scharfer Zucht zu halten, weil es vielleicht mehr aussagen könnte, als man laut machen will; eine Vorsicht, welche die wahre Würde freylich nicht nöthig hat. Diese wird die Natur nur beherrschen, nie verbergen; bey der falschen hingegen herrscht die Natur nur desto gewaltthätiger *innen,* indem sie *außen* bezwungen ist.*

---

* Indessen giebt es auch eine *Feyerlichkeit* im guten Sinne, wovon die Kunst Gebrauch machen kann. Diese entsteht nicht aus der Anmaßung, sich wichtig zu machen, sondern sie hat die Absicht, das Gemüth auf etwas wichtiges *vorzubereiten.* Da wo ein großer und tiefer Eindruck geschehen soll, und es dem Dichter darum zu thun ist, daß nichts davon verloren gehe, so stimmt er das Gemüth vorher zum Empfang desselben, entfernt alle Zerstreuungen und setzt die Einbildungskraft in eine Erwartungsvolle Spannung. Dazu ist nun das *Feyerliche* sehr geschickt, welches in Häufung vieler Anstalten besteht, wovon man den Zweck nicht absieht, und in einer absichtlichen Verzögerung des Fortschritts, da, wo die Ungeduld Eile fodert. In der Musik wird das Feyerliche durch eine *langsame* gleichförmige Folge starker Töne hervorgebracht; die Stärke erweckt und spannt das Gemüth, die Langsamkeit verzögert die Befriedigung, und die Gleichförmigkeit des Takts läßt die Ungeduld gar kein Ende absehen.

Das *Feyerliche* unterstützt den Eindruck des großen und erhabenen nicht wenig, und wird daher bey Religionsgebräuchen und Mysterien mit großem Erfolg gebraucht. Die Wirkungen der Glocken, der Choralmusik, der Orgel sind bekannt; aber auch für das Auge giebt es ein *Feyerliches,* nehmlich die *Pracht,* verbunden mit dem *Furchtbaren,* wie bey Leichenzeremonien, und bey allen öffentlichen Aufzügen, die eine große Stille, und einen langsamen Takt beobachten.

Contributors

JANE V. CURRAN is the Chair, Department of German, Dalhousie University, Halifax, NS, Canada. Her books include *Horace's* Epistles, *Wieland and the Reader: A Three-Way Conversation* (London: WS Maney & Son, 1995) and *Goethe's* Wilhelm Meister's Apprenticeship: *A Reader's Commentary* (Camden House, 2002). She has co-edited, with Hans-Günther Schwarz, *Denken und Geschichte: Festschrift für Friedrich Gaede* (Munich: iudicium, 2002) and published articles and reviews in *Philosophy and Rhetoric, International Journal of the Classical Tradition, Simpliciana, Germanic Notes and Reviews, Monatshefte, British Journal for Eighteenth-Century Studies, Amsterdamer Beiträge zur Neueren Germanistik,* and *Seminar.*

CHRISTOPHE FRICKER is a D.Phil candidate at St John's College, Oxford. He is an editor of *Castrum Peregrini* magazine. He has edited, with Manuel R. Goldschmidt, *"Unser ganzes Geheimnis liegt im Du": Wolf van Cassel; 1946–1994* (Amsterdam: Castrum Peregrini, 2001) and, with Jan Bonin, *Dunkeldeutschland — Zehn Jahre deutsche Einheit in ihrer Provinz* (Potsdam: Verlag für Berlin-Brandenburg, 2000). He has also published poetry and translations of verse (Dick Davis, Edgar Bowers, English Renaissance poems).

FRITZ HEUER teaches at the Institut für Deutsch als Fremdsprachenphilologie, Universität Heidelberg, Germany. He has published *Darstellung der Freiheit: Schillers transzendentale Frage nach der Kunst* (Cologne: Böhlau, 1970) and edited, with W. Keller, *Schillers* Wallenstein (Darmstadt: WBG, 1977). His articles in *Philosophisches Jahrbuch* and the *Deutsche Vierteljahresschrift* deal with Schillers plan for an "Analytik des Schönen," with the grotesque, and with Universal History.

ALAN MENHENNET is a Professor Emeritus in the Department of German, University of Newcastle, Newcastle upon Tyne, UK. He has written *Order and Freedom: Literature and Society in Germany from 1720 to 1805* (London: Weidenfeld & Nicolson, 1973); *The Romantic Movement* (London: Croom Helm, 1981); *Grimmelshausen the Storyteller: A Study of the "Simplician" Novels* (Camden House, 1997); and *The Historical Experience in German Drama: From Gryphius to Brecht* (Camden House, 2003).

DAVID PUGH is the Head of the Department of German, Queen's University, Kingston, Ontario, Canada. His books include *Dialectic of Love: Platonism in Schiller's Aesthetics* (Montreal/Kingston: McGill-Queen's UP, 1996) and *Schiller's Early Dramas: A Critical History* (Camden House, 2000). He has written numerous articles on Schiller, published in Gerhart Hoffmeister, ed., *On the Eve of Revolution: The French Revolution and the Age of Goethe* (Hildesheim: Olms, 1989); Wolfgang Wittkowski, ed., *Revolution und Autonomie: Deutsche Autonomieästhetik im Zeitalter der Französischen Revolution* (Tübingen: Niemeyer, 1990); *Oxford German Studies* 18/19 (1989/90); W. Daniel Wilson and Robert R. Holub, eds., *Impure Reason: Dialectic of Enlightenment in Germany* (Detroit: Wayne State UP, 1993); *Colloquia Germanica* 24 (1991); Friedrich Gaede, Patrick O'Neill, and Ulrich Scheck, eds., *Hinter dem schwarzen Vorhang*, Festschrift für Anthony W. Riley (Tübingen: Francke, 1994); Gerhart Hoffmeister, ed., *Weimar Classicism: A Reassessment* (Bristol: Mellen, 1995). Jeffrey High, ed. *Die Goethezeit: Werke — Wirkung — Wechselbeziehungen,* Festschrift für Wilfried Malsch (Göttingen: Schwerin), 2001; and Steven Martinson, ed., *A Companion to the Works of Schiller* (Camden House, forthcoming).

Index